Edward Shreeves
Editor

The New Dynamics and Economics of Cooperative Collection Development

The New Dynamics and Economics of Cooperative Collection Development has been co-published simultaneously as *Collection Management*, Volume 28, Numbers 1/2 and 3 2003.

Pre-publication REVIEWS, COMMENTARIES, EVALUATIONS . . .

"**A** generous sharing of the proceedings of the Second Conference on Cooperative Collection Development. For those who were enchanted by the conference program and lineup of speakers, but unable to attend, this book extends to them the best thinking and best practices discussed at the conference. Of particular interest to me was Ross Atkinson's paper noting the evolution of collection development to collection management, and finally to knowledge management."

Caroline Early, MLS
Head, Collection Development
National Agricultural Library

The Haworth Information Press
An Imprint of The Haworth Press, Inc.

The New Dynamics
and Economics of Cooperative
Collection Development

The New Dynamics and Economics of Cooperative Collection Development has been co-published simultaneously as *Collection Management*, Volume 28, Numbers 1/2 and 3 2003.

Collection Management Monographic "Separates"

Below is a list of "separates," which in serials librarianship means a special issue simultaneously published as a special journal issue or double-issue *and* as a "separate" hardbound monograph. (This is a format which we also call a "DocuSerial.")

"Separates" are published because specialized libraries or professionals may wish to purchase a specific thematic issue by itself in a format which can be separately cataloged and shelved, as opposed to purchasing the journal on an on-going basis. Faculty members may also more easily consider a "separate" for classroom adoption.

"Separates" are carefully classified separately with the major book jobbers so that the journal tie-in can be noted on new book order slips to avoid duplicate purchasing.

You may wish to visit Haworth's website at . . .

http://www.HaworthPress.com

. . . to search our online catalog for complete tables of contents of these separates and related publications.

You may also call 1-800-HAWORTH (outside US/Canada: 607-722-5857), or Fax 1-800-895-0582 (outside US/Canada: 607-771-0012), or e-mail at:

docdelivery@haworthpress.com

The New Dynamics and Economics of Cooperative Collection Development, edited by Edward Shreeves (Vol. 28, No. (1/2)(3), 2003). *Explores state-of-the-art techniques and new possibilities for cooperative collection development.*

Electronic Collection Management, edited by Suzan D. McGinnis (Vol. 25, No. 1/2, 2000). *A practical guide to the art and science of acquiring and organizing electronic resources.*

Creating New Strategies for Cooperative Collection Development, edited by Milton T. Wolf and Marjorie E. Bloss (Vol. 24, No. (1/2)(3/4), 2000). *Discusses current initiatives in cooperative collection development and points the way to expanding the scope of this activity in the future.*

Cooperative Collection Development: Significant Trends and Issues, edited by Donald B. Simpson (Vol. 23, No. 4, 1998). *Shows how the art of cooperation requires librarians' ability to comprehend and support "big picture" goals and the skills to incorporate "common good" objectives into local activities so that there is constructive and affirmative benefit to your own programs and services.*

Government Information Collections in the Networked Environment: New Issues and Models, edited by Joan F. Cheverie (Vol. 23, No. 3, 1998). *Explores the challenging issues related to effective access to government information.*

Going Digital: Strategies for Access, Preservation, and Conversion of Collections to a Digital Format, edited by Donald L. DeWitt (Vol. 22, No. 3/4, 1998). *"This excellent book presents a comprehensive study of crucial issues confronting librarians and archivists today. . . . From the first article to the last, it is a compelling read!" (Carol A. Mathius, MLIS, CA, Archivist, Head of Special Collections, Nicholls State University, Thibodaux, Louisiana)*

Collection Development: Access in the Virtual Library, edited by Maureen Pastine (Vol. 22, No. 1/2, 1997). *"Documents unequivocally that collaboration–between library and customer, library and vendor, and among libraries–is essential for success in today's academic library." (Kathryn Hammell Carpenter, MS, University Librarian, Valparaiso University, Indiana)*

Collection Development: Past and Future, edited by Maureen Pastine (Vol. 21, No. 2/3, 1996). *"An important navigational tool for steering through the turbulent waters of the evolving collection development environment. I highly recommend it." (Blake Landar, PhD, Philosophy, Classics, and Religion Bibliographer, University of Florida)*

Electronic Resources: Implications for Collection Management, edited by Genevieve S. Owens (Vol. 21, No. 1, 1996). *"Discusses the strengths and weaknesses of electronic resources, as well as the implications these resources have on collection management. Also provides guidance on incorporating electronic resources into library collections." (Reference and Research Book News)*

Practical Issues in Collection Development and Collection Access, edited by Katina Strauch, Sally W. Somers, Susan Zappen, and Anne Jennings (Vol. 19, No. 3/4, 1995). *With surveys, studies, and first-hand accounts of "how we did it," this book shows how fellow professionals view the evolving world of information selection, maintenance, access, and delivery.*

Access Services in Libraries: New Solutions for Collection Management, edited by Gregg Sapp (Vol. 17, No. 1/2, 1993). *"Develops a theoretical foundation for the growing phenomenon of access services in public and academic libraries–an approach to the increasingly complex problem of making materials available to patrons." (Reference and Research Book News)*

Euro-Librarianship: Shared Resources, Shared Responsibilities, edited by Assunta Pisani (Vol. 15, No. 1/2/3/4, 1992). *"A rich compendium of information about European studies, especially in relation to librarianship. . . . A worthwhile volume that will be helpful to Western European Studies librarians for many years to come." (Western European Specialists Section Newsletter)*

International Conference on Research Library Cooperation, The Research Libraries Group, Inc. (Vol. 9, No. 2/3, 1998). *"A useful . . . look at selected cooperative schemes in Britain, Europe and the United States and propose guidelines for the future." (Library Association Record)*

Reading and the Art of Librarianship: Selected Essays of John B. Nicholson, Jr., edited by Paul Z. DuBois and Dean H. Keller (Vol. 8, No. 3/4, 1986). *"A selection from over 300 completely delightful essays, representing the late author's wide and varied interests. There is much food for thought in these pages, a lively collection that is personal, intimate . . . a passionate look at the world of books." (Academic Library Book Review)*

Collection Management for School Library Media Centers, edited by Brenda H. White (Vol. 7, No. 3/4, 1986). *"A wealth of information concerning managing a school library media center collection. . . . Readable, interesting, and practical." (The Book Report: The Journal for Junior and Senior High School Librarians)*

The State of Western European Studies: Implication for Collection Development, edited by Anthony M. Angiletta, Martha L. Brogan, Charles S. Fineman, and Clara M. Lovett (Vol. 6, No. 1/2, 1984). *"An exceptionally well-edited volume . . . lively and engrossing. . . . An informative and thought-provoking overview of the current state of Western European studies and its possible future directions." (Special Libraries Association)*

The New Dynamics
and Economics of Cooperative
Collection Development

**Papers Presented at a Conference
Hosted by the Center for Research Libraries
Cosponsored by the Association of Research Libraries
with the Support of The Gladys Kreible Delmas Foundation
November 8-10, 2002, Atlanta, Georgia**

Edward Shreeves
Editor

The New Dynamics and Economics of Cooperative Collection Development has been co-published simultaneously as *Collection Management*, Volume 28, Numbers 1/2 and 3 2003.

The Haworth Information Press®
An Imprint of The Haworth Press, Inc.

New York • London • Victoria (AU)
www.HaworthPress.com

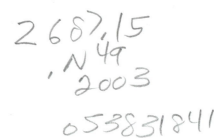

Published by

The Haworth Information Press®, 10 Alice Street, Binghamton, NY 13904-1580 USA

The Haworth Information Press® is an imprint of The Haworth Press, Inc., 10 Alice Street, Binghamton, NY 13904-1580 USA.

The New Dynamics and Economics of Cooperative Collection Development has been co-published simultaneously as *Collection Management*™, Volume 28, Numbers 1/2 and 3 2003.

The development, preparation, and publication of this work has been undertaken with great care. However, the publisher, employees, editors, and agents of The Haworth Press and all imprints of The Haworth Press, Inc., including The Haworth Medical Press® and The Pharmaceutical Products Press®, are not responsible for any errors contained herein or for consequences that may ensue from use of materials or information contained in this work. Opinions expressed by the author(s) are not necessarily those of The Haworth Press, Inc. With regard to case studies, identities and circumstances of individuals discussed herein have been changed to protect confidentiality. Any resemblance to actual persons, living or dead, is entirely coincidental.

Cover design by Brooke R. Stiles.

Library of Congress Cataloging-in-Publication Data

The new dynamics and economics of cooperative collection development : papers presented at a conference hosted by the Center for Research Libraries; cosponsored by the Association of Research Libraries with the support of The Gladys Kreible Delmas Foundation, November 8-10, 2002, Atlanta, Georgia / Edward Shreeves, editor.
    p. cm.
    "Co-published simultaneously as Collection management, volume 28, numbers 1/2 and 3, 2003."
    Includes bibliographical references and index.
    ISBN 0-7890-2490-X (alk. paper) – ISBN 0-7890-2491-8 (pbk. : alk. paper)
    1. Cooperative collection development–Congresses. 2. Research libraries–Collection development–Congresses. 3. Digital libraries–Collection development–Congresses. 4. Cooperative collection development–United States–Case studies–Congresses. I. Shreeves, Edward. II. Center for Research Libraries (U.S.) III. Association of Research Libraries. IV. Collection management.
  Z687.15.N49 2003
  025.2'1–dc22
                                             2003025623

Indexing, Abstracting & Website/Internet Coverage

This section provides you with a list of major indexing & abstracting services. That is to say, each service began covering this periodical during the year noted in the right column. Most Websites which are listed below have indicated that they will either post, disseminate, compile, archive, cite or alert their own Website users with research-based content from this work. (This list is as current as the copyright date of this publication.)

(continued)

*Exact start date to come.

Book reviews are selectively excerpted by the Guide to Professional Literature of the Journal of Academic Librarianship.

(continued)

Special Bibliographic Notes related to special journal issues (separates) and indexing/abstracting:

- indexing/abstracting services in this list will also cover material in any "separate" that is co-published simultaneously with Haworth's special thematic journal issue or DocuSerial. Indexing/abstracting usually covers material at the article/chapter level.
- monographic co-editions are intended for either non-subscribers or libraries which intend to purchase a second copy for their circulating collections.
- monographic co-editions are reported to all jobbers/wholesalers/approval plans. The source journal is listed as the "series" to assist the prevention of duplicate purchasing in the same manner utilized for books-in-series.
- to facilitate user/access services all indexing/abstracting services are encouraged to utilize the co-indexing entry note indicated at the bottom of the first page of each article/chapter/contribution.
- this is intended to assist a library user of any reference tool (whether print, electronic, online, or CD-ROM) to locate the monographic version if the library has purchased this version but not a subscription to the source journal.
- individual articles/chapters in any Haworth publication are also available through the Haworth Document Delivery Service (HDDS).

The New Dynamics and Economics of Cooperative Collection Development

CONTENTS

ABOUT THE EDITOR

Edward Shreeves, PhD, currently Director for Collections and Information Services at the University of Iowa Libraries, has been involved in collection management for more than two decades. In his present position since 1989, he previously worked as Medieval and Renaissance Bibliographer at the UCLA Library.

Dr. Shreeves is the author of several articles on collection management topics appearing in *Library Trends*, including "Is there a future for cooperative collection development in the digital age?" (Winter, 1997), "Between the Visionaries and the Luddites: Collection Development and Electronic Resources in the Humanities" (Spring, 1992), and most recently, "The Acquisitions Culture Wars" (Spring, 2000). He has also published articles or book reviews in *College and Research Libraries*, *The Journal of Academic Librarianship*, and *Library Acquisitions: Practice and Theory*.

Dr. Shreeves has been active in the Association for Library Collections and Technical Services of the American Library Association, for which he served as Chair of the Collection Management and Development Section in 1996-97 and Chair of the Chief Collection Development Officers of Large Research Libraries in 1994-95. From 1999 through 2001 he co-chaired the Interinstitutional Task Force on Scholarly Communications of the Iowa Regental Universities, and has taken an active role in discussions about the future of scholarly publishing. He is the Chair of the Collections and Services Advisory Panel of the Center for Research Libraries, and recently served on the Task Force on Collection Assessment for the Center. Dr. Shreeves completed the 2001 Senior Fellows program at UCLA.

He holds a BA with high honors from the College of William and Mary and an MSLS and PhD in Classics from the University of North Carolina.

PART I:
INVITED
AND CONTRIBUTED
PAPERS

Uses and Abuses of Cooperation in a Digital Age

Ross Atkinson

SUMMARY. This paper reviews some of the standard issues relating to cooperative collection development, first with respect to traditional materials, and then from the standpoint of an environment increasingly dependent upon licensed electronic resources. Some options for cooperation in a licensed environment are suggested. A few issues relating to a shift from collection management to knowledge management are explored, and some further suggestions are presented as to how services based upon some concepts of knowledge management might be improved through inter-institutional cooperation. The paper concludes with a recommendation to replace some of the current competition among libraries with a more competitive stance toward other information intermediaries. *[Article copies available for a fee from The Haworth Document Delivery Service: 1-800-HAWORTH. E-mail address: <docdelivery@haworthpress.com> Website: <http://www.HaworthPress.com> © 2003 by The Haworth Press, Inc. All rights reserved.]*

KEYWORDS. Cooperative collection development, knowledge management, digital libraries

This paper is yet another addition to the seemingly interminable discussion of cooperative collection development. Many collection development officers of a certain age no doubt feel, as I do, that they have been reading and talking about cooperation for most of their adult lives. Oceans of ink

Ross Atkinson is Associate University Librarian for Collections, Cornell University, Ithaca, NY 13053 (E-mail: RA13@cornell.edu).

[Haworth co-indexing entry note]: "Uses and Abuses of Cooperation in a Digital Age." Atkinson, Ross. Co-published simultaneously in *Collection Management* (The Haworth Information Press, an imprint of The Haworth Press, Inc.) Vol. 28, No. 1/2, 2003, pp. 3-20; and: *The New Dynamics and Economics of Cooperative Collection Development* (ed: Edward Shreeves) The Haworth Information Press, an imprint of The Haworth Press, Inc., 2003, pp. 3-20. Single or multiple copies of this article are available for a fee from The Haworth Document Delivery Service [1-800-HAWORTH, 9:00 a.m. - 5:00 p.m. (EST). E-mail address: docdelivery@haworthpress.com].

Digital Object Identifier: 10.1300/J105v28n01_01

3

have been spilled in arguments over the rationale and practicability of co-operation–how future cooperative agreements might work, and why past ones have not. What is in fact so fascinating about cooperative collection development is why it is so plausible in theory–and yet so problematic to implement in practice. Times are now changing so rapidly and so radically, however, that one more examination of a few key issues would seem warranted. Let us fan again, therefore, some of these old embers, and see if they can yet shed some light on this new age.

CONVENTION AND COMPETITION

If the "classic and traditional" purpose of cooperative collection development (Shreeves 1997, 383) is primarily to improve local library services, then we must ask at the outset what scales libraries use, such that they can gauge the qualities of those services and determine whether they are in fact improving. Clearly there are many such scales–use and user studies, collection evaluations–but there are two especially important methods of assessing effectiveness that are rarely discussed. First, there are management conventions, by which I mean values and precepts that condition how library administrators perceive the quality of library services. Operations that conform to these conventions are viewed as functioning well, while those that do not are suspected of deficiencies. I want to emphasize that these are not management principles, which would imply a kind of eternal validity, but rather conventions, i.e., concepts of purpose and effectiveness that change over time, depending upon consensus and fashion. We must try to identify such conventions whenever considering such complex management issues as cooperation, therefore, to help us understand why certain decisions are made and certain attitudes prevail.

The other seldom discussed but unquestionably powerful method libraries use to assess the quality of their services is to look at each other. Libraries need each other–because without each other, they cannot tell what they are. The identity and individuality of any library is understandable only as a relation to every other one. How well I think my library is doing depends to a substantial degree on my perception of how yours is doing. Such comparison is, needless to say, highly selective and subjective, but its effect is undeniably real. There is a fundamental, encompassing, essential and inevitable competition among libraries–although it is considered gauche in the current environment to dwell upon these competitive relationships publicly. The exact opposite situation obtains with respect to cooperation: to discuss inter-institutional cooperation, frequently and at length, is much encouraged–and some might even say that the primary purpose of cooperation is in fact to provide libraries with something to talk with each other about. The problem is that the present custom of ignoring or concealing underlying competition greatly impairs the ability of libraries to set (let alone achieve) cooperative goals, because cooperation is only practicable–indeed, only conceivable–within the context of competition. This is because true cooperation, the kind of cooperation that produces clear and mutually beneficial results, is always necessarily a kind of temporary suspension of competition among near equals within jointly defined rules or parameters.

If there is one convention most central to cooperative collection development, it is surely what we can call the *Law of Local Access Optimization.* Every service a library develops, every action it takes, every dollar it spends, has but one purpose–and that is to enhance local access to and use of relevant information. Any library resource used for any other purpose than the enhancement of local access and utility is *mis*used. The library receives local funding, to create local programs that meet local needs. No library would or could spend local funding to meet regional or national needs–unless, in so doing, it could more effectively and demonstrably meet local needs. That is the reality of our situation, and it is from that point that any discussion of cooperation must proceed.

There are of course many implications of the Law of Local Access Optimization, but we should note two in particular. The first is what we can call the rule of *value over cost.* Cooperation entails my expenditure of some of my resources to meet the needs of your users, and vice-versa–but the value of the services my users receive must exceed what I am investing in the cooperation, otherwise I would simply use my resources to meet the needs of my users. The second implication of the Law of Local Access Optimization is the requirement for *relational equilibrium.* A cooperative program, if successful, is indeed a tide that raises all boats–but it does not change the size, wealth or power of those individual boats in relation to each other. Cooperation can and should result in increased effectiveness for participating libraries, when measured against libraries outside of the cooperative group–but cooperation may not significantly change the relationship of those libraries within the cooperative group to each other. The purpose of cooperation will and can never be to make all libraries within the cooperative group equal: their differential relationship to each other must be maintained, for cooperation to be possible.

TRADITIONAL COOPERATION

With these realities in mind, let us focus on a few characteristics of traditional cooperative collection development. We can begin by resuscitating an old dichotomy: *synergism* and *complementarity* (Atkinson 1990, 100). Synergistic cooperation entails a conscious change in behavior on the part of each participant, such that all participants together create a sense of a consortial collection that meets some of the needs of all members. Complementarity, on the other hand, is the more passive form of cooperation, which focuses mainly on ensuring that effective methods for interlibrary lending are in place–and it might indeed be objected that complementarity does not really qualify as cooperation at all, at least from the standpoint of collection development. Complementarity means that each partner buys what its local users need. This does, of course, result in substantial overlap–but it also permits the acquisition of some unique items; if pursued on a sufficiently broad scale, complementarity may ultimately result in a cumulative collection that contains many materials that might be needed by most members. From the complementary perspective, therefore, there is no need to invest in the (often considerable) expense of synergism: the simple pursuit of self-interest will be sufficient to produce the desired "cooperative" result. Members of the Research Libraries Group did in fact struggle mightily and nobly for more than a decade, trying to put into effect a large scale program of synergistic cooperation–only finally to move more toward complementarity in the early 1990s. This is not to say, of course, that synergism is never successful. Synergistic programs have indeed been very effectively implemented– but they are normally restricted, operating mainly at the regional level. (Two of the most successful examples are the Triangle University Libraries, for which see Dominguez and Swindler 1993, and OhioLink, for which see Dannelly 1997.)

What types of synergism are in fact possible? Let us try to lay out an abstract typology (see Figure 1). *Prospective synergism*, we can say, is the division of responsibilities in advance for the acquisition of designated categories of materials, while *retrospective synergism* involves dividing responsibility for maintaining materials already acquired. We

FIGURE 1. Types of Synergistic Cooperation

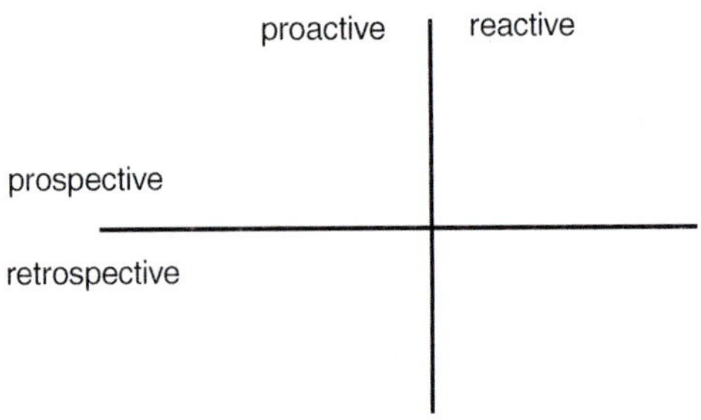

should also think in terms of proactive and reactive methods of cooperation. We can then refer to *prospective/proactive*, which is indeed the most standard notion of cooperation, such as the Farmington Plan: each institution takes responsibility for a different category of material, so that each member can support some of the needs of the other members with respect to that category. (In order to achieve this kind of cooperation, of course, there must be a relatively clear understanding and agreement among the partnering institutions at the outset as to the parameters of the subjects and the definitions of the collection levels.) *Prospective/reactive*, on the other hand, would be a matter of each institution collecting independently for a predetermined period–and then pausing at some point to divide responsibility for some subset of the materials that remain. All members could, for example, define Harrassowitz slips as the cooperative universe; then, after a period of selection, the group could create a list of the titles that no member of the group had so far acquired, and then divide responsibility for purchasing some or all of those.

For *retrospective/proactive* cooperation, each member institution would assume responsibility in advance for maintaining (preferably indefinitely) a particular category of its collection. If one institution in the group agreed, for example, to retain all of the materials it held on a particular subject, all other members would have the option to discard any of those materials and to depend in future upon the holdings of the designated institution. (The library assuming this responsibility might also need to agree to accept the transfer from partner institutions of any materials on the subject that it does not already hold.) The *retrospective/reactive* approach, finally, could be highly chaotic, if not very carefully controlled. As I see it, this method in its basic form would be primarily a matter of any member having the opportunity to withdraw any title held by any other member of the group. One way to provide some control over such an arrangement would be to give all members the option of annotating each others catalog records, so that an institution would know when it has been given responsibility by another member for maintaining a particular title for the partnership. The understanding might be that no member could withdraw an item that another member is depending upon that institution for–unless, of course, the member wanting to withdraw could find yet another member of the partnership holding that item. Needless to say, without carefully crafted rules, the race would be to the swift–and such an arrangement could quickly get out of hand, were many of the partners suddenly compelled for some reason to undertake serious weeding.

Most cooperative collection development focuses on the prospective approach. We can try to model the basic mode of prospective cooperation as seen in Figure 2. The entire pyramid represents what I prefer to call the

FIGURE 2. Prospective Cooperation

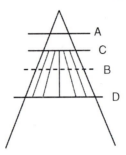

"anti-collection," i.e., those materials that are not in the local collection, and are therefore candidates for selection. As a selector, I should be able to prioritize the objects in this anti-collection according to their relative value to my local users, at least at the time of selection. There is no question that I am going to purchase what I consider to be the very most important material, i.e., down to Level A. Publications below Level A are a somewhat lower priority, so I set some citations aside, see how my budget holds up, and compare materials published over time–but by the end of the year, I know that I will have selected down to Level B. Prospective synergism, at its most rudimentary, is simply a matter of spending initially only down to Level C–and using what funding is saved (by not buying down to Level B), to contribute to the purchase of materials below Level C (and, indeed, below Level B, otherwise such cooperation would not be worthwhile, by virtue of the "value over cost" rule described above). Since the anti-collection has no perceivable bottom, the partnership needs to define a base for cooperation, which we can call Level D. The consortial agreement would be to divide responsibility among the members for purchasing materials between C and D. Since no one wants to buy exclusively down toward Level D, and everyone wants to buy up toward Level C–and since selection responsibilities need to be distributed clearly and systematically–the C-D area is usually divided into "vertical" segments by designated categories, such as subject, publisher, geographical area, or language, so that each member can assume responsibility for one or more segments.

While some refinements and special agreements are, of course, invariably needed, this is, to a great extent, all there is to prospective cooperation. Why, then, we must ask–this concept being so straight forward–is it so insurmountably difficult to put into practice? Ask any selector, and you will quickly find out. The fact is that this clean, neat, abstract model may in fact bear little resemblance to the concrete reality of day-to-day collection building. For a selector to define such levels for himself or herself is difficult enough; for a group of selectors at different institutions to agree upon such divisions can be very problematic. It is for this reason that selectors and collection development officers may often conclude that such a division of responsibilities would be a clear transgression of the "value over cost" rule, i.e., that the resource expense of trying to define such levels in the real world would likely exceed what would actually be saved through the resulting cooperative program.

This negative perception of cooperation, however, is also driven, at least in part, by what we might call the *tactical fallacy*, which is something to which all of us who work in organizations are unavoidably prone. It is the assumption that the purpose of the organization is equivalent to the operations it performs–e.g., cataloging, or reference, or, in our case, selection. As collection development officers, we may well feel, therefore, that the primary purpose of the library is to build and maintain collections. The fact is, of course, that none of those functions, including collection building, are the library's actual purpose. All such operations are rather always a means to an end–and that end is local user access. We who build collections may often make the mistake, therefore, of reification: the assumption that reality consists of things or relationships among them. The purpose of collection development, we may feel, is to create a thing–the perfect (within resource constraints) collection. The time has now finally arrived, however, to begin to refocus our sense of purpose, to stop regarding the collection as a thing, and to acknowledge that the local collection, as beautiful as it may be, is rather primarily a method or means–increasingly only one among several–to provide effective access to locally needed information.

Another inexorably evolving trend that has impaired cooperation in some ways is what we can call the denigration, repudiation, or demise of the *completeness syndrome*. (This is another one of the management conventions mentioned earlier that condition so profoundly our views of service quality.) By this, I mean the partial disappearance of the sense that managing well is equivalent to doing a complete job. In the span of my own career, I subjectively date the true beginning of the demise of the completeness syndrome from the decision made by Richard Dougherty, the Director at the University of Michigan, to eliminate the Michigan cataloging backlog by having Michigan catalogers create brief (read: less complete) records (see Marko and von Wahlde 1986). As I well recall, this was felt at the time, of course, by some members of the library profession, to border on treason. The best record is the most complete record, and the whole point of cataloging was to create the best possible records. The completeness of the record *was* the service. But Dougherty presumably felt otherwise. He presumably felt that to leave some information out of Michigan catalog records was a reasonable price to pay to get the materials, to which those records referred, on to the Michigan shelves. Over the years, of course, that view for many reasons has gradually become the more prevailing one–but that was the first starkly visible example, for me, at least, of the demise of the completeness syndrome, which we now see manifested wherever we look. To take an abstract example relating to collection development, a library could subscribe to a certain number of monographic series, making certain that it acquires every number in those series; alternatively, the library could use some of the funding it spends on ensuring completeness to purchase yet more series, giving up in return its ability to ensure that it receives every number. Which approach should a library take? Twenty years ago, there would have been, I think, little question: what would be the point of subscribing to a series, one would have asked back then, if some numbers were going to be missed? Good management, good service, was measured and defined by having assembled a complete set. But we now operate in a new age, which no longer views completeness as the ideal. We are in general now much more inclined to purchase access to greater numbers of resources at the expense of completeness in records or collections. There can be no doubt, moreover, that the final nail in the coffin of the completeness syndrome has been the World Wide Web–where undeniably significant publications come into being, change, and then disappear, without libraries (at least so far) being able effectively to capture and maintain their evolving content. Such circumstances rule out entirely the prospect of ever developing a truly complete collection.

   This demise of the completeness syndrome damaged synergism. If we read publications on cooperative collection development from the 1980s, we note that the primary rationale for cooperation was that no library could collect comprehensively (see, for example, Mosher 1985, 21-4). Today, on the other hand, not only do we accept that not even a consortium can collect comprehensively–we feel in many cases that, generally speaking, no consortium should try to. Such an effort would not be cost-effective: it would not be good management or good service, and would be an irresponsible use of resources. This position leads directly therefore to complementarity. Since we cannot acquire everything, each library should simply acquire what it needs; all libraries together will therefore acquire most of what is important–and if a few important materials are not acquired, that is acceptable.

THE ONLINE ENVIRONMENT

Cooperation in the traditional environment is a matter of sharing. One library decides not to purchase something, with the understanding that it can rely on another library for access to that item. Now that we are moving increasingly into an online environment, however, such a method of cooperation is no longer an option for many of the most important materials. If my library cannot afford the *Web of Science*, my users are obviously not going to be able to rely on your "copy." From the standpoint of cooperation, therefore, the single most important development in the new era is the adoption of licenses that prohibit cooperation and define sharing as theft.

Publishers have been obliged in the traditional environment to allow libraries to share materials within strict, legal parameters. In the online environment, publishers have argued, technology would allow users to share everything, which would obviously be entirely impractical from the commercial perspective. The answer for publishers, therefore, has been to create licenses that in many cases allow libraries to share nothing–and libraries have for the most part accepted such restrictions and signed such licenses. While we recognize only too well that these licenses are highly problematic, we do need electronic access to high-use materials, and we have been prepared to accept these restrictions as part of the price of that access. We do need to continue to protest and oppose such licenses, therefore, as part of the broader battle against third-party ownership of scholarly information–but the prosecution of that battle will doubtless take some time.

Even when forced to submit to the oppression of licenses, there are still a variety of opportunities for libraries to cooperate. To begin with, we can still effect cooperative programs for traditional materials. We are still at liberty in the traditional environment to apply any of the methods we have developed over the years for cooperative collection development. While these methods have not worked nearly as effectively as we had hoped in the past, there may be a new willingness to try them now. Because libraries seldom receive additional funding to acquire new and needed electronic materials, for example, we might consider freeing up such funding by cooperating on the acquisition of traditional materials. The major problem, I hasten to note, in taking such an approach (aside from the obvious perversity of increasing cooperation in order to move more rapidly into an environment in which cooperation is prohibited) is that, while the literature of some subjects is becoming increasingly digital, the publications of other disciplines remain primarily traditional. That being the case, the transfer of funding from traditional to digital materials could in effect shift support from some subjects to others. At the present time, the humanities could be severely damaged in such an arrangement, therefore, were effective safe-guards not taken.

A second opportunity for cooperation in the new environment might take the form of information exchange in what we might call the "regressive mode." Some publishers, in other words, will permit ILL operations to print off articles from electronic journals and fax them to other libraries. We need to work to retain that capacity in our licenses.

Another opportunity for cooperation in a restrictive licensing environment could be the sharing of auxiliary resources (by which I mean resources other than information resources). Such auxiliary resources come in three basic forms: money, space and time. We have traditionally concentrated on sharing information resources, or indirectly the money that purchases them–but we can certainly also share other resources, such as storage and even disk space. Above all, however, we can share what may be our scarcest resource, time–specifically, selector time. The greatest redundancy among research libraries may be in the area of human resources. We do need to ask at some point whether every institution must have a selector for every subject–and to consider whether some (parts of) local collections might be built by selectors at other institutions.

We can, finally, also engage in cooperation through joint buying and negotiation of license agreements, although labeling this activity "cooperative" is admittedly questionable. Cooperation (at least in its synergistic form) should mean that each partner changes its behavior somewhat in order to contribute to the creation of the consortial whole. Cooperative buying often entails no such change of behavior, nor any such sense of a whole. It would be different, of course, if more consortia were prepared to negotiate as a cohesive group; all members would agree, for example, to purchase an item at a particular, fair price–and if a higher price were offered, all members would agree not to purchase it. That would indeed be synergistic cooperation. Whether it would also be restraint of trade is something that needs to be tested.

KNOWLEDGE MANAGEMENT

Joe Branin has recently observed that, in the same way that collection development shifted to collection management some fifteen or twenty years ago, collection management now needs to transform into knowledge management (Atkinson 2002, 162-3; see also Branin, Groen and Thorin 2000). I must note, to begin with, that I do disagree that collection development did in fact evolve into collection management in the 1980s–despite the heralding of that transformation with great fanfare in the library literature. Collection development, we must remember, involves primarily looking outside of the collection at the anti-collection. The purpose and practice of collection management, on the other hand, is to apply the same skills and values used for collection development to the maintenance and improvement of the collection already in place–through, e.g., preservation, weeding, or advice on cataloging. Collection management is indeed now a standard practice–but this has come about, I believe, only relatively recently, as a result of the significantly increased dependence on offsite storage: it is that new requirement to transfer substantial parts of our collections off campus, creating a bifurcation of the collection (a spatial core and periphery), that has forced collection development to turn its attention back to its own collections, and to move finally into an era of true collection management.

What, then, is knowledge management, as it relates to libraries? There is, to be sure, a vast quantity of published information on the subject of knowledge management–but most of that literature relates to business. The purpose of knowledge management, as explained in the business literature, is to assist commercial organizations in making use of their knowledge as a strategic asset, to enhance productivity and competitiveness. Knowledge, in the knowledge management literature, is often divided into two categories: *explicit knowledge* (e.g., in files and databases), and *tacit knowledge* (in the minds of staff and consultants). (See, for example, Nonaka and Konno 1999 on the subject of "ba," i.e., a combined physical, virtual and mental space for sharing knowledge.) In some cases, applying knowledge management to libraries may be viewed primarily as emulating such business practices, in the sense of developing methods to move information among library staff more effectively. (As an example, see Jantz 2001.) In other cases, I infer that knowledge management may entail an expansion of the content for which libraries should be responsible, to include more informal materials (e.g., Web sites, working papers, technical reports, lecture notes, data sets). This may be manifested most clearly in the rapidly developing interest in local repositories (Crow 2002).

We must ask, however, whether either of these paths is sufficiently transformative to warrant the level of effort that would be needed to bring it about. One way to achieve a deeper transformation might be to apply some version of the so-called cognitive model of information services (Yates-Mercer and Bawden 2002, 21). To do that, we might stipulate for this discussion that knowledge is something you have, while information is something you exchange. Knowledge, let us say, cannot be shared: it is private and constantly changing, based in part upon new information received. Information takes the form of sign (symbol) strings–which people exchange, in order to enhance their knowledge. What concepts might be needed, then, to set out on a course of effective transformation? Perhaps at least one further stipulation. We noted above the problem of the tactical fallacy, i.e., the false assumption that the library's purpose is its operations–while in fact that purpose is access, and library operations are merely a means to bring about that end. Let us now move that concept up one more level, and define what we can call a *strategic fallacy*, which is the false assumption that the library's purpose is access. The real purpose of the library is in fact the production of information by local users–and access is only a means to that end. We can then stipulate that the primary rationale for the library is to improve the capacity of local users to produce new and significant information.

This being the case, we must bear in mind the information production cycle. For our purposes, we can use the model in Figure 3. Information is identified in the universe, it is retrieved, it is understood, used, and applied as knowledge–and then new information is produced and inserted into the universe, so that the cycle can continue. The library, if it is serious about moving into knowledge management, must be prepared to provide services not only at the information level (identification, retrieval), but also at the knowledge level (understanding, application, production).

If this is–if this be–library knowledge management, how then could cooperation further such a service? Let me make three suggestions.

1. Amplification of Local Production. Academic libraries know very little about the information being produced on their local campuses. There is, to be sure, a general understanding about who is doing research in which areas, but I suspect we know very little detail about local research, especially at larger institutions. If libraries seriously intend to effect a system of knowledge management services, they must now

FIGURE 3. Information Production Cycle

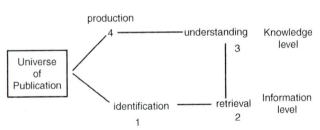

find a way to acquaint themselves with that detail. Libraries need to assemble dynamic information databases that summarize and track local research–and those databases should be shared with other institutions. Needless to say, issues of privacy would have to be taken very carefully into account–and some of this work may best be done in consultation and cooperation with scholarly societies. The main point, however, is that synergism, in a knowledge management environment, may be not so much a matter of libraries working together, as the creation by libraries of some kind of connecting services that will allow scholars at separate institutions to work much more effectively with each other (see Lougee 2002, 9-11).

A further facet of such a goal of amplification should be an increased willingness by libraries to take more responsibility for the information produced at their institutions. That information may have been formally published, but the library should still be ultimately responsible for ensuring that it remains accessible one way or another over time. The library also has a responsibility at the citation level–ideally ensuring that all information cited in local publications remains accessible. This should be the case especially for electronic information: if Web pages, for example, are cited in publications produced at a library's institution, then that library should be responsible for ensuring that those Web pages remain accessible indefinitely–preferably in the form they took at the time of the publication.

2. Boundary Definition. Research libraries as a group should define those objects of information that are essential for research on each subject: they need in effect to circumscribe core materials, which is to say they need to agree that any library supporting research on a particular subject should provide access at minimum to particular objects. Cooperation is not merely a matter of ensuring access to unique materials, therefore, but also of defining those standard materials needed by all researchers. Core definition can be, of course, highly problematic–for the same reason it is so difficult to define the levels in Figure 2. It is time now, however, to make an attempt at core definition, because values and conventions have changed–including especially the completeness syndrome. Some specialists will inevitably believe that some items should not be included in such a core, while others will certainly feel that some items not in the core should be; but the core boundary can be agreed upon anyway, if perfection or completeness is no longer a prerequisite.

Research libraries must also ensure, needless to say, sustained access to materials beyond the core. In order to do that, we need to *decouple selection from acquisition.* To select something should no longer be understood as necessarily equivalent to buying it. To select something should rather be to acknowledge that the item is (or will likely be) needed to do research on a particular subject. The job of selection, therefore, does not end with the local budget. Merely because a library cannot afford to purchase particular objects needed by local users does not mean that the library is not responsible for ensuring access to them. Libraries must not succumb to the siren-song of complementarity. We must not imagine that, when we each run out of money, we have done all we can–and that we must each then simply trust to the invisible hand of collection development that needed but unaffordable information will be accessible somehow, someplace, in the future. The building of local collections in all formats must be coordinated. This is the job of large and small libraries alike, because scholars at smaller institutions will need the same information for research as scholars at larger ones. The only difference is that larger institutions will be able to provide better (in the sense of faster) access than smaller ones, because larger institutions can afford to purchase more materials for immediate access.

 3. Differentiating the Means of Production. In a knowledge management environment, the library (information services) is a means for the production of information. In discussing the means of production, Marx drew one particularly useful distinction between the tools of production (*Arbeitsmittel*) and the materials of production (*Arbeitsgegenstand*) (Shaw 1978, 10-13). If you are going to build a wooden box, you need (a) a hammer, saw and nails, and you need (b) some wood. These are two very different categories from the standpoint of economics and production. It is the same with the use of information objects for knowledge production. There is a difference between objects you work with, and those you work on. Those you work with may be defined as secondary literature, while those you work on are primary literature. There is a danger that research libraries may begin to lose their grasp on the concept of primary literature–mainly because, as libraries race to put in place an effective digital library, they are working most closely with those disciplines that have significant portions of their materials in digital form, and most of those disciplines are in the sciences. The problem, of course, is that the sciences, regardless of their terminology, do not have primary literature. Scientific literature is not something you work on, but rather something you work with. The main purpose of scientific literature is for scientists to communicate with each other about the work they are doing. And the work they are doing is not *on* literature, not on information objects, but is rather for the most part on natural (or social) objects, that they then describe *in* the literature. We need to find a means, therefore, to protect primary literature in an increasingly on-line environment, because there are many disciplines that need primary literature for their practitioners to engage in the production cycle. (Some of this work has, to be sure, already begun, most notably in the Early English Books Online project. See Mark Sandler's paper in this volume.) Primary and secondary literature require different treatment and different service options. Format, for example, can play a key role in primary literature, and needs therefore to be protected when possible. The format of secondary literature, on the other hand, is often relatively unimportant. Above all, however, there is a difference in the use and value of primary and secondary information. We are rapidly beginning to build collections that are mainly use-driven. This works well for secondary literature, such as science serials. Libraries must acquire high-use secondary materials, because those materials are where the action, the essential conversation, is; indeed, the more used a secondary object is, the more valuable it is. The opposite is sometimes the case, however, with primary literature: the less used it has been, the more valuable it can sometimes be. We need, therefore, to find a way to accommodate and safeguard access to very low use materials, and the only effective means to that end is likely to be retrospective synergistic cooperation.

CONCLUSION

Previously I have suggested four areas in which libraries might cooperate in an online environment, even when forced to bear the yoke of highly restrictive licensing. I have furthermore suggested a simple concept of knowledge management, and I have identified three opportunities for cooperation, by applying such a concept. What then are the chances, we must ask in conclusion, that libraries will actually take advantage of these or similar cooperative opportunities in the near future? Frankly, if nothing changes, practically zero. There is no evidence (that I can see) that libraries are any more prepared at this time than in the past to engage in cooperative collection efforts. The reason is that traditional axes of competition remain in play.

Assume each point on the horizontal axis, in Figure 4, is a library, and each point on the vertical axis is another kind of information intermediary (e.g., publishers, printers, booksellers, database providers, software programmers). It has been and remains the custom and practice of libraries, especially research libraries, to cooperate with the in-

FIGURE 4. Axes of Competition

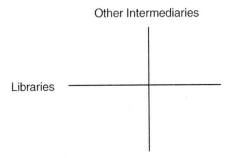

termediaries on the vertical axis, in order to compete more effectively with other libraries on the horizontal axis.

Why then should we assume this will change? Libraries certainly have not hesitated to sign licenses prohibiting cooperation–probably primarily as a result of what we have defined above as the Law of Local Access Optimization: I need those databases and electronic journals on my campus, because others have them on their campuses–and if my users do not have electronic access to those materials, then my users will not be competitive. I am therefore prepared to pay whatever price I must, to provide such local access–and if part of that price is not to share those materials, then so be it.

There are, of course, other, related reasons that libraries have been so willing to sign such licenses. One of those reasons may be that licenses tend to reinforce the relational equilibrium. Licensing, by prohibiting cooperation, effectively freezes all institutions in their present positions in relation to each other; this ensures, among other things, that the large and the small, the rich and the poor, remain in their respective places. The most powerful reason, however, that libraries have been so ready to sign licenses prohibiting cooperation, may be that such licenses provide us in collection development with something to say to our libraries, to our users, to our institutions, and above all to each other, as to why we are not cooperating. It is not our fault, we can say: the reason we are not cooperating does not have to do with the library, let alone with collection development. The reason, we can say, is external and beyond our control. It is the publishers who are responsible for our lack of cooperation: we in libraries are merely the victims of the avarice of capitalism.

These are the excuses that licenses allow us to make to each other–but are we indeed that self-deceiving? Are we really possessed by such timidity, such impotence? If we are, then there is no reason that libraries, or at least their collection development components, should not and will not become increasingly subordinated to other information service providers, the further we move into an online environment. But if we are now prepared to accept full responsibility for providing the best possible local services, then the library community in general and collection development in particular have only one choice: it is to shift the action on the axis of competition from the horizontal to the vertical. Libraries have the ability to cooperate with each other very effectively–if they want to–while the businesses on the vertical axis are for the most part incapable of doing so. Cooperation is, somewhat paradoxically, one of the few competitive advantages libraries have. Such cooperation does indeed entail significant risks for those libraries bold enough to engage in it–but those risks are in fact negligible, in comparison with the dangers libraries will surely encounter by continuing to insist that they should each face the future alone.

REFERENCES

Atkinson, Ross 1990. "Preservation and Collection Development: Toward a Political Synthesis," *Journal of Academic Librarianship* 16 (2), 98-103.

Atkinson, Ross 2002. "ARL Conference on Collections and Access . . . : A Brief Report," *Library Collections, Acquisitions, & Technical Services* 26 (2), 161-5.

Branin, Joseph, Groen, Frances and Thorin, Suzanne 2000. "The Changing Nature of Collection Management in Research Libraries," *Library Resources and Technical Services* 44 (1), 23-32.

Crow, Raym 2002. *The Case for Institutional Repositories: A SPARC Position Paper,* Washington, DC: The Scholarly Publishing & Academic Resource Coalition. http://www.arl.org/sparc/IR/ir.html.

Dannelly, Gay N. 1997. "Cooperation is the Future of Collection Management and Development: OhioLINK and CIC" in *Collection Management for the 21st Century: A Handbook for Librarians,* ed. G.E. Gorman and Ruth H. Miller (Westport, CT: Greenwood), 249-62.

Dominguez, Patricia Buck and Swindler, Luke 1993. "Cooperative Collection Development at the Research Triangle University Libraries: A Model for the Nation," *College and Research Libraries* 54 (6), 470-96.

Jantz, Ronald C. 2001. "Knowledge Management in Academic Libraries: Special Tools and Processes to Support Information Professionals," *Reference Services Review* 29 (1), 33-9.

Lougee, Wendy Pradt 2002. *Diffuse Libraries: Emergent Roles for the Research Library in the Digital Age,* Washington, DC: Council on Library and Information Resources.

Marko, Lynn and von Wahlde, Barbara 1986. "BRC (Brief Record Cataloging) at Michigan," *The Journal of Academic Librarianship* 11 (6), 339-40.

Mosher, Paul H. 1985. "A National Scheme for Collaboration in Collection Development: The RLG-NCIP Effort," *Resource Sharing & Information Networks* 2 (3/4), 21-35.

Nonaka, Ikujiro and Konno, Noboru 1999. "A Knowledge Management Ecology: The Concept of 'Ba'–Building a Foundation for Knowledge Creation," in *The Knowledge Management Yearbook 1999-2000*, Boston: Butterworth-Heinemann, pp. 37-51.

Shaw, William H. 1978. *Marx's Theory of History*, Stanford, CA: Stanford University Press.

Shreeves, Edward 1997. "Is There a Future for Cooperative Collection Development in the Digital Age?" *Library Trends* 45 (3), 373-90.

Yates-Mercer, Penelope and Bawden, David 2002. "Managing the Paradox: The Valuation of Knowledge and Knowledge Management," *Journal of Information Science* 28 (1), 19-29.

Worldwide Rural Research & Education Network (WRREN): A Stakeholder Model for Digital Project Development

Rebecca Bichel

SUMMARY. Rural Sociology Online (RuSOL) is an innovative, digital venture of the Rural Sociology Society (RSS), Penn State Press, Pennsylvania State University Libraries and Pennsylvania State University Library Computing Services to create an online source for scholars, students and policy experts who specialize in rural issues. RuSOL will provide useful resources to the scholarly community while offering insight into the role that digital technology can play in the world of scholarly communication. The portal will provide digital access to current and past issues of *Rural Sociology*, the flagship journal of RSS, working papers of the Society, books in the *Rural Study Series*, conference proceedings, data, bibliographic information, collections of scholarship not publishable in today's economic environment, policy briefs, links to relevant web sites, and additional content as appropriate. Each of the partners brings special strength to this venture: Pennsylvania State University is a public, land-grant university; Penn State's College of Agricultural Sciences has a strong Rural Sociology Program; University Libraries has strengths in agricultural and rural issues; and Penn State Press has an ongoing relationship with the Rural Sociologi-

Rebecca Bichel is Social Sciences Librarian, Social Sciences Library, 208 Paterno Library, University Park, PA 16802-1809 (E-mail: rmb26@psulias.psu.edu).

[Haworth co-indexing entry note]: "Worldwide Rural Research & Education Network (WRREN): A Stakeholder Model for Digital Project Development." Bichel, Rebecca. Co-published simultaneously in *Collection Management* (The Haworth Information Press, an imprint of The Haworth Press, Inc.) Vol. 28, No. 1/2, 2003, pp. 21-32; and: *The New Dynamics and Economics of Cooperative Collection Development* (ed: Edward Shreeves) The Haworth Information Press, an imprint of The Haworth Press, Inc., 2003, pp. 21-32. Single or multiple copies of this article are available for a fee from The Haworth Document Delivery Service [1-800-HAWORTH, 9:00 a.m. - 5:00 p.m. (EST). E-mail address: docdelivery@haworthpress.com].

cal Society through publication of the Society's *Rural Studies Series.* SPARC (Scholarly Publishing and Academic Resources Coalition), an alliance of research libraries, library organizations and research institutions, is another critical partner in its support of projects such as RuSOL that promote a more competitive scholarly publishing marketplace. *[Article copies available for a fee from The Haworth Document Delivery Service: 1-800-HAWORTH. E-mail address: <docdelivery@haworthpress.com> Website: <http://www. HaworthPress.com> © 2003 by The Haworth Press, Inc. All rights reserved.]*

KEYWORDS. Rural Sociology Online, Pennsylvania State University, scholarly publishing

OVERVIEW

Pennsylvania State University (PSU) Libraries is a partner in developing a unique online information community to advance communications, research and education in the field of rural sociology. The Worldwide Rural Research & Education Network (WRREN), a not-for-profit enterprise, is being developed collaboratively by Penn State (including University Libraries, Penn State Press, and PSU Computing Services) and the Rural Sociological Society (RSS).

Our vision is that WRREN will become a significant force in the advancement of rural interests and concerns by increasing access to scholarly and professional communication in rural sociology and related issues. WRREN will become a dynamic information community for scholars, students, policy experts, practitioners, and citizens concerned with rural issues–a global universe of more than 100,000 potential online users–many of whose informational needs are crucial but presently unmet.

Although unique in our field, WRREN will follow in the path of several successful initiatives in other disciplines, including Columbia International Affairs Online (CIAO) (www.ciaonet.org), Project Muse (www. nelinet.net/cpp/eroffers/pro_muse.htm) and ChemWeb.com (www.chemweb. com). WRREN is distinctive not only for its subject scope but also for its partnership of stakeholders.

STAKEHOLDERS

WRREN is being developed through the joint cooperation of representatives of the Rural Sociological Society (RSS), Penn State Press, Pennsylvania State University Libraries and PSU Computing Services. Each of these stakeholders brings valuable expertise to the initiative.

The Rural Sociological Society (RSS) publishes *Rural Sociology*, the premiere journal in rural sociology. The professional society offers insights into scholarly uses of online portals, suggesting how WRREN could benefits its members. RSS has committed to WRREN being the sole online provider of *Rural Sociology*, providing current and back content of the journal. The Penn State Press publishes the *Rural Studies Series* and other important monographs dealing with rural issues. They will make these titles available through WRREN. Collectively, these two stakeholders offer valuable publishing expertise on monographs and serials in the field of rural sociology.

University Libraries offers expertise though our knowledge of information access issues and searching patterns of users. Through our familiarity with other online portals and databases, we are able to offer insights into models of online delivery that are successful for patrons, so we can build in structures from the beginning that facilitate ease of use and maximum information access. PSU Computing Services brings expertise in technical project development and support to the project. The representatives have worked with University Libraries in the past with digital product development, and so are aware of the unique technical needs of information projects. By having information, technology and publishing professionals, as well as a professional society at the table during development, we are able to create a digital product that reflects multiple interests and expertise.

There are a number of pitfalls that can characterize online information projects that this unique partnership allows WRREN to avoid. Portals may lack for content, dependent upon a variety of publishers, corporate, academic and scholarly, with many, often conflicting, demands. Agreements can be limited by publishers' prior contracts with other online providers. Such limitations hinder the value of online portals that are in other ways well-designed and valuable. Alternatively, librarians routinely encounter databases with a wealth of online texts but terrible interfaces. WRREN avoids these problems by having a development team with information and technical expertise, as well as depth of content.

ROLES OF STAKEHOLDERS

WRREN's founding partners are committed to making significant investments of time, resources, and the subsidization of start-up costs. The RSS/PSU collaboration represents a joining of two eminent organizations, each with a unique position and set of capabilities that can be combined to their best advantage in creating and operating WRREN. The parties have agreed that each as co-founders will perform or share in the performance of and responsibility for all activities and functions required for the development and operation of WRREN, including financing; development of a business plan; design, content and quality assurance; acquisition, assembly, digital conversion, and aggregation of content (their own and that of other organizations); editorial management and control for the site; acquisition and/or development of operations and applications software; production, technology, and resource operation and maintenance; establishment and implementation of standards of various types; pricing, marketing, sales, and distribution; customer and user support; creation of licenses and other forms of contracts or agreements for customers, users, and other parties; on-line hosting of Internet access; authorized user access and user support; archiving, preservation, and migration of digital content; and administrative, personnel, accounting (including calculation, reserves for and periodic disbursement of royalties to which certain parties may be entitled), and related functions required to operate WRREN in accordance with best practices. Within this context, we have outlined principal roles for each.

Principal Role of Penn State

Penn State (incorporating the University's Library, Press, and Computing Services) will perform generally and overall as aggregator and operator of the WRREN portal, and as its design, content, and quality manager, central production and technology facility maintenance, aggregator, seller, and distributor, online host, and archive of digital content, some aspects of which may be performed by third parties. Penn State will perform all administrative, personnel, accounting, and related functions required to operate WRREN as a distinct entity within the University's system.

Principal Role of RSS

RSS will perform as an advisor to Penn State at the highest level of decision-making regarding the development, creation, and operation of WRREN. RSS will provide editorial and scholarly expertise, through an editor and editorial board, and will engage in quality assessments of various publishers and information sources, content acquisition and outreach to potential participating societies' executives and other content-owners' decision-makers. Furthermore, of course, RSS will be the lead and likely most prominent provider of proprietary content to be disseminated via WRREN.

Governance

Representatives from RSS and PSU will comprise a governing body to set policies and practices and to make decisions at the highest level. The charter and composition of this body remains to be determined. Additional parties of high stature and complementary objectives are being invited to join WRREN, where their participation will strengthen the initiative's scope, value, appeal, and visibility, and enrich its content. The Southern Rural Sociological Association is one such party among, potentially, five to ten others that will each be designated as a Charter Participant of WRREN. Each such organization will be identified prominently in all public communications issued by WRREN and on the web site. Each will be invited to designate one representative to a Participants' Council, which will communicate occasionally by telephone, by e-mail, or in person to review and consider major strategic and substantive matters related to the development of and business planning for WRREN. (This is an advisory group, not a governing body.) Charter Participants will be encouraged to publicize and promote WRREN to their respective constituencies, and perhaps even to contribute assets (such as membership lists) to marketing and promotional efforts conducted by Penn State Press.

WRREN's core R&D and planning team is comprised of Peter Potter (project supervisor), Editor-in-Chief, Penn State Press; Ken Pigg, Chair, Social Sciences Unit, Department of Rural Sociology, University of Missouri-Columbia, and Treasurer, RSS; and Bonnie MacEwan, Assistant Dean for Collections, Penn State University Libraries.

Rick Johnson, Enterprise Director of SPARC, provides advice and assistance on an as-needed basis. SPARC's role in helping to launch WRREN will become more central as we move further along. Some months ago, PSU engaged Howard Goldstein, a consultant who brings to our project substantial experience in start-up scholarly communications initiatives. Howard works with the core team and will be principal author of the Business Plan in close consultation with Ken, Peter, Bonnie and other concerned parties.

An academic advisory group, with representatives from the University and the Society, has recently begun to consider the many different possibilities and priorities for WRREN content and services from a scholarly viewpoint. Two other advisory groups will also be formed. A technology group will develop recommendations for a technology and technical solutions plan, and a librarians' group will advise on such issues as institutional pricing models and site licenses. The Participants' Council, mentioned above, serves as a de facto publishers' advisory group.

It is especially important to engage leaders in various constituent areas in a meaningful exchange of information, ideas, and opinions to help shape WRREN and its plans. Some time after launch, and as ongoing operations proceed, the role of these groups will likely change.

THE PRODUCT

Through their partnership, PSU and RSS will perform as a value-added consolidator and online disseminator of a comprehensive, multi-dimensional digital resource. Parts of the WRREN information community will be open for free use by all researchers; other parts will be accessible on a fee-only basis to authorized users. Research libraries at universities and colleges will be the largest paid subscriber market segment. WRREN will have added visibility and credibility in this market, particularly in North America and Europe, through an endorsement and assistance from the Scholarly Publishing & Academic Resources Coalition (SPARC), a unit of the Association of Research Libraries (ARL).

WRREN will be an Internet host and portal to a wide variety of information resources pertinent directly, and in some cases vitally, to the large body of scholars, students, policy experts, and practitioners concerned with rural issues both in the United States and around the globe. This will meet a great need for increased awareness and more effective and economical access across the international community including those in smaller institutions and in less-developed areas.

WRREN will be comprised of multiple components of complementary information, drawn from various publishers and sources, and chosen for their relevance to the interests of the intended audiences. Some components will be included in the inauguration of public online access, and others will be added over time. Some will be accessible free of charge, but most of the core published research will be accessible only by subscription, or through other purchase mechanisms, in order to sustain WRREN's ongoing operations and meet the incremental income requirements of participating content owners. It is, however, also our intent to provide access to WRREN to those audiences without substantial institutional or other financial support.

A content advisory group is considering the many different possibilities for WRREN products and services. Their recommendations will contribute to a refinement of our plans for building the information community.

Currently we hope to provide the following types of content and services.

Journals of Scholarly Societies

WRREN has set as the highest priority the inclusion of scholarly journals in the discipline. *Rural Sociology*, the RSS journal, is a leading peer-reviewed journal in the discipline. Current issues and back years will be aggregated in a hyperlinked database. The RSS journal will be the centerpiece with, eventually, all of its back years dating to 1936 converted to electronic form. Other leading journals of similar relevance and quality will also be included, with their current issues and at least three years of back issues (potentially more, based on individual situations). Other participating content-owners will include the Southern Rural Sociological Association (SRSA), publisher of *Southern Rural Sociology*, with whom we have an agreement in principle. Other potential partners include the National Rural Health Association, the Centre for Rural Social Research, and the Community Development Society.

Southern Rural Sociology is the official journal of the Southern Rural Sociological Association (SRSA). The SRSA is a section of the Southern Association of Agricultural Scientists, an organization of researchers and Extension staff in 1862 and 1890 land grant colleges and universities in the South. The SRSA is not, however, limited in its membership to people who work at land grant institutions. Membership of the SRSA is drawn from a range of social science interests and disciplines, as well as from the ranks of those involved in promoting social change. As an academic refereed journal, *Southern Rural Sociology* was established in 1983 to stimulate research on a wide range of rural issues that relate to the South. Areas of interest include rural economic restructuring, rural development, rural households in transition, the sociology of community, health, and poverty, rural labor market participation, agricultural restructuring, natural resource and environmental issues, agricultural and natural resource commodity systems, globalization of the agro-food system, race, gender, and class inequality.

The National Rural Health Association (NRHA) is a nonprofit association composed of individual and organizational members who share a common interest in rural health. NRHA's *Journal of Rural Health* is a quarterly journal offering original research encompassing evaluations of model and demonstration projects to improve rural health, statistical comparisons of rural and urban differences, and mathematical models examining the use of health care services by rural residents. Summaries of recently published rural health research discuss the objectives, geographical focus, database, and methods and outcomes of the research.

The Centre for Rural Social Research (CRSR) contributes significantly to rural Australia and is recognized as the Australian national centre for rural and regional social research. Publishing activities at the CRSR provide a vital source of information on rural social issues, particularly its unique nationally refereed journal *Rural Society*. *Rural Society* is a refereed, academic journal, which covers topics such as: the rural media; small town development; rural gender issues; agricultural restructuring; heritage and tourism; youth and ageing in rural areas and many other rural related topics.

The international Community Development Society (CDS), founded in 1969, is a professional association for community development practitioners and citizen leaders around the world. CDS members represent a variety of fields: education, health care, social services, government, utilities, economic development practitioners, citizen groups, and more. *The Journal of the Community Development Society* is devoted to improving knowledge and practice in the field of purposive community change. The *Journal's* purposes are to disseminate information on community development theory, research, and practice.

Our initial goal is to secure electronic publishing rights to leading journals, including those with an international focus. Some of these journals are already available online. For those journals for which WRREN is not exclusive electronic distributor, the strength of WRREN will be in the advantages of its aggregation and cross-journal functionality, rather than in exclusivity.

Monographs

Books of interest to the field from university presses, scholarly societies, and other publishers are a high priority, including in particular the *Rural Studies Series* published by Penn State Press and sponsored by RSS. While emphasizing current in-print editions, some older books (even out-of-print books) might be included at some point. Various technological solutions to delivery of full text are to be examined. In some cases, WRREN may make full texts available electronically for download in PDF; in others WRREN will act as an e-commerce transaction facility, processing the online user's order for drop shipment of the printed book by the publisher.

Working Papers

Selected publications of research institutes, government agencies and foundation-funded research projects represent a potentially integral component of the information community. Virtually all of these materials exist in digital form (although forms will vary), and many may already appear online elsewhere, but not in a centralized set. For example, we hope to include the issue papers of the National Rural Health Association, currently freely available on the Association's web site. These papers include the NRHA's position and policies on federal programs and issues impacting our nation's rural health care delivery system.

Policy Briefs, Issue Updates, Legislative Alerts, Etc.

Selected publications may include current legislative and regulatory activity alerts from the Census Bureau, the Economic Development Administration, the Congressional Rural Caucus, the United States Department of Agriculture, and from non-governmental organizations, such as the Rural Policy Research Institute (RUPRI). Additionally, RSS can expand its role as publisher by commissioning five to ten original papers annually on important topics from eminent researchers.

Web Subject Directory

WRREN will facilitate the greatest number and widest variety of Internet links reasonably possible to and from pertinent web sites and resources (such as societies, institutes, agencies, associations, development centers, universities, publishers, abstracting and indexing services). Again, this would reinforce our community stature and add to the site's functionality and user convenience. This subject directory would be free to all online users.

Conference Proceedings

We hope to include the proceedings of annual meetings of RSS and other societies. Such publications are currently indexed in Sociological Abstracts and other databases but are not easily available.

Pedagogical Resources

Including course syllabi and other teaching materials reinforces the intended value of WRREN as a central resource for rural studies education. Individual scholars may be encouraged to share their course packs and other teaching materials with the community.

News and Updates

Postings of news and other current non-research information of community interest would present participating society publishers with an additional communications venue and increased visibility for their activities and programs. For RSS, this could be as simple as an electronic version of *The Rural Sociologist*, published four times a year to provide information and comment of interest to members of the Rural Sociological Society; however, we may be able to enhance this with regular updating and bulletin-board features. Access by all online users would be free.

Preprints

. Scholars wanting quicker and potentially wider access to their papers by other researchers are more frequently posting preprints of articles or papers on the Internet, on both their own web sites and elsewhere. These papers are identified as un-refereed and may, as often is the case, precede publication in a peer-reviewed journal. Preprints, posted within a "rolling repository" (with appropriate criteria for inclusion and oversight) may be a potentially rich complementary resource for WRREN. Access by all online users would be free.

Maps and Country Data

We are considering including maps, country information, and statistics, and perhaps even State Department travel advisories, to expand the WRREN information community. At a minimum, we plan to provide lists or indices of such materials with links to those available on other web sites.

Scholars' Commons

We are considering inclusion of an interactive online discussion facility (e.g., chat room), either moderated (by volunteers) or not, where visitors can exchange information and views or post notices of interest to the community.

FUNCTIONALITY AND ONLINE USER BENEFITS

Penn State and RSS will create an electronic information resource that not only is comprehensive and highly relevant to researchers in our field, but that also provides contemporary features and functionality to best serve the members of RSS and the entire community. The very creation and operation of the online service presents great benefits. WRREN will offer a consolidated, readily accessible body of information, all within a single location. Moreover, through this web resource, researchers throughout the world have access to vital information that otherwise would remain difficult or impossible to find and retrieve. With an aggregated collection, it becomes remarkably easy to navigate from one journal article to another, even when the articles appear in separate journals. (Also, for the authors, editors, and publishers, for whom visibility and impact are of paramount importance, WRREN presents an unparalleled venue for dissemination.)

The search page for WRREN will be designed with a two-tier level search interface. The Basic Search will allow users to do a quick keyword search across all content on the web site. The Enhanced or Advanced Search will allow users to perform more sophisticated searches, either in specific types of sources (journals, monographs, papers) or across all types. Users will also be able to limit a search to a specific title, such as *Rural Sociology*. Finally, users will be able to designate specific fields within which to search, e.g., author, title, abstract, or full-text.

The following presents the basic goals (subject to refinement) we will pursue for WRREN's core content component, the journals. We intend to offer the highest practical levels of functionality for online users, meeting the expectations of both basic and advanced searchers for precision, convenience, and efficiency.

- Search by: journal, volume, issue; document type; date range; author; keywords; abstract; full-text; title
- Browsable
- Keyword searches across any and all journals by year, title, and issue based on strings within title, author, abstract, and article full-text
- Display of a list of hits (search results) in the form of titles and authors, with the user option to view abstract, full-text HTML, and full-text PDF
- Separate online delivery of abstracts and full-text articles in HTML
- Many basic pages/templates

- Opening page with links to current journal issues, available issues (archive), information about each journal and publisher, information about WRREN
- Online help screens and FAQ
- Feedback (e-mail) function
- Current issues page with links to current tables of contents of journal issues
- Archive "drill-down" pages indicating available volumes/issues for each journal
- Individual HTML abstract displays
- Individual full-text article displays
- Search page for simple queries as well as more complex Boolean searches
- List of hits in the form of titles and authors linked internally to abstracts, full-text HTML, and PDF files
- External linking including to/from other online publications and content (external to WRREN), other database aggregators, A&I databases, participating societies, and other participants and/or sites of interest

A comparable level of functionality, relative to cost-benefits, will also be pursued for other content components, such as monographs, adapted to their respective types and electronic formats.

The Economics and Management of Digital Resources in a Multi-Campus, Multi-Library University: Introduction

Cecily Johns

SUMMARY. The three papers that follow detail the funding issues that underlie a multi-campus shared digital collection; the implementation of an experiment to determine costs incurred and avoided, usage and user preferences when print journals are relocated to storage and users must rely on the electronic versions; and finally, campus perspectives on UC libraries' collaborative environment, the co-investment models used to fund shared collections and University-wide participation in an extensive and complicated research project. *[Article copies available for a fee from The Haworth Document Delivery Service: 1-800-HAWORTH. E-mail address: <docdelivery@ haworthpress.com> Website: <http://www.HaworthPress.com> © 2003 by The Haworth Press, Inc. All rights reserved.]*

KEYWORDS. Digital collections, cooperative collection development–economic aspects, University of California (system)

Since the inception in 1997 of the California Digital Library (CDL), a collaborative library of the ten campuses of the University of Califor-

Cecily Johns is Associate University Librarian, Davidson Library, University of California, Santa Barbara, Santa Barbara, CA 93106-9010 (E-mail: johns@library.ucsb.edu).

[Haworth co-indexing entry note]: "The Economics and Management of Digital Resources in a Multi-Campus, Multi-Library University: Introduction." Johns, Cecily. Co-published simultaneously in *Collection Management* (The Haworth Information Press, an imprint of The Haworth Press, Inc.) Vol. 28, No. 1/2, 2003, pp. 33-35; and: *The New Dynamics and Economics of Cooperative Collection Development* (ed: Edward Shreeves) The Haworth Information Press, an imprint of The Haworth Press, Inc., 2003, pp. 33-35. Single or multiple copies of this article are available for a fee from The Haworth Document Delivery Service [1-800-HAWORTH, 9:00 a.m. - 5:00 p.m. (EST). E-mail address: docdelivery@haworthpress.com].

Digital Object Identifier: 10.1300/J105v28n01_03

nia, the issue of funding shared digital resources and providing access to these materials has been a major focus. The primary method of funding has been a co-investment model that relies both on contributions from the campus libraries, usually proportionate to campus library materials budgets or FTE, and a contribution from the California Digital Library. CDL uses its funds to facilitate campus decisions in transition from print to electronic. The University's goal from the outset was to provide access to the resources that UC scholars need, secondarily to stabilize costs, and finally to influence the marketplace.

One means to this end was to establish the California Digital Library. The CDL was launched as a result of an extensive strategic planning process by a task force of faculty and academic administrators (the Library and Planning and Action Initiative) from several UC campuses who concluded that the primary goal for UC should be to seek innovative and cost-effective means to achieve comprehensive access to scholarly and scientific communication for all members of the University community.

As a part of this planning process, the University established the Systemwide Library and Scholarly Information Advisory Committee with broad representation from the University community to monitor and advise the University on issues related to library services and scholarly communication (SLASIAC). This group carried on the advisory and planning role begun by the Library Planning and Action Initiative task force. In 2000 SLASIAC approved a resolution that endorsed the implementation, beginning no later than January 2001, of experiments that will help the University "to explore the feasibility of reliance on the electronic copies of these journals to meet the various usage requirements of the UC community" (http://www.slp.ucop.edu/consultation/slasiac/).

Planning began soon after to mount an extensive research project that would help the University community increase its understanding of strategies for managing its digital and print collections and particularly to determine user preferences for print vs. electronic resources. To further this goal the University applied for and was awarded a grant from the Mellon Foundation beginning in January 2001. The primary objectives of the Collection Management Initiative (CMI) were to study behavior and attitudes of users when print journals for which electronic content is available are relocated to remote storage, gather usage data for both print and electronic versions of the same journal, and compile cost data to determine the costs of consultation, processing and bibliographic control of journal volumes destined for storage, transportation and storage of print journals, and the myriad costs, including print subscriptions, license agreements for ejournals, and system infrastructure.

What the University of California learns from this study will be used to develop strategies for managing mixed collections of print and digital materials. One of these strategies will be a shared print journal collection, sometimes referred to as an archive, consisting of information resources collectively managed and accessible University wide. Initial planning by the University Librarians has determined that such resources may be collectively purchased or electively contributed and that items in the shared collection will be collectively owned. Access and security policies with regard to specific shared materials are currently under discussion but the creation of such an archive will allow UC libraries to consider cancellation or remote storage with more confidence.

The University of California libraries have a long history of strategic planning that has led to collaborative approaches to shared collection building and seeking solutions to the complex issues surrounding the management of digital and print collections. The CDL was established as an outgrowth of strategic planning in order to create a University-wide digital collection and to gain experience with the challenges of developing and integrating a mixed format collection. The papers that follow detail the funding issues that underlie a multi-campus shared digital collection; the implementation of an experiment to determine costs incurred and avoided, usage and user preferences when print journals are relocated to storage and users must rely on the electronic versions; and finally, campus perspectives on UC libraries' collaborative environment, the co-investment models used to fund shared collections and University-wide participation in an extensive and complicated research project.

Collection Management Strategies in a Digital Environment

Cecily Johns

SUMMARY. This article discusses the issue of costs related to managing print and digital collections in an environment of increasing digital content that replicates the University's collective print collections. The University of California, with funding from the Mellon Foundation, has been administering an experiment to determine user acceptance and costs incurred when print journals are placed in remote storage and users must rely on the digital versions. As part of the grant project, the University has been gathering cost information and planning future scenarios for preserving a limited number of print copies in storage and relying on electronic versions. The article describes the project briefly and how it relates to the funding issues of supporting digital and print collections. *[Article copies available for a fee from The Haworth Document Delivery Service: 1-800-HAWORTH. E-mail address: <docdelivery@ haworthpress.com> Website: <http://www.HaworthPress.com> © 2003 by The Haworth Press, Inc. All rights reserved.]*

KEYWORDS. Digital collections, cooperative collection development–economic aspects, University of California (system), Collection Management Initiative (University of California)

Cecily Johns is Associate University Librarian, Davidson Library, University of California, Santa Barbara, Santa Barbara, CA 93106-9010 (E-mail: johns@library. ucsb.edu).

[Haworth co-indexing entry note]: "Collection Management Strategies in a Digital Environment." Johns, Cecily. Co-published simultaneously in *Collection Management* (The Haworth Information Press, an imprint of The Haworth Press, Inc.) Vol. 28, No. 1/2, 2003, pp. 37-43; and: *The New Dynamics and Economics of Cooperative Collection Development* (ed: Edward Shreeves) The Haworth Information Press, an imprint of The Haworth Press, Inc., 2003, pp. 37-43. Single or multiple copies of this article are available for a fee from The Haworth Document Delivery Service [1-800-HAWORTH, 9:00 a.m. - 5:00 p.m. (EST). E-mail address: docdelivery@ haworthpress.com].

http://www.haworthpress.com/web/COL
Digital Object Identifier: 10.1300/J105v28n01_04

BACKGROUND

Collection Management Strategies in a Digital Environment, also known as the Collection Management Initiative (CMI), is the formal title of a two-year grant project funded by the Andrew W. Mellon Foundation. The grant was awarded to the University of California on January 1, 2001 and extends through December 31, 2002. Mellon expressed an interest in funding experiments that would test academic and research libraries' ability to manage their collections that increasingly consist of a mix of print and digital materials. In early 2000, the University initiated a planning process to develop a research grant to develop strategies for managing digital and print collections. The University was awarded a planning grant by the Mellon Foundation to develop a fuller proposal for a research project. In support of these efforts, a University-wide committee made up of faculty and academic administrators who advise the University on library planning issues approved a resolution endorsing "the implementation, beginning no later than January 2001, of experiments that would help the University increase its understanding of strategies for creating a durable, reliable archive of its digital collections and of issues arising from the development and implementation of these strategies." See URL http://www.slp.ucop.edu/consultation/slasiac/ for the complete text of Resolution A. The final research grant from Mellon was awarded in late 2000 to begin in January 2001.

The University of California is particularly well suited to undertake such a complex and extensive research project. Several factors, including a history of collaboration, an infrastructure and extensive digital collections, supported the University's application to the Mellon Foundation:

- A long history of collaboration, as evidenced by resource-sharing agreements among the nine campuses; a patron initiated online "Request" service, which is increasingly replacing the more staff-intensive campus Interlibrary Loan operations for UC owned materials; and an overnight courier service to deliver books and journals among the campuses.
- An infrastructure to support access and resource sharing that combines a union catalog (the Melvyl catalog) of library holdings for all UC campuses with over 150 online reference databases and indexes with citations linked to full-text digital resources.
- Extensive shared digital and print collections. For example, all the journal titles selected for the study are held in print form by more

than one campus of the University and digital versions are available on all the campuses.

- Two regional storage facilities that house "seldom used" library materials from all campus libraries, one housed in northern California and one in the south.

In addition to an infrastructure that supports and encourages resource sharing among the campuses, UC was seeking long term solutions to collection management issues that would relieve pressure on physical facilities and capital budgets and would leverage the University's investment in extensive digital collections. Among the motivating factors that led to the University taking on such a complex project are:

- Overcrowded physical facilities: Many UC libraries are currently full or nearly full. The University does not anticipate sufficient additional funding for new buildings over the next decade that would satisfy library space needs on every campus. Financial support for capital expenditures on UC campuses is dependent on bond issues and a strong economy. Even if capital funding were abundant, libraries must compete for funding with proposals for new classroom buildings and faculty office space.
- Need to address urgent seismic safety deficiencies and replace deteriorating campus infrastructure: The University of California has a compelling interest in managing existing library facilities to accommodate continually-growing collections, while relieving demands on its overtaxed capital program.
- Projected increase in enrollment: Over the next ten years UC is anticipating an enrollment increase of 60,000 new students that will most certainly impact the priorities for capital expenditures.

OBJECTIVES FOR THE PROJECT

The overarching goal of the project is to explore issues associated with integrating and managing research library journal collections composed of print and digital formats. The study will evaluate the factors that affect reliance on digital resources to relieve pressure on physical facilities and capital budgets.

The specific objectives of the grant are to:

- Study the behavior and attitudes of users when selected print journals for which electronic access is provided are relocated to a re-

mote storage facility and primary use is of the electronic version, and ascertain the variety of factors affecting the acceptability of digital publications as a substitute for the equivalent print publications
- Design and test processes for consultation and decision-making for selection, processing, relocation and administrative management of print materials relocated to remote storage
- Document the costs incurred and avoided for maintaining selected journal titles for which electronic access is provided when paper copies of the journals are relocated to a storage facility and primary use is of the electronic version
- Document the change in usage of digital and print versions of selected journal titles when print is relocated to storage
- Assess the institutional implications for library organization and operations, including facilities planning, capital budgeting, systems and resource management
- Evaluate institutional strategies and policies for archiving of research library materials in a mixed print/digital environment.

CRITERIA FOR THE SELECTION OF JOURNALS

The following criteria were developed by project staff during the planning phase to inform the selection process and to aid librarians who were consulting with faculty, students and colleagues on their campuses in the decision-making process.

- All journals selected must be available in digital form on all campuses
- The print journal must be held in more than one library in the UC system to enable us to gather usage data for print runs on library shelves as well as usage data for print journals relocated to a storage facility
- Sufficient use data must be available from the electronic journal publisher in order to obtain use by title and use by campus
- The choice of journals should allow us to study a variety of factors influencing use, including disciplinary and content characteristics, such as graphics, language, and article length
- The sample of journal titles must include titles for which current issues are available in digital form and titles for which the digital version is available only retrospectively in back runs (e.g., JSTOR titles), so that we can gather cost, usage and behavioral data for both publishing models
- The sample of journal titles should include multiple publishers of electronic journals.

PHASES OF THE GRANT

The grant covers a two year period (from January 1, 2001 to December 31, 2002) and is being implemented in three phases:

- Phase 1: Consultation and decision-making including the identification of journal titles to be included in the study and the campuses that will participate (January 1-September 30, 2001)
- Phase 2: Implementation of the actual experiment when print journals are relocated to storage and the gathering of data of ongoing (October 1, 2001-September 30, 2002)
- Phase 3: Evaluation of Institutional Strategies, Policies, and Programs for archiving and management of collections in the print and digital environment (July 1-December 30, 2002). Note that Phase 2 and 3 overlap.

Phase 1 posed the most difficult challenges to the campuses and to the grant staff. The selection of journal titles and the related bibliographic work that was needed to match journals from two campuses was more difficult than had been anticipated. Originally, Phase 1 was scheduled to last six months but was extended to nine months. At this writing, the campuses are completing Phase 2, the yearlong period during which journals are located in storage and staff are collecting usage and cost data.

IMPLEMENTATION OF THE EXPERIMENT

In order to create the necessary conditions for the experiment and to set the stage for data gathering, librarians on the campuses of the University of California worked with project staff to identify 300 journal titles. Libraries on all nine campuses participated in the study.

One copy of a print journal run, called "an experimental journal" for purposes of the study was placed in storage. A second print copy, called "a control journal," was identified and maintained on library shelves on another campus. Use data for the experimental journals, the control journals and the ejournals is being gathered during the yearlong study.

Once the journal titles were selected, print volumes and issues for which electronic content was available, were relocated to remote storage. These journals will remain in storage for a year while use data are gathered. Even though the experimental print journals are in storage, the library will bring a volume or issue back or supply a photocopy upon request.

USE DATA

The definition of use of an experimental journal is defined as "each request by a library patron at the owning campus library for a volume or unbound issue or for a copy of an article contained in a study volume or issue." As an example, *French Historical Studies*, volume 22 (1999) to the present, held on the Irvine campus, was relocated to the University's Southern Regional Library Facility at the beginning of the study. A control copy of the same journal, *French Historical Studies*, is housed on campus in the library at UCLA. During the study use data will be gathered for that copy of the journal as well. The definition of use for control journals is "each instance of re-shelving of a volume or an issue" during the study period.

Use data for print and digital copies of the 300 journals in the study has been collected for the first and second quarters of the experiment. Print use data only is available for the third quarter.

BEHAVIOR AND PREFERENCE DATA

A critical part of the research for the grant will be to gather information about user attitudes and preferences when primary access to journals is the digital version. Grant staff has utilized various methodologies to gather user preference data, including face-to-face interviews that will inform the design of a broad survey to gather information about user preferences and behavior.

COST DATA

Dr. Michael Cooper, School of Information Management and Systems, UC Berkeley, was engaged as a consultant to the project (Cooper, 1989 & 1991). He developed an extensive research framework for acquiring and analyzing relevant costs in the following categories:

- Access and circulation costs (applicable in varying ways to both print and digital use, including print use from storage for the "experimental journals," and including costs both to the library and the user)
- Selection, transfer and processing of titles for storage
- Ongoing storage costs for print journals (campus and storage)

During Phase 1, grant staff gathered cost data from each campus library that participated in the study, including the costs of management activity, preparation for the relocation of journals, selection of titles, bibliographic record changes, processing, publicity to library users about the project, and staff training. Campus librarians completed a survey form indicating the number of hours devoted to each activity and the level of staff that performed those tasks. In addition, cost data were gathered from the regional library storage facilities in order to determine the cost of processing and storing print materials. Special studies may be required to capture costs of activities not included in this survey.

These data are being translated into unit costs in order to more effectively project expenditures and savings in the future. For example, as a result of the study, staff will be able to estimate costs for selecting titles and relocating journal volumes to storage, including loading volumes into boxes or trucks, transporting volumes, updating records, recataloging and shelving and handling at the storage facility. Ongoing costs of storing print journals has been estimated in terms of acquisitions, processing, circulation, requests from the campus, retrieval and return to the campus as well as additional transportation costs.

In addition, cost avoidance and cost savings are being estimated in terms of recovered space in campus libraries were journals to be relocated to storage or discarded, centralized processing in lieu of multi-campus processing operations, and savings of print subscriptions and binding costs. To estimate potential savings as a result of canceling print subscriptions, an analysis was done to estimate savings were print journals to be cancelled. The analysis focused on the publishers and providers of the journals selected for the Collection Management Initiative project. In spite of restrictions in license agreements the analysis showed that substantial savings can be achieved.

During the final phase of the project various planning and management groups within the University will assess what we have learned during the study and develop University-wide strategies, policies and programs for archiving and managing collections in both print and digital form. Cost data gathered as part of the CMI study will be invaluable for planning future strategies for managing print and digital collections effectively.

LIST OF SOURCES

UC Office of the President, Collection Management Initiative website, http://www. ucop.edu/cmi/welcome.html.

Cooper, Michael D. "The Sensitivity of Book Storage Strategy Decisions to Alternative Cost Assumptions," *Library Quarterly*. 61:4 (October 1991) 414-428.

Cooper, Michael D. "A Cost Comparison of Alternative Book Storage Strategies," *Library Quarterly* 59:3 (July 1989) 239-260.

The Economics and Management of Digital Resources in a Multi-Campus, Multi-Library University: The Shared Digital Collection

Beverlee French

SUMMARY. This article discusses funding issues underlying the support of a shared collection of digital resources in a University of ten campuses, seven of which are ARL libraries and one, a health sciences campus. The California Digital Library (CDL), a co-library of the campuses of the University of California (UC), has developed a number of co-investment funding models that are the basis for sharing the financial responsibility for providing access to the rich array of digital resources now available on all ten campuses. Publishers of electronic products employ a number of business models in order to calculate the total cost for the University, including models such as a unit cost based on student FTE, the cost of print plus an electronic access fee, and a flat fee plus ongoing access fees. In order to share the costs fairly among UC libraries, the CDL, in collaboration with the campuses, has adopted strategies for sharing costs among the campuses, called "co-investment models." *[Article copies available for a fee from The Haworth Document Delivery Service: 1-800-HAWORTH. E-mail address: <docdelivery@haworthpress.com> Website: <http://www.HaworthPress.com>.]*

Beverlee French is Director for Shared Content, California Digital Library, Office of the President, University of California, 415 20th Street, 4th Floor, Oakland, CA 94612-2901 (E-mail: beverlee.french@ucop.edu). © Beverlee French. Printed with permission.

[Haworth co-indexing entry note]: "The Economics and Management of Digital Resources in a Multi-Campus, Multi-Library University: The Shared Digital Collection." French, Beverlee. Co-published simultaneously in *Collection Management* (The Haworth Information Press, an imprint of The Haworth Press, Inc.) Vol. 28, No. 1/2, 2003, pp. 45-54; and: *The New Dynamics and Economics of Cooperative Collection Development* (ed: Edward Shreeves) The Haworth Information Press, an imprint of The Haworth Press, Inc., 2003, pp. 45-54. Single or multiple copies of this article are available for a fee from The Haworth Document Delivery Service [1-800-HAWORTH, 9:00 a.m. - 5:00 p.m. (EST). E-mail address: docdelivery@haworthpress.com].

KEYWORDS. Digital collections, cooperative collection development–economic aspects, University of California (system), California Digital Library

INSTITUTIONAL BACKGROUND

In contrast to many state systems with one or two "flagship" campuses, the University of California is a ten-campus system in which each campus has significant academic stature. Over the last forty years, university administration and then funding has been increasingly decentralized to the campus chancellors. Line items in the state budget for UC libraries have disappeared in favor of complete campus control over resource allocation.

History of Planning and Collaboration

Throughout this time, collaboration in collection building and resource sharing has occurred both voluntarily and as a result of systemwide funding and initiatives. Earliest efforts focused on intercampus transport of materials.[1] A "master plan" in 1977[2] brought the system the concept of "one university, one library," a union catalog of holdings, shared regional library facilities, and a small fund taken "off the top" for shared purchases of expensive items–initially spent primarily on microform sets and eventually on locally loaded databases.

The University's current library planning framework and the California Digital Library (CDL) emerged from the budget crisis of the 1990s. Although mitigated by robust resource sharing arrangements, increasing quantities of knowledge and high inflationary costs found all UC libraries providing an ever-shrinking portion of knowledge to its faculty and students. Librarians, led by Richard Lucier of San Francisco, engaged faculty and administrators to launch a new planning process that is ongoing. Among the recommended strategies in the 1998 Library Planning and Action Initiative Task Force Report: "The University's knowledge network includes robust campus collections supporting the core academic programs of each campus, specialized collections distributed among the campuses to support the advanced research and teaching needs of the University, and a single digital collection to serve the University's common and specialized information needs."[3]

Role of central infrastructure and funding. With much better economic conditions, and in spite of the overwhelming institutional preference for campus funding, the foregoing report resulted in the establishment and funding of the California Digital Library as a collaborative library of the ten campuses. A new organizational infrastructure was built upon the existing one that had been created for the union catalog and shared databases. Some new funding is used to catalyze collective investments and is critical to the successes that the system has realized in building a shared digital collection through co-investment.

LICENSING STRATEGIES

CDL funding enabled establishment of a small organizational infrastructure for consultation, licensing, acquisitions, and cataloging. Licensing electronic journals by publisher–all UC subscribed titles for all campuses–became the primary strategy for resource sharing of journal literature. Continuing to build shared databases and other resources complemented this effort but this paper focuses on journals because of their complexity in a collaborative and mixed print and digital environment. The philosophy behind this strategy is that all UC faculty and students should have access to the resources they need. It is not as easy, in fact, to share digital content as it is to share physical items because of licensing restrictions. A second objective was to try to stabilize costs. Finally, given the university's size and clout, we deliberately set out to influence the marketplace. The CDL and campuses have also made access to digital archives (e.g., JSTOR) a priority even when the content is widely held in paper. These backfiles contribute to users' convenience and offer potential space savings for campuses. The University is facing a "tidal wave II" of increased enrollments, exerting extreme pressure on state and campus capital resources.

Licensing principles.[4] The CDL has followed a number of licensing principles that were first developed by the all-campus Collection Development Committee and refined over time. Some of the most important are:

> Electronic pricing should be independent of print: Prefer electronic and access pricing independent of print, with print available at a discount. Cost of electronic *should* be less than the cost of print. Maintenance of print subscriptions in order to access the electronic product should not be required. These principles are consonant with ICOLC's preferred practices.[5] There has been substantial variation in results, depending on such factors as the extent of historic print holdings.

Important and non-negotiable:

• Perpetual license and archiving. Permanent rights to use information paid for and ability to copy data for purpose of preservation. Especially critical for ejournals.

- Linking to and from content. To maximize the value of content, linking at the citation level in abstracting/indexing databases has been critical.
- Completeness of content. Include all editorial content found in print equivalent (e.g., incomplete content is one of the reasons that CDL still has no contracts with some priority society publishers). To increase overall sustainability of scholarly resources, we do not want to invest in the same content multiple times, e.g., print and electronic. Adhering to this principle will be particularly difficult in fields such as art where there is user demand for online versions but they are incomplete, often without images or perpetual ownership.
- Interlibrary loan (by at least printing out and mailing).
- Walk-in users–to library facilities–must be allowed (in addition to all UC faculty, students, and staff regardless of their location).
- Site definitions. A single site is no less than a campus.
- Indemnification. The UC Regents require indemnification.

Co-Investment. As previously noted, additional new funding was critical to launching a collaborative model so quickly. All agreed that we could maximize the impact of systemwide funding by using it as a catalyst, a strategy summarized as follows:

- *The CDL uses funds strategically to further the goal of creating a shared digital collection that is available to all UC faculty, students, and staff regardless of their campus affiliation.* For an expensive digital resource with no print counterpart, the CDL negotiation and contribution enables large campuses to participate with savings over single campus pricing and small campuses to acquire otherwise unaffordable resources.
- *Campus collection decisions are integral to all investments; there is no systemwide collection without co-investment.* The CDL advisory structure assures that CDL funding is aligned with campus priorities and sufficient in specific cases to reach the goal above. Co-investment models are devised by the campuses and are generally proportionate to library materials budgets.
- *CDL uses its funds to facilitate campus decisions in transition from print to electronic.* For example, the CDL funds the systemwide "electronic premium" when e-costs are based on campus library print investments. This mitigates the difficulties of paying for print and digital content simultaneously.

- *CDL uses its funds to promote sustainability.* To maximize flexibility in CDL funds, they are often used for one-time purchases to reduce ongoing access fees to campuses.

By using CDL funds strategically in conjunction with campus co-investments, we have maximized the overall shared digital collection. Secondly, decisions are best when those closest to users confirm their interest with funding. The overarching goal of CDL's efforts has been for everyone–students and faculty on all campuses–to have access to all resources recommended for the shared digital collection.

Although all agree on the general principles of cost sharing, applying them is an art. The models have generally followed some kind of proportional share based on the size of materials budgets often combined with each campus's "historic expenditures."

UNIVERSITY OF CALIFORNIA LIBRARIES COST-SHARING MODELS

Primary goals:

- To allow as many UC users as possible to benefit from centrally licensed electronic information;
- To divide costs fairly and reasonably according to criteria on which all participants can agree;
- To take into account the diverse size of the campuses, their libraries, academic programs, budgets, and potential use of electronic resources.

Among the variables considered in these discussions were:

- Current costs for equivalent content or potential cancellation savings;
- Relative campus size as measured by collection budgets or FTE;
- Potential or actual use of the resource, based on estimates or experience;
- Availability of systemwide funds at the CDL level;
- Hybrids combining any of the above.

COST-SHARING MODEL ENDORSED BY COLLECTION DEVELOPMENT COMMITTEE

If the cost for any campus is less than $1,000, or if the total systemwide cost is less than $10,000, the actual cost will be paid by each campus. *Otherwise:*

1. Costs of licenses for digital resources will be shared among participating campuses in proportion to size of the collection budgets.
2. No campus shall pay more than the amount it would pay via independent negotiation with the provider.
3. In cases where the systemwide discount is not high enough to satisfy principle 2, CDL may contribute the difference, dependent on
   funds available and the strategic importance of the resource.
4. For resources that are already widely held, a "base" cost, roughly
   equivalent to the minimal campus cost for the content, in print or
   CD-ROM, will be subtracted from the total amount to be shared
   BEFORE the proportional campus shares are calculated.

A campus that does not contribute its share to the systemwide license
of a given resource, will not be given access to that resource, unless the
potential demand from that campus is likely to be minimal for programmatic reasons, e.g., UCSF (UC's health sciences campus) in many
cases, generally negotiated zero to a cost.

There have been limits to the strategy. Appropriate resources, recommended for systemwide access, are not available to some campuses because of the "no contribution, no access" policy.

RESULTS

Nearly 7,000 journal titles from some 30 publishers are now licensed
as a shared collection and are generally available for all campuses. Some
large publishers and societies remain on the list of priorities but are prob-
lematical because of pricing, content, or other aspects. Although the systemwide licensing began with STM publishers, social science and humanities publishers were added to priorities by 2000 as more of this
content became digital.

Added content and imputed value. If UC holds five subscriptions of
each of the ~7,000 titles, then the subscriptions gained by campuses
would total 28,000.[6] CDL has generally only negotiated for *UC-held* titles (and in fact this was an initial principle), but there are a number of
cases in which UC has access to all of the publisher's titles. For other digital purchases, central negotiations and leveraging the total size of the institution resulted in discounts from "list prices" for single campuses.[7]

Price caps. In a number of cases, we have agreed to multi-year contracts in order to win some predictability and control of price increases.
Some of the large ejournal contracts include price increase caps of 5-8%.

Electronic pricing/print savings. Most prices for systemwide electronic access to journals are based on UC's "historic spend." A number of contracts have been "flipped" and now have electronic pricing with print available at a discount. It is a CDL goal to include the option of receiving a single print archive as part of electronic pricing, and there are a number of such contracts. Realizing these potential savings is tied closely to collaboration of print collections and is of course not a sustainable solution, but in the short term offers some fiscal relief.

Co-Investment. CDL contributions to ejournal packages have benefited both large and small campuses. Sometimes CDL funds a systemwide charge for extension of all subscribed content to all campuses. As noted above, a value could be imputed for the added content for smaller campuses (and even for large) and CDL's contribution might appear to benefit small campuses most. In other models CDL contributions constitute a kind of "e-premium" that even a single campus might incur, and CDL is "paying the difference" between the electronic pricing and the print. In those cases, the CDL contribution in straight dollars is clearly much larger for large campuses than for small.

With co-investments from CDL and the campuses, the ejournal contracts comprise, for print and digital commitments, a sizable proportion of UC materials expenditures. They do not comprise the same proportion of each campus's budget because of the effect of "historic spends" on the cost-share models presently in place. Patterns of historic investment are fairly proportionate for large and diverse packages such as Elsevier but for premier society publishers (e.g., American Physical Society, IEEE), historic expenditures were similar across all campuses regardless of size. The effect is that smaller campuses have a larger proportion of their total budgets committed to co-investments. The assumption is that small campuses have always had a higher percentage of their budgets allocated to serials and to "core" materials, but there is a perception of increasingly limited flexibility because of these contracts.

Use. We are only beginning to learn about the new dynamics of information use in the electronic arena and have not yet used it as a factor in cost sharing. It is proving very time consuming to analyze, especially the use of ejournal titles. With 35 pieces of information for every title in a recent analysis of selected publishers and nine campuses, working further with these data is daunting. It appears that convenience stimulates use of journal articles but there are still many unknowns about use–should we be adding HTML to PDF use, perhaps the same person uses both versions of the same article? We also have to trust the publishers for the use data.

Use data by campus and title and interlibrary loan trends suggest that systemwide licensing has been an effective resource sharing mechanism. *Interlibrary loan trends.* Licensing priorities included publishers that were well represented in interlibrary loans amongst campuses. The early 1990s had produced high and steady increases every year in the sharing of journal articles. In 1999, the CDL introduced an automated patron-initiated request system to its core databases, expanded since through use of SFX technology. During this time, intercampus book (returnable) borrowing rose by 43% while intercampus photocopies (non-returnables) declined by 6.5% to a total of 62,822. The "Request" service is blocked if full-text is known to be available. These patterns suggest that systemwide licensing of ejournals has mitigated demand that might otherwise have occurred for intercampus journal article requests.

CHALLENGES OF THE SHARED DIGITAL COLLECTION

Interdependency. As noted above, there is no shared digital collection without co-investments from all campuses and the size of that fiscal interdependency is now quite large, both in total dollars and as a proportion of total materials budgets. Ejournal packages, especially as titles move in and out, new titles are created, and pricing is tied to print subscriptions, also entail a staggering amount of detailed serials work on a large scale. A number of challenges have arisen that have been or must be dealt with collectively. The University's Collection Development Committee has generally agreed that the benefits of collaboration outweigh the difficulties and has committed itself to collective decision making.

New titles. How does a collective select new titles within packages? Campuses have agreed on principles and decision-making practices that allow for agility and ultimate savings but are not automatic. In many cases, the CDL has negotiated terms for brand new, "start-up" journals that collectively are favorable. New electronic only titles should be some percentage (at best 75%) of the average number of "historic" subscriptions in UC. Thus, we should be able to add new titles to the shared digital collection at lower cost than if the "normal" number of campuses placed subscriptions. The CDL can initially fund such titles in order to activate them quickly.

Deselection. Budget outlooks are very poor and because of the decentralized budgets, the severity of the downturn may be unevenly experienced by campus libraries. How are we collectively going to trim costs? There are at least two challenges: First, inevitably there will be resources to which everyone has contributed and that continue to be of high value to users that campuses most pressed by funding shortfalls will want to drop out of. This is not a buying club. Such action could have serious implications to other campuses, may not lower overall costs to the university, and will incur the costs of renegotiation for a subset of campuses. It will make little sense to eliminate content from the shared digital collection for which the remaining campuses on their own might spend collectively more than the previous shared total expenditure. Related to this issue is the challenge of appropriate cost-sharing models as more and more pricing is for digital content. Will we maintain shares, partially based on print expenditures in the year of the first contract, forever? Can we handle some disagreements over what to retain in the shared digital collection by sharing costs differently? At this point materials budgets have been fairly close to enrollment proportions but they may increasingly diverge. How can we assure that each institution funds its "fair share" of shared collections and what are the factors to consider–enrollment, enrollment growth, faculty growth?

For journals, the old way of savings was to cut journals, title by title, at each campus, often with some communication amongst campuses lest we cancel the only copy of something deemed important for our shared collections and resource sharing. If we are to drop titles from packages these will have to be collective decisions. To that end, the Collection Development Committee is beginning to work on principles of deselection by analyzing title-by-title use data. This exercise sounds simple but has significant costs because of complex bibliographic details such as title changes and inconsistent use data. The cost of each title to the system is somewhat artificial–it is an artifact of the historic expenditure. When pricing is for e-content, will it matter what the system spent in 1996? Or is it whatever we can negotiate?

Decisions to trim content, especially from packages, are complicated by a number of factors including whether it is worth it in terms of cost for remaining content. There will also be substantial collection development, technical and public services costs incurred by deselection of titles in the shared digital collection. Any decisions to drop titles from a shared digital collection must be accompanied by the will and coordination to trim print subscriptions as well or the publisher may gain rather than lose revenue. These are issues on which agreement may be more difficult to obtain than our decisions to make initial commitments.

Print archive. The relationship of a shared digital collection to print subscriptions has already been alluded to above in the discussion of the interdependence of business models and the possibility of subverting a digital cancellation strategy by campus print subscription behavior. It is becoming increasingly difficult to make both collective and individual decisions without coordinating a shared print collection. Many contracts are now available for the electronic with print available at a discount. Some electronic only subscriptions include an archival print copy. Other business models for electronic only compare favorably to total system expenditures for print but can only be affordable if substantial print cancellations occur. Without an infrastructure to build a journal repository, receive issues, house and make them available, it is impossible to accept the free print archive, to make decisions on some shared digital models, and for individual campuses to make their decisions on print cancellations.

NOTES

1. For discussion of the earliest systemwide planning efforts, see Kerr, Clark. *The Gold and the Blue: A Personal Memoir of the University of California, vol. 1, Academic Triumphs*. Berkeley: University of California Press, 2001, p. 362.

2. *The University of California Libraries: a plan for development, 1978-1988*. Berkeley: Office of the Executive Director of Universitywide Library Planning, University of California Systemwide Administration, 1977.

3. *Library Planning and Action Initiative Advisory Task Force Final Report, University of California*. Oakland: University of California (www.slp.ucop.edu), March, 1998. p. 10.

4. See "Checklist of Points to be Addressed in a CDL License Agreement," http://www.cdlib.org/about/publisher_info_pub/.

5. See http://www.library.yale.edu/consortia/2001currentpractices.htm.

6. This is a hypothetical figure, not actual. Presently there are nine campuses.

7. Campus staff also use the CDL organizational infrastructure, tools, and principles for multi-campus negotiations.

The University of California's Collection Development Collaboration: A Campus Perspective

Phyllis S. Mirsky

SUMMARY. This article presents the campus perspective for various funding models in a consortial environment. The co-investment models range from sharing costs proportionately to the CDL supporting all but the cost of print. The article discusses the individual campus funding issues and how each campus library collaborates to develop cost models. *[Article copies available for a fee from The Haworth Document Delivery Service: 1-800-HAWORTH. E-mail address: <docdelivery@haworthpress.com> Website: <http://www.HaworthPress.com> © 2003 by The Haworth Press, Inc. All rights reserved.]*

KEYWORDS. Digital collections, cooperative collection development–economic aspects, University of California (system), University of California, San Diego

Phyllis S. Mirsky is Deputy University Librarian, University of California, San Diego, UCSD Libraries, 9500 Gilman Drive #0175, La Jolla, CA 92093 (E-mail: pmirsky@ucsd.edu).

The author would like to acknowledge the contributions of the following University of California colleagues in the preparation of this paper: Jo Anne Boorkman, UC Davis; Christine Bunting, UC Santa Cruz; Julia Kochi, UC San Francisco; and Alan Ritch (formerly UC Santa Cruz and UC Berkeley).

[Haworth co-indexing entry note]: "The University of California's Collection Development Collaboration: A Campus Perspective." Mirsky, Phyllis S. Co-published simultaneously in *Collection Management* (The Haworth Information Press, an imprint of The Haworth Press, Inc.) Vol. 28, No. 1/2, 2003, pp. 55-61; and: *The New Dynamics and Economics of Cooperative Collection Development* (ed: Edward Shreeves) The Haworth Information Press, an imprint of The Haworth Press, Inc., 2003, pp. 55-61. Single or multiple copies of this article are available for a fee from The Haworth Document Delivery Service [1-800-HAWORTH, 9:00 a.m. - 5:00 p.m. (EST). E-mail address: docdelivery@haworthpress.com].

Digital Object Identifier: 10.1300/J105v28n01_06 *55*

INTRODUCTION

When the University of California launched the California Digital Library in 1997, it was just one more step in an evolutionary process begun 30 years earlier. The 1960s saw tremendous growth in enrollments and the launching of three new campuses at Irvine, San Diego and Santa Cruz, bringing the total number of campuses to nine. Resource sharing was a key component of early library planning including extensive interlibrary loan and transportation services between the smaller campuses and UCLA and Berkeley. In fact, funding was made available to the new campuses to support these activities.

By the 1970s, however, this period of growth had slowed and the projected enrollment growth numbers were reduced dramatically. If the libraries were going to be able to continue to receive state funding for collections and facilities, it would have to be within the context of coordinated planning. In 1977, with the articulation of the "One University, One Library" concept, a new age of library cooperation was launched for the University of California. With the development of the Melvyl Union Catalog and the construction of two regional library storage facilities, a framework was now in place for expanding the resource sharing activities of the University's libraries.

The California Digital Library (CDL), building on two decades worth of these collaborative activities and itself the result of collaborative planning, was able relatively quickly to establish its policies and programs. Although the focus of this paper is on collection development, the CDL has, in fact a much larger mandate, which both reinforces the collaboration and extends the capabilities of the individual campuses to support research and scholarship.

Initial efforts, however, were directed to the licensing of electronic journals. By emphasizing and reinforcing the institutional unity of the UC system in the face of vendor perceptions and insistence that we were nine separate universities, we were able to significantly reduce the license cost and administrative overhead by unifying our negotiations. In addition, CDL turned to one of the campuses, UCSD, to serve as its acquisitions arm. It funded the creation of a UC Shared Acquisitions Unit, which provides a variety of services to both the CDL and to the campuses. But at least as important as these budgetary economies was the growing conviction that we were serving with equal determination the whole of the UC community.

A key strategy was involvement of staff from all of the campuses to be part of the effort. I've usually used the term "co-opt" to describe the approach but it is meant in a positive sense. Basically, for many campus librarians, there is a shared sense of ownership of the process. Collection development, always a local effort, took on a broader context. Yet the need to involve local bibliographers and selectors was essential. A process for collecting and prioritizing information about desired resources was launched. In addition, the growing awareness of the shared aspects of the endeavor slowly developed and now has been institutionalized with the appointment of a resource liaison for each "product." The role of the resource liaison is to monitor the assigned digital resource for technical and content performance, including usage data. In addition, the resource liaison works with colleagues on the other campuses to identify and recommend enhancements and identify appropriate online and vendor-provided educational materials.

What Are the Special Features of the University of California's Model for Collaborative Acquisition of Electronic Resources?

* Co-investment using a variety of models
* Use of centralized funding to leverage campus funding
* Contracting out by CDL to one of the campuses (UC San Diego) to cover the bulk of the processing including acquisition and cataloging
* Collection development principles drive the collection decisions
* Bibliographers/selectors determine priority for acquisitions.

Because it was not possible for CDL to manage all the acquisitions that were a high priority for the bibliographers, a parallel system of acquisitions was established. Dubbed "Tier II," this approach relied on the existence of a UC framework for the licensing of electronic resources, including principles and sample licensing agreements. With this assistance, a bibliographer on one of the campuses was empowered to take the lead in negotiating for the licensing of a resource. This might be on behalf of all the campuses or for only a subset of the campuses. Once the "deal" was finalized, it was turned over to the Shared Acquisitions office to handle the financial arrangements, which usually included the transfer of funding from the campuses that participated.

What Have Been the Implications for the Campus Libraries?

Licensing

* Using the clout of the full UC system, we have been able to negotiate better licensing terms and pricing than we could have on our own. The

disadvantage is that the process takes longer than it might as a single institution.
- Large campuses had to slow down some local efforts at licensing to permit the systemwide efforts to proceed. As we were first getting started, some of the campuses went ahead and signed individual licenses (usually due to local pressures) but this is no longer an issue; in most instances a systemwide contract superseded the local one and in some instances local funding was reimbursed for the difference.
- Centralized licensing removed a big burden from the campuses, some of which would not have been able to handle it locally.

Co-Investment

- Loss of control by "buying in" to the Big Deals leaves fewer discretionary dollars available to develop unique campus collecting areas. The priorities of the system are not always the same as the priorities of the individual library.
- Commitments to maintain print subscriptions, in order to retain electronic access, has been difficult for some campuses as there is wide variation in campus funding for libraries. Therefore some libraries have had more difficulty in fully participating in some of the "packages."
- Flexibility in co-investment models permitted us to try different models on for size. The ability to uniquely fashion and combine these models has proven interesting. Ironically, the most prevalent co-investment model finally agreed to was a percentage based on the overall materials budget. Since one of the basic principles was that no library should be disadvantaged by participating, in those few instances where the model resulted in a library paying more than they would have going it alone, the formulas were adjusted.
- Overhead costs of collaboration have included the need for a bibliographer from one of the campuses to serve as the expert on that product and coordinate public services issues with the publisher and the users. Librarians are encouraged now to think beyond their campus and take a more collective approach–many have become involved in speaking to vendors about systemwide pricing possibilities and licensing conditions.
- Liaisons from each of the campuses were identified to work directly with the Shared Acquisitions Office, especially to facilitate the co-investment aspect of the program. This usually meant the transfer of funds from a campus to a central pot in order to fund the resource.

Collection Development

- Having centralized funding to leverage or offset was essential; CDL paid the "delta" between what the libraries were paying for the print and what the electronic packages cost; commitment, however, remained at the local library to maintain that level of expenditure. The ability to have centralized funding to purchase "heritage" collections (one time costs) increased tremendously the amount of back files available to the University of California.
- Though the initial push was on resources in support of the sciences, access to substantial humanities and social science resources is now available.
- The CDL has built on the collaboration of the established bibliographer groups. It has definitely taken up more of the bibliographers' time as opportunities for shared purchases increase. When looking at new digital resources, groups tend to think in terms of whether a resource would be appropriate for systemwide access.

Bibliographic Access

- A Shared Cataloging Program was established by CDL at UC San Diego to provide centralized cataloging records for the electronic resources. This has been especially useful and has decreased duplicative efforts.
- Trying to explain the difference between locally available resources and those available systemwide can be confusing.

What Lessons Have We Learned?

Timely and effective communication is imperative in order for this type of endeavor to work. Being able to use the technology to support this communication has been essential to the success of our collaboration. A "staff only" website exists with access to all the documents that inform the process. Model licensing agreements, principles for licensing, survey documents of bibliographers' priorities for licensing and many others are easily brought together in one place. Regular distribution of an electronic newsletter keeps everyone informed of developments and activities. Alerts regarding problems at vendor sites keep public service personnel informed in a timely manner.

The collaborative approach has been successful–in a very short period of time a large number of licenses have been developed, innovative vendor models pursued, and access to digital content radically increased. There continue to be challenges. We have raised faculty and student expectations that all resources will eventually be available at their desk tops. Librarians have taken on expanded roles as instructors in searching for and presenting digital resources. The campuses have had to take on additional roles to support the required infrastructure, e.g., establishing and managing proxy servers.

Finally, as articulated by my colleague, Alan Ritch, three fundamental principles underlie and have been confirmed by our approach:

- utilitarianism (the greatest good for the greatest number)
- egalitarianism (from each according to his ability, to each according to his needs)
- universal access to scholarly information.

COLLECTION MANAGEMENT INITIATIVE

The launching of the Collection Management Initiative (CMI) project was a lot of work for all concerned and was frustrating at times. The process of selecting journals, verifying bibliographic information, and matching experimental with control titles between two campuses took much more time than we had anticipated. The initial planning and preparation phase of the Mellon project had to be extended by three months. Those of us with experimental titles had the added effort of removing the volumes from the shelves and sending them to storage facilities.

Once the journal titles were assigned to each campus for either experimental or control status, the study went along smoothly at all campuses and, in essence, became a "non-event." Through the CMI, we gained a lot of information about people's behavior when they have alternatives to paper. Many of us had assumed that access to the electronic versions would suffice for most of our users and these predicted results were generally reinforced during the project.

Our biggest challenges are not behind us but ahead of us. Now that we have some empirical usage data, we can begin the process of moving print titles off-site and rely on the electronic. The difficult task of deciding which titles to move now takes center stage. In a collaborative environment, this is a local decision with systemwide implications, and therefore, must be addressed in a collective manner. Issues we've never dealt with before include how many print copies are necessary in the system when the electronic version is so readily available and rapid delivery of print is a given. How will digital archiving be addressed and what is the role of the University of California in this effort? What is the responsibility of the University of California in preserving print copies and how does that fit into national efforts?

So, though we have answered some of the questions we had hoped to in undertaking the study, we now find a new set awaiting our attention.

The Role of WorldCat in Resources Sharing

Anna H. Perrault

SUMMARY. The 30th anniversary of WorldCat was celebrated in 2001. At that time, there were 45 million records with over 750 million location listings, spanning over 4,000 years of recorded knowledge in 377 languages. In the anniversary year, a bibliometric study was begun under the auspices of an OCLC/ALISE research grant. A 10% systematic random sample of the database was analyzed utilizing the OCLC iCas software to profile the monographic contents of WorldCat by type of library, subject and language parameters. The profile reveals the extent of global publications made accessible through the OCLC international network. Several findings of the study can be examined as possible barriers to successful cooperation in collection development and resources sharing. One of the major problems analyzed in the study is the timeliness in the availability of bibliographic records for current publications. This paper explores the feasibility of using WorldCat as a cooperative collection development tool as well as additional measures which might be derived from analyzing bibliographic records. The results can be used to stimulate discussion on

Anna H. Perrault is Associate Professor, School of Library and Information Science, University of South Florida, Tampa, FL (E-mail: perrault@chuma1.cas.usf.edu).

Grateful acknowledgement is given to OCLC, Inc. for the OCLC/ALISE Research Grant that supported this research.

[Haworth co-indexing entry note]: "The Role of WorldCat in Resources Sharing." Perrault, Anna H. Co-published simultaneously in *Collection Management* (The Haworth Information Press, an imprint of The Haworth Press, Inc.) Vol. 28, No. 1/2, 2003, pp. 63-75; and: *The New Dynamics and Economics of Cooperative Collection Development* (ed: Edward Shreeves) The Haworth Information Press, an imprint of The Haworth Press, Inc., 2003, pp. 63-75. Single or multiple copies of this article are available for a fee from The Haworth Document Delivery Service [1-800-HAWORTH, 9:00 a.m. - 5:00 p.m. (EST). E-mail address: docdelivery@haworthpress.com].

Digital Object Identifier: 10.1300/J105v28n01_07

the role of WorldCat as an international resource on the universe of publication available for research and resources sharing worldwide. *[Article copies available for a fee from The Haworth Document Delivery Service: 1-800-HAWORTH. E-mail address: <docdelivery@haworthpress.com> Website: <http://www.HaworthPress.com> © 2003 by The Haworth Press, Inc. All rights reserved.]*

KEYWORDS. Collection analysis, collection assessment, collection evaluation, cooperative collection development, bibliometric studies, cooperative cataloging

INTRODUCTION

The history of cooperative collection development is familiar to those engaged in the acquisition of information materials and the building of library collections. Most histories of cooperative collection development in the United States use the Farmington Plan (1942) as the beginning point of the cooperative collection development movement in the 20th century. The introduction of electronic resources at the end of the 20th century brought new formats and new challenges to cooperative collection development. There was also a renewed intensity of effort as the effects of price inflation in published works in the 1970s and 1980s made Cooperative Collection Development an ever more desirable, if elusive, goal. There were several conferences and volumes devoted to cooperative collection development at the end of the 1990s. In just a few years, there was an issue of *Library Trends*,[1] several monographs (*Collection Management for the 21st Century*,[2] *Cooperative Collection Development: Significant Trends and Issues*,[3] *Creating New Strategies for Cooperative Collection Development*[4]), and conferences, the CRL 50th Anniversary conference at Aberdeen Woods in November 1999, among them, all devoted to resources sharing and cooperative collection development. At the first Aberdeen Woods conference, one of the goals was to develop a new agenda for cooperative collection development. There were a number of papers at that conference which focused on new models of cooperative collection development in the electronic environment. There was also an international focus in that several papers concentrated on the necessity for global cooperation in the 21st century, arguing that the Internet has fostered the concept of a "global information commons." This paper is based upon that idea of global cooperation in collection building and resources sharing and offers suggestions for overcoming barriers to cooperative collection development. It utilizes findings from the author's "Global Collective Resources: A Study of the Monographic Bibliographic Records in WorldCat,"[5] which is published on the OCLC Office of Research website (www.oclc.org/research/reports/perrault/ intro.pdf).

The first part of the paper reports findings from the WorldCat study and poses suggestions arising from those findings. After that the standardization of measures for cooperative collection development and the role of databases in facilitating implementation of those measures are discussed.

GLOBAL COLLECTIVE RESOURCES

The WorldCat study was conducted by extracting a 10% systematic random sample of the monographic bibliographic records in the WorldCat database in February 2001. The sample contained 3,378,272 usable records. The first stage analysis was conducted via the OCLC iCAS product which was developed by WLN to provide collection analyses and peer comparisons of library collections. The WorldCat study profiles the monographic bibliographic records in the database by parameters of imprint year, subject, language, adult/juvenile, and unique titles/overlap. Libraries were divided into five types of library groupings: research, academic, public, special/other, and school. The sample was of the WorldCat database and thus includes the international membership of OCLC.

Among the findings of the study are that the universe of materials under bibliographic control in WorldCat show a high level of diversity of resources with 53% of records in the analysis having only one library location symbol. The unique records in the WorldCat sample are almost evenly divided between records with call numbers and records without usable call numbers. The research libraries have 63.5% of total records as unique records. The other four types of library groupings have low percentages of unique titles and higher overlap among the four. The profile of the research libraries grouping by imprint year and subject divisions closely parallels the profile of WorldCat.

Of all the records in the study, approximately 65% are for English language monographs with 35% being foreign language publications. The six foreign language groupings analyzed in the study–Chinese, French, German, Japanese, Russian, and Spanish–together account for 67.5% of all foreign language records in the sample.

One of the most significant findings was identified at the outset during the preparations for the iCAS analysis. It was apparent that over one-third of the records in the sample did not have usable call numbers for subject analysis. Since the call number, Dewey, LC or NLM, is used to perform subject analysis of the records, over one-third of the records could not be used in the subject analysis. Analysis of the records without usable call numbers to determine the characteristics of that subset of the sample became an added dimension to the study.

A major finding of the WorldCat study germane to the topics of resources sharing and cooperative collection development is that for the research, academic and public library groupings, by nearly every measure, the number of bibliographic records declines rather precipitously in the latter or most current imprint years in the study. The number of records with call numbers declined 72 percentage points between 1992 and 2000, while the number of records without usable call numbers declined 88 percentage points in the same time frame. The decline in the number of records annually in the 1990s is most acute in the research libraries aggregated collections. The major differences between the research libraries and the academic libraries' groupings are in the records without call numbers. Most of the measures show a peak in the early 1990s, around 1992 and 1993, and the number of records declines from that point forward. It seems reasonable to assume that acquisitions and cataloging lag combined could be the reason for the decline in the number of current records. To look at the decline and also to further examine the records without usable call numbers, a special analysis was run of those records in the 10% sample which had ISBN numbers. A look at the findings from the ISBN analysis illustrates the downtrend in the number of records in the 1990s.

Figure 1 shows the trendlines for those records with ISBN numbers published within the last decade in the study. The ISBN records are analyzed by categories of English language titles, both with and without call numbers, and all non-English titles, with and without call numbers.

It is easy to see that the category with the lowest number of ISBN records, the bottom line in Figure 1, is that of English language records without usable call numbers. Titles with ISBN numbers are mostly from mainstream publishers and are more likely to be cataloged and classified. Hence, it stands to reason that the category of English language records without usable call numbers would have the lowest number of records with ISBN numbers. In fact, "mainstream" publications can be operationally defined as those titles with ISBN numbers.

FIGURE 1. WorldCat Records with ISBN Numbers, 1990-2000

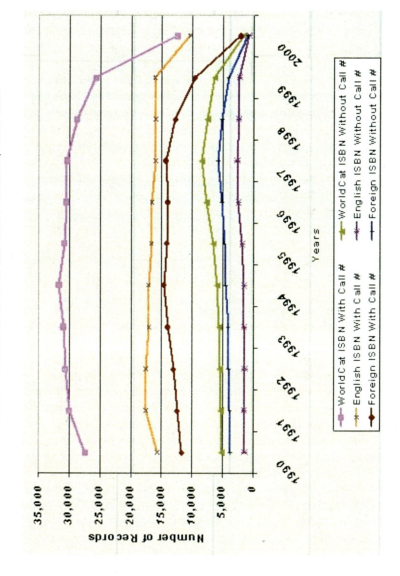

The next line up from the bottom of the graph is that of non-English (foreign language) titles without call numbers. Not all foreign language titles would have a Dewey, LC or NLM call number, so it is understandable that more foreign language than English language titles with ISBN numbers did not have usable call numbers in the records. The third line from the bottom in Figure 1, is a total of the lowest two lines. Thus, those records with ISBN numbers but no usable call number formed the smallest grouping of records with ISBN numbers in the sample.

The top three trendlines in Figure 1 track those bibliographic records with both ISBN numbers and call numbers. The lowest of the three is foreign language records with call numbers. The number of English language titles with both call numbers and ISBN numbers is higher than the number of non-English titles. Again, not a surprising finding. It can be seen that these two lines for English and non-English records with both call numbers and ISBN numbers do not have exactly the same pattern for the imprint years shown. The English language records with call numbers begin to trend downward in 1992, but the decline is slight and the number of records in 1990 and 1998 are very close to the same number. On the other hand, the foreign language records trend upward and remain in the same range until after 1997, but then drop precipitously. From these data, it appears that English language records with call numbers and ISBN numbers are added to the database in a more consistent and timely manner than the other categories of records analyzed. The decline for records with ISBN numbers is most severe in foreign language records with call numbers, and in all records without call numbers. Thus it appears that mainstream publications in English are the only category of materials added to the database in a timely manner. So we can see that the records which have neither ISBN number nor call number, those materials which are more unique and really establish the diversity of the universe of resources, are added in an incremental manner over a longer period of time.

There are some indications from the WorldCat data analysis that the national libraries and large research libraries internationally which began contributing records in the 1990s are responsible, in large part, for the foreign language records in WorldCat in the last decade in the study. From the first Aberdeen Woods conference, it seems safe to conclude that research libraries in the United States now depend more and more upon research libraries abroad to acquire the publications from their respective countries. The WorldCat study results encourage the belief that these same libraries do appear to be contributing the bibliographic records for publications from their own country to the WorldCat database.

The availability of bibliographic records for recent publications, especially for foreign language publications, might possibly look better if vendor records had been included in the WorldCat analysis. In the 1990s, many of the major book vendors in the U.S. and Europe began transmitting their database records to OCLC. These records are not included in the 10% sample because they would not have library location holdings even though they may have call numbers. Because the WorldCat study analyzed the sample records by type of holding library, one of the criteria for inclusion in the study was that the records had to have at least one library location symbol. For resources sharing it is necessary to have library holding symbols attached to the bibliographic record. Thus, the findings from the WorldCat study show the availability of titles for resources sharing.

In order to discuss the "Role of WorldCat in Resources Sharing," the implications of these findings for resources sharing and coordinated cooperative collection development are considered next.

WorldCat AND RESOURCES SHARING

In reviewing the present role of WorldCat and implications for the future, it is useful to give some historical background on OCLC and ILL. BD, that is, Before Databases, the process of interlibrary loan was one of detective work and intuition. It was necessary to verify the existence of an item before one attempted to secure the item from another library. The tools for verifying titles were printed catalogs and bibliographies. These tools were mainly of two types: they were by country from the book trade or they were produced from the cataloging records of libraries. In the United States we had *PTLA*, *Books in Print*, and *Cumulative Book Index* from the book trade and the *Library of Congress Union Catalog*. There were the *British National Bibliography* or *British Library Catalogue; Bibliographie de la France* or the *Bibliothèque Nationale Catalogue*. The national bibliographies of the most industrialized countries often swept theses and dissertations, government documents, reports, and other grey literature into the comprehensive of "everything published in" a particular country. During this period, it was much easier to verify the existence of a title than to actually obtain a copy because not all of the tools had library location symbols. Nonetheless, bibliographic coverage was quite comprehensive, at least for the industrialized countries. But only large research libraries owned the full complement of the bibliographies and catalogs needed for the verification work. This is one example of how, before databases, a scholar could be disadvantaged if he or she were not working in a research institution.

When the OCLC Catalog began in 1971 with a few thousand records, the task was to build up a cataloging database by adding current publications but also records for the existing universe of retrospective publications. After 30 years, the database can now be said to have reached critical mass with respect to the universe of publication. But unlike the printed bibliographies, an item does not appear in WorldCat unless at least one library owns it. With the exception of vendor records, as long as there is a bibliographic record in WorldCat for an item, there is at least one library holding symbol. So in a way, we have the opposite situation of Before Databases (BD). BD we had fairly good bibliographic control of what items were in existence whether or not any library held a copy. Now, to most library staff, if a bibliographic record for an item is not found in WorldCat or other databases, that item, for all library practical purposes, does not exist. We have shifted the responsibility of bibliographic control from comprehensive country-specific printed bibliographies and other tools not originated by libraries to dependency upon libraries to contribute cataloging records. This brings us to the implications of the decline in the number of bibliographic records within the last, most current decade of publication.

For purposes of resources sharing, the retrospective wealth, numbers and variety of resources represented in WorldCat provide the wherewithal for over 8 million ILL transactions annually. For resources sharing purposes, WorldCat is where the action is and this action is increasingly international. OCLC has revolutionized the process of resources sharing, but the same cannot be said for cooperative collection development. Whereas, the great majority of ILL is either for retrospective monographs or journal article photocopies, cooperative collection development centers around current acquisitions. And we have seen that the universe of publication is not fully represented in records for recently published materials. One of the major purposes of cooperative collection development is to ACQUIRE things. Cooperative collection development is focused on the present and what will be acquired for the future. Given the findings from the WorldCat study and other similar bibliometric studies, it seems there are problems for which we need to seek solutions.

The next section contains suggestions for approaches to problems pointed up by the findings of the WorldCat study.

COOPERATIVE COLLECTION DEVELOPMENT

The problem of contributing current bibliographic records to WorldCat was addressed in 1999 when the OCLC Users Council adopted a resolution on "Shared Commitments to the Principles of Cooperation." The thrust of the resolution was to re-affirm and strengthen OCLC's commitment to cooperation and resource sharing. A letter was sent to all member libraries and networks urging compliance with the responsibility to contribute all current, Roman-alphabet cataloging records and holdings to OCLC. The letter stated that "these actions, fully supported by Users Council, are intended to safeguard and strengthen WorldCat as the preeminent, international union catalog and the foundation for global library collaboration."[6] While it has only been three years since the Users Council resolution, as of the time of data extraction in February 2001 for the WorldCat study, it does not appear that there has been an effort on the part of member libraries to increase the availability of bibliographic records for recently published materials.

Indeed, there is evidence to conclude that cataloging has become a diminished activity in research libraries. Wilder's study of "New Hires in Research Libraries," found a 45% decline in the hiring of new catalogers between 1985 and 2000.[7] This finding certainly dovetails with the declines in the cataloging of new publications, especially those without ISBN numbers, found in the WorldCat study.

The findings of the WorldCat study indicate that current imprints with ISBN numbers are not where the problem lies in the addition of records for recently published titles. The drop in the number of records for recently published titles may be as much a problem of becoming aware of the existence of those titles as of timely cataloging. This is the old chicken and egg syndrome. How do we find out about the existence of publications? We check WorldCat, vendor databases and other electronic indexes and databases. But how do records for publications get in the database? This points up how dependent we are upon the electronic bibliographic databases. While there was a drastic decline in the hiring of catalogers, there was an encouraging 61% increase in the hiring of subject specialists, leading one to hope that there are professionals to hunt for appropriate titles in addition to the obvious ones with ISBN numbers.[8]

Suggestion Number One

Cooperative collection development agreements should have the responsibility for timely cataloging and classifying of materials as well as the acquisition of them.

It is pretty useless to resources sharing partners for a library to claim to have the definitive collection of materials in a certain subject area if the bibliographic records to identify the items in those collections do not exist. Acquisitions is only the first step in cooperative collection development. Bibliographic control is the other half of the equation. Perhaps not enough attention has been paid to the supplying of bibliographic records as a corollary of cooperative collection development agreements.

Suggestion Number Two

Creation of incentives for cataloging current materials.

When OCLC was first founded, a great deal of attention was paid to building up the database. Policies were set to give incentives for adding bibliographic records for retrospective resources Now perhaps incentives are needed to both acquire current materials *without ISBN* numbers and catalog and classify those items. Maybe adding a record for a current item without an ISBN number could be free? Could it actually become profitable to add records for certain kinds of materials? But only if added, say, within two years of publication date. Would it be possible to create a competitive mentality whereby instead of waiting for a record to show up in the database, librarians actually would vie to be the first to enter a record?

In 2001 at the ALA Annual conference in San Francisco Phyllis Spies, Vice President, Worldwide Library Services for OCLC, gave a presentation entitled, "Key Barriers to International Resource Sharing and OCLC Actions to Help Remove Them." One of those barriers was described as the "lack of a critical mass of online metadata for the world's libraries," and one of the solutions to overcoming that barrier was the suggestion to provide "contribution" credits to encourage shared cataloging on OCLC. Other suggestions were to load more non-U.S. library catalogs into WorldCat and to link WorldCat to more country/region based union catalogs.

The point here is that in spite of all these efforts, it appears that only records for mainstream publications are appearing in WorldCat within the most current five years. Perhaps one of the problems is that only these materials are being acquired on a current basis. It may be that more attention needs to be focused on the timely identification and acquisition of local materials and other publications which enrich the diversity of bibliographic databases.

Suggestion Number Three

Can database scans be run for records in WorldCat without library holdings to identify titles still in need of an owner?

The bibliographic records contributed by vendors and other pre-publication cataloging might be useful in cooperative collection development for identifying titles no library owns. In other words to get maximum benefit from the vendor contributed records it would be useful to know, say, three years after publication date, those records still without at least one library holding symbol, that is, those records which have not been converted into real bibliographic records because no library owns the title. This would be a measurement of what is not being purchased. Creating lists of this type might be a real challenge for cooperative collection development arrangements because those titles not owned would become . . . whose responsibility?

These suggestions are made to encourage the acquisition, cataloging, and classifying of recently published materials, with an emphasis on titles which are not mainstream publications that will add to the variety of resources represented in WorldCat. There are other ways in which the records in WorldCat can be utilized in resources sharing and cooperative collection development. One of these avenues is in the provision of data for measuring the impact or success of consortial agreements.

CRL WORKING GROUPS

Several working groups were formed out of the first CRL Aberdeen Woods conference in 1999. One of these is the CRL/Big Twelve Plus Working Group for Quantitative Evaluation of Cooperative Collection Development Projects. The measures drafted by this group include a number of performance measures for which the data need to be produced from library systems management reports, consortial data reports, or databases such as WorldCat. The point is to create standardized measures and to monitor changes in those measures over time. Success can only be judged in improvements in the number and variety of resources being provided to users. Routine management reports can be designed to provide data for those measures which track the diversity of resources, currency of resources, retrospective depth of resources, etc.

A few of these measures suggested by the CRL/Big Twelve Plus Working Group for Quantitative Evaluation of Cooperative Collection Development Projects are:

- The number of non-serial and serial titles by subject and time period.
- The number of unique titles by subject and time period.

- The mean number of holding libraries per title (on the average, how many libraries in the consortia own each title).
- The median age of collections by subject.

The OCLC iCAS product either already provides the means to assess consortial progress or could be adapted to provide the measures from WorldCat data. There have been several state assessment projects conducted utilizing the iCAS product. It is also being used abroad. For example, CURL (the Consortium of University Research Libraries in the British Isles) began a collection analysis project using the iCAS software in June 2001. Besides using the product within a consortium, the possibility also exists of comparing the aggregated holdings of different consortia across standardized measures.

There are now a number of library systems that have incorporated such measures as median age or number of unique titles into the system management reports. Consortial databases have also been programmed to provide the number of libraries owning each title and identifying unique titles. If we had a sufficient number of consortia reporting standardized measures, these measures could become benchmarks for libraries and consortia to utilize in collection comparisons.

Up to this point, the annual report statistics from OCLC have not focused on providing data to assist in cooperative collection development, but this could be done. The International Consortium of Library Consortia (ICOLC) could adopt measures and work with the bibliographic utilities to provide these annually as benchmarks. IFLA has for many years had a goal of universal availability of publications. It now seems possible to attain this goal with international databases and international agreements.

CONCLUSION

In an article on the international growth of OCLC in 1998, Phyllis Spies, stated, "OCLC offers the opportunity to facilitate the identification and location of materials on a global basis. OCLC and its member libraries are building the global information infrastructure. This collaborative effort allows people around the world to gain access to the rich scholarly resources of libraries that heretofore may have been inaccessible due to the lack of automation and/or isolation of a country. In the 21st century, OCLC and its member libraries have the opportunity to achieve the long established library goals of universal bibliographic control and universal access to publications."[9] WorldCAT as the preeminent international bibliographic database has a role to play in providing the means for formulating cooperative agreements in this global effort.

OCLC has continued to work with libraries to load national collections into WorldCat. The list of these libraries is becoming very long and the international representation in WorldCat continues to grow. The number of international book vendors and publishers contributing records to WorldCat also continues to grow.

It is the responsibility of the OCLC membership and those who wish to engage in cooperative collection development to ensure that the international universe of publication is represented in WorldCat.

NOTES

1. *Library Trends* 45 (Winter 1997).

2. *Collection Management for the 21st Century*, ed. G.E. Gorman and Ruth H. Miller. Westport, CT: Greenwood Press, 1997.

3. *Cooperative Collection Development: Significant Trends and Issues*, ed. Donald B. Simpson. New York: The Haworth Press, Inc., 1998.

4. *Creating New Strategies for Cooperative Collection Development*, ed. Milton T. Wolf and Marjorie E. Bloss. New York: The Haworth Press, Inc., 2000.

5. Perrault, Anna H. "Global Collective Resources: A Study of the Monographic Bibliographic Records in WorldCat," Report of a study conducted under the auspices of an OCLC/ALISE 2001 Research Grant. (http://www.oclc.org/research/reports/perrault/intro.pdf) (http://www.oclc.org/res/).

6. Ibid.

7. Wilder, Stanley J. "New Hires in Research Libraries: Demographic Trends and Hiring Priorities," *ARL Bimonthly Report* 221 (April 2002): 1.

8. Ibid., p. 2.

9. Phyllis B. Spies. "OCLC Worldwide," *OCLC Newsletter* (September/October 1998): 23.

Practical Cooperative Collecting for Consortia: Books-Not-Bought in Ohio

Julia A. Gammon
Michael Zeoli

SUMMARY. One of the essential goals of OhioLINK is to increase the diversity of resources available to member libraries. OhioLINK and YBP Library Services have worked closely together to achieve this goal. In this paper we discuss what has come to be known as the *Not-Bought-In-Ohio Report (NBIO Report)*. This report is in fact a mechanism designed to report in a shared electronic environment which English language monographs have not been purchased by any OhioLINK library and to enable the efficient purchasing of these materials. Beyond presenting observations regarding the contents of the *NBIO Report*, we also discuss the evolution of the *NBIO Report* and the underlying OhioLINK history: we

Julia A. Gammon is Head, Acquisitions Department, University of Akron, University Libraries, Akron, OH 44325-1708 (E-mail: jgammon@uakron.edu). She is also Chair, OhioLINK Collection Building Task Force. Michael Zeoli is Regional Manager, Collection Management and Development Group, YBP Library Services, 999 Maple Street, Contoocook, NH 03229 (E-mail: mzeoli@ybp.com).

The authors would like to express their gratitude to the OhioLINK Collection Building Task Force members, both past and present, who had the vision, and to David Swords, of YPB Library Services, who provided information for the time-line in Appendix 2 and was the inspiration behind this paper.

[Haworth co-indexing entry note]: "Practical Cooperative Collecting for Consortia: Books-Not-Bought in Ohio." Gammon, Julia A., and Michael Zeoli. Co-published simultaneously in *Collection Management* (The Haworth Information Press, an imprint of The Haworth Press, Inc.) Vol. 28, No. 1/2, 2003, pp. 77-105; and: *The New Dynamics and Economics of Cooperative Collection Development* (ed: Edward Shreeves) The Haworth Information Press, an imprint of The Haworth Press, Inc., 2003, pp. 77-105. Single or multiple copies of this article are available for a fee from The Haworth Document Delivery Service [1-800-HAWORTH, 9:00 a.m. - 5:00 p.m. (EST). E-mail address: docdelivery@haworthpress.com].

believe that *getting to* the *NBIO Report* is an important and informative story. An important *leitmotif* in the history of this project has been the value created in the partnership between OhioLINK and YBP Library Services (YBP). *Partnership* in its fullest sense is the *sine qua non* in developing effective systems and practices for the consortial environment. By allying forces, the vendor and consortium obtain a pool of material and intellectual resources, and a sense of common purpose, capable of creating far greater and enduring value than either of the constituents could imagine if left to operate individually. Working together OhioLINK and YBP have been able to inform and enhance each other's practices, strategies and development agendas. *[Article copies available for a fee from The Haworth Document Delivery Service: 1-800-HAWORTH. E-mail address: <docdelivery@ haworthpress.com> Website: <http://www.HaworthPress.com> © 2003 by The Haworth Press, Inc. All rights reserved.]*

KEYWORDS. OhioLINK, YBP Library Services, cooperative collection management, vendor-library partnership, *Not-Bought-In-Ohio-Report*, library consortia, collection assessment

No Library of One Million Volumes can be all BAD

–From a cover, *Antiquarian Bookman*

Have I done something for the common good? Then I share in the benefits. To stay centered on that. Not to give up.

–Marcus Aurelius, *Meditations*. Book 11, 4

INTRODUCTION

In a passage from a paper presented in this forum in 1999, Carol Pitts Diedrichs, Assistant Director for Technical Services and Collections at Ohio State University, foreshadows what has become the subject of our paper. Responding to an article by Edward Shreeves[1] in which he posits the defining of "core" and "peripheral" materials as the "traditional stumbling blocks to successful cooperative collection projects"[2] she writes:

Again, the OhioLINK project flies in the face of this traditional model. These stumbling blocks have been eliminated by jumping forward to skip the process of defining who will collect what, to identifying, instead, what has been missed completely and purchase that material. OhioLINK has not yet taken the step to deal with the issue of purchasing the missing material, but it is easy to imagine that as the next potential step in the process particularly where central funding might be used for that purpose.

We are here to report that Ohio *has* "taken the step to deal with the issue of purchasing the missing material." We will discuss the mechanisms that have grown out of what has come to be known as the *Not-Bought-In-Ohio Report (NBIO Report)* enabling the *sharing* or *distribution*[3] of the contents as well as the efficient purchasing of these materials. Beyond the obligation of presenting our observations regarding the contents of the *NBIO Report*, we would also like to discuss the evolution of the *NBIO Report* and the underlying OhioLINK history as we firmly believe that *getting to* the *NBIO Report* is an important and informative story. This has been a voyage of discovery and much experience has been acquired along the way.

An important *leitmotif* in the history of this project has been the value created in the partnership between OhioLINK and YBP Library Services (YBP). *Partnership* in its fullest sense is the *sine qua non* in developing effective systems and practices for the consortial environment, as we hope will become clear in the following pages. We would also offer this as evidence of a paradigm shift[4] in the library-vendor relationship which, again, "flies in the face" of common belief–held both among vendors and librarians–that in many respects the enterprises of vendors and libraries are at odds with one another (breeding skepticism and suspicion). Dan Halloran, states:[5]

> Consortia participants are unlikely to reduce their total number of book purchases (good news), but there are no operational economies of scale for the book vendor when he enters into a contract with a consortium (bad news). [. . .] So, for the book vendor, the attraction of a consortial contract may be the assurance of a volume of business over some period of time. For the consortium, it's the expectation of standardized discounts (at the most favorable rate) for all members, as well as shared access to purchase information.

The revealed truth beyond speculated "attractions" and "expectations" is that by allying forces the vendor and consortium obtain a pool of material and intellectual resources, and a sense of common purpose, capable of creating far greater and enduring value than either of the constituents could imagine if left to operate individually. Working together OhioLINK and YBP have been able to inform and enhance each other's practices, strategies and development agendas. From YBP's point of view, the attraction and value of this relationship is most successfully measured in terms of the advances in systems development, approval plan strategies, and a host of experimental consortial projects, rather than in mere dollars earned.[6] Among OhioLINK libraries, the value of the relationship with YBP can be measured more successfully in terms of new electronic services (and their ability to inform these), a willing partner in consortial projects, access to the largest approval plan universe of titles available, and excellence in service, rather than simply in terms of discount.

One of the concepts that stands at the base of the OhioLINK consortium mission, and of this project in particular, lies in increasing the diversity of resources available to member libraries. In 1997, following the lead of an often cited report by Anna Perrault[7] which observed that "the core of titles academic research libraries select in common is increasing, resulting in less diversity in title and subject coverage among those libraries," Tom Sanville, Executive Director of OhioLINK, studied the availability of recent imprints requested in Ohio.[8] He discovered that the number of unfilled requests was growing, while contemporaneously the number of duplicate holdings of 5 or more copies of individual titles was also increasing.[9] He presented his findings to the Library Advisory Council (LAC), a committee of Ohio Library Directors responsible for defining and organizing consortial missions for OhioLINK, who attributed this phenomenon to the homogeneity of approval plans. It is hard to support or deny the validity of this common indictment of the lack of "individuality" of approval plans without examining the details of the particular approval plans functioning in the state at the time, but there is good reason to question this assumption based on the results of several recent studies. Studying approval plan overlap among TRLN (Triangle Research Library Network) libraries, Kim Armstrong, Program Officer, Triangle Research Libraries Network, and Bob Nardini, Senior Vice President at YBP, write that:

> The percentage of titles held by only one library, 50% following approval plan shipments, fell to 11% after other types of purchases. Titles held by all three TRLN libraries, 14% due to ap-

proval plan shipments, rose to 64%. The change is most dramatic in F History, where approval plan shipments placed no titles in all three libraries. Yet Table 2 shows that all three libraries in fact acquired 72% of the titles in F, while only 10% were held in the end by just one TRLN library. [. . .] These results run contrary to the opinion held by some librarians, that is, that approval plans homogenize library collections. In the case of the TRLN libraries, the relative uniqueness resulting from approval plan shipments in fact was largely erased by discretionary purchases.[10]

In a study[11] of approval titles purchased among 70 or so libraries in Ohio from YBP during one week of March 1999, we observed that of 726 unique titles, 606 were collected by five or fewer libraries. Just 67 titles sold more than 7 copies, after which the numbers drop sharply ending with 2 titles selling 12 copies each. Unfortunately, these numbers also include purchases made from YBP notification slips and firm orders (not just books shipped directly on approval plans). This raises the tantalizing question of how many of the duplicates resulted from library orders. Though we do not have the answer to this question, it seems clear that whatever problems there may be in collecting duplicates, it is unlikely to be the homogenizing handiwork of approval plans. Also, returning to the ideas of "core" and "peripheral" mentioned at the beginning of our introduction, one can begin to understand, given the relative narrowness of the universe of widely duplicated titles, the difficulty of defining these concepts, across multiple institutions.[12] However this may be, it is true that this common belief in the homogenizing effects of a consortial approval plan served early on to instigate the study of a consortial approval plan in Ohio, and this has led not only to a general accumulation of knowledge and experience, but also to the *Not-Bought-In-Ohio Report* which functions to increase the diversity of titles available in Ohio.

Before we lose the trail of our real quarry, let us take a look now at the genesis of the *NBIO Report*.

OhioLINK AND THE COLLECTION BUILDING TASK FORCE: BACKGROUND HISTORY

In this section we would like to briefly present background information on OhioLINK in order to understand the scale of our undertaking. We would also like to retrace some of the key events leading to the formation of the Collection Building Task Force (CBTF) and, subsequently, birth of the *NBIO Report*. The following description of OhioLINK and additional information is available on the OhioLINK website:[13]

> The Ohio Library and Information Network, OhioLINK, is a consortium of Ohio's college and university libraries and the State Library of Ohio. Serving more than 500,000 students, faculty, and staff at 80 institutions, OhioLINK's membership includes 17 public universities, 23 community/technical colleges, 39 private colleges and the State Library of Ohio. OhioLINK serves faculty, students, staff and other researchers at member institutions via 120 campus-based library systems and networks, and the Internet.
> OhioLINK offers access to more than 31 million library items statewide. To date, the OhioLINK Central catalog contains more than 8 million unique master records from its 80 institutions, encompassing a spectrum of library material including law, medical and special collections. The catalog systems throughout the state provide capacity for more than 4,500 simultaneous users. The OhioLINK central catalog also is available to outside users via the Internet. OhioLINK offers user-initiated, non-mediated online borrowing through its statewide central catalog. Our students and faculty have the ability to electronically request items while searching the OhioLINK central catalog. It also provides a delivery service among member institutions to speed the exchange of library items.

Resource sharing throughout the State of Ohio was the primary goal in the founding of OhioLINK. Having built a strong delivery system for sharing resources, a combined catalog and shared online system, and established a history of cooperation, the critical infrastructure necessary to pursue cooperative collection management had been put in place. Carol Pitts Diedrichs, in the article we cited at the beginning of our paper, presents an excellent in-depth account of the design and implementation of OhioLINK's "consortial approval plan."[14] Based on her article, and the firsthand experience of one of the authors as a member of Collection Building Task Force (CBTF), a summary follows.

As already mentioned, Tom Sanville, Executive Director of OhioLINK, tracking trends in collection building in Ohio, noted that during the mid to late 1990s the collections of OhioLINK member libraries were becoming more homogeneous. Sanville found that there was duplication in recent imprints, that is, 5+ copies of a title were available in the OhioLINK shared catalog at the time of a patron request. Yet, there were requests for other materials that went unfilled; and this number was growing. In 1997, these figures were presented to OhioLINK's Library Advisory Council (LAC), the operational governing body of the consortium composed of library directors, and, upon further discussion and observation, the hypothesis was launched that the increasing rate of duplication was the result of similarity in approval plan profiles (regardless of vendor).

LAC asked the OhioLINK Cooperative Information Resources Committee (CIRM) to charge a task force to investigate the feasibility of a consortial approval plan. In fall 1997, this small task force met with vendors to gain their perspective on the feasibility of such a project. While issues were raised by both vendors and OhioLINK member libraries, none appeared insurmountable. In January 1998, the initial CIRM Approval Plan Task Force membership was expanded and began to work in earnest.

The task force surveyed the libraries to collect information on approval plan expenditures, discounts, vendors, as well as, interest in participation should the idea go forward. Interestingly, in the survey results showed that libraries interested in participating fell into two camps: (1) those who were *willing* to join with no vendor yet selected and, (2) those who would *not* sign on until the vendor was determined. Those who were willing to sign on in good faith, the "risk-takers," became responsible for the design of the Request for Proposals (RFP). In just ten months OhioLINK signed a contract with YBP Library Services[15] on behalf all the libraries, and approval plan profiling began with the University of Akron in 1998. Others followed quickly in succession. As we write, approximately 70 libraries of all sizes and interests across the state have become YBP customers, and nearly as many YBP approval book or slip plans are in place. The importance of this achievement in carrying forward the consortium's mission cannot be underestimated (and, indeed, the consortium will make efforts to defend and increase this level of participation among its members) as we hope will be come clear in the following pages.

At the 2001 OhioLINK summit meeting on collection building came a new charge for the reformed, revised and reconstituted CBTF. The charge includes:

- Actively seek to reduce unnecessary duplication of print materials in order to free funds for increasing the depth and breadth of the OhioLINK collection.
- Increase the involvement in and coordination of local collection development activities.
- Expand the amount spent on cooperative central OhioLINK purchases.

- Expand the central war chest idea in both dollar amount and type of material purchased (move beyond books).
- Explore expanding the book approval plan to other vendors, including those dealing with non-English and non-U.S. imprints.
- Encourage YBP to actively market the statewide approval plan to local institutions as part of a movement to an "all in" approval plan in the future.

One of the first tasks to be initiated this fall was an active marketing plan for "reselling" involvement in the coordination of collecting around the state through a series of regional meetings called the *OhioLINK-YBP Road Show*. The purpose was to educate and re-educate new and old staff on the benefits of collection building across the state through YBP. Demonstrations were offered by Ohio librarians on how YBP services–including approval plans, but also, and importantly, technical services–could be used to greatest effect; these educational presentations will be ongoing.

But let us return to the subject of the *NBIO Report*. Some of the very early ideas that the CBTF discussed were ways to reduce duplication across the state while increasing the diversity of the collection, as we have said. But how does one do this and not give the impression that OhioLINK is telling libraries what to buy? How can the constructive nature of our interest be made clear? One way was to make available information on titles that were not represented in the collections of any library in the state. The CBTF felt that if collection managers in Ohio knew what was *not* being purchased, buying patterns and purchasing decisions could be altered for the benefit of all. We sought answers to the following questions:

- What titles were not being purchased?
- What titles required ILL to find a title from an out-of-state source?
- What titles were heavily represented statewide?
- What titles were frequently unavailable due to high circulation?

One could call this "negative" collection building by finding out what is not there. Finding out what one does not have is relatively easy, but getting to this point is not. Neither is getting beyond this point. These form the interesting chapters surrounding the *Not-Bought-In-Ohio Report*.

DEBUNKING THE MYTH OF THE "SUPRA-PROFILE": COOPERATION AND COORDINATION

Not infrequently (and occasionally, still, even in Ohio), we encounter the belief that OhioLINK and YBP have created a "supra-profile," that is, a monolithic overarching approval plan which responds with a single voice to the needs of the individual member libraries while at the same time efficiently coordinating collecting statewide. Let us debunk the myth and state explicitly that there is no YBP-OhioLINK "supra"-approval plan; references to its existence are greatly exaggerated!

So why not a supra-profile? On the surface, it might seem reasonable to believe that a state with a history of cooperation going back to the early years of the Ohio College Library Center (OCLC) could draw on the collective intelligence of its members to develop guidelines for the writing of a "supra" approval profile designed to determine the locations and to calculate the numbers of many new titles to be distributed in Ohio. In one sense, YBP already does this in its internal purchasing process, which involves ordering a prescribed number of copies of a title from a publisher based on previous approval sales of similar titles from that publisher. For each approval title, YBP has already made an estimate of how many of copies of each title are likely to be sold in Ohio. But not so fast! The road to a statewide approval plan is as difficult as the twelve tasks of Hercules complete with the killing of the man-eating Stymphalian birds (perhaps the vultures at Denison?) and the cleaning of the Augean stables.

Complexity

The first obstacle in attempting to design a supra-profile is simply one of scale for both the library and the vendor. The number of participating institutions (80 at last count), multiplied by the number of participating collection managers, divided by the geographical boundaries of a large midwestern state present a significant level of complexity. Then take these simultaneously active and geographically distributed participants and create a coherent system by which they can each interact with some portion of the number of new monographs being profiled by YBP's approval program each year (56,000 new titles in 2001-2002), and arrive at decisions that benefit both their individual libraries and the OhioLINK collective.

Modularity

Too often these cooperative efforts bog down under the overwhelming weight of complexity. We have met with some preliminary success in breaking the complexity problem down into "modular" units by limiting the scope of cooperative collecting projects. OhioLINK's committees and members are pursuing multi-campus coordination of collecting in specific subject areas. The CONSORT libraries (The College of Wooster, Denison University, Kenyon College, Ohio Wesleyan University), with the absence of Oberlin College, have been conducting a number of experiments in cooperative collection development over the past several years and have had interesting results and made good progress. The collecting of all playscripts among the group is one successful project. They have also investigated Philosophy and Asian Studies. Attempts have been made to coordinate the engineering profiles at Wright State University, Ohio State University, and the University of Toledo. A religion group has recently met to coordinate purchases in the southern part of the state. The assignment of purchasing music scores by specific composers is carried out by one group of libraries. Most recently, another task force called the Working Group on Subject Groups is moving towards integrating the collecting by subject on multiple campuses. There is also interest in coordinating the purchasing of continuation/standing order titles across the state through YBP. Not limited to just print materials, another task force is looking at the purchase of digital video materials and other audiovisual materials. By breaking cooperative collecting initiatives into coherent "modular" units, it is easier to reach a practical coordination of collecting that truly does reduce duplication and extend the combined budgets of the participants to allow for the coverage of titles that would otherwise be unlikely to be represented in their collections.[16] We can imagine that the success of these cooperative efforts, eventually reaching an optimum density within the state, might be measured in terms of sufficient but not excessive duplication, the satisfaction of 99% of ILL (both traditional and patron-initiated borrowing) requests from within the state, and full coverage of all approval plan titles with academic merit.

Technology

OhioLINK had reached a certain level of maturity in terms of technological and human infrastructure at the point it went looking for a vendor.[17] Reviewing the responses to the RFP, OhioLINK discovered that very few vendors had developed ways to share information across a group of users in a real time. Nor had vendors developed the technological and human infrastructure to work with large consortia. The need for a vendor to develop new technology in support of OhioLINK initiatives was recognized early on as essential in a cooperative venture of this scale. Whoever was selected as the vendor of choice for OhioLINK would be faced with a steep technology development agenda. Success would require speed, and greatly improved access to information and reporting mechanisms.

YBP has made significant efforts to develop technology in support of OhioLINK cooperative collection development initiatives and has benefited from its partnership with OhioLINK as a result. One of the earliest developments was the "GobiTween" screen. When a library calls up an individual title in GOBI, YBP's interactive online utility for acquisitions and collection development, the user is presented not only with the local history for that title at that institution, but also with the history of that title among Ohio libraries represented in YBP's database. An Ohio library can see who else has received a notification slip, which libraries received the book directly on approval or have placed an order, which libraries may have received the title as part of a standing order, and which libraries may have blocked or returned the book. This tool is used most often by selectors reviewing their weekly approval notification slips, but has also proven useful to acquisitions, for example in avoiding duplication.

GobiTween was developed to support Ohio's expressed intention of trying to limit the number of copies of an individual title purchased in the state, thereby freeing up funds with which to purchase less well represented titles. This has worked to some extent; however, in some instances, the fact that one institution has thought a book good enough to add to its collection, has functioned to encourage other libraries to purchase the title as well, thereby defeating to some degree one of the original intentions of GobiTween.

Similarly, YBP developed the ability to print numbers on each paper notification slip reflecting how many books and how many notification slips were sent to Ohio libraries via approval plans for that particular title (a function which has been replicated electronically in GOBI Edition 2). Again, the goal was to support cooperative collecting efforts in the state by offering data to help selectors determine when "enough" copies of a given title may have been purchased in the state, so that the funds could be directed towards more "exotic" titles. Since this tool does not list the individual names of institutions receiving the book, the anxiety of influence is greatly reduced, and so may function better in leading to the acquisition of fewer duplicate copies.

Finally, GOBI Edition 2 (GE2), released late in 2002, represents an enormous leap forward in online vendor interfaces. For the purpose of this article we want to point out the fact that GE2 incorporates many features specifically designed to facilitate consortial initiatives (some of these will be discussed in the section on the *Not-Bought-In-Ohio Report*). The GE2 development team traveled around the United States in order to involve libraries in the design process. YBP systems developers spent a week at various libraries across Ohio seeking information on use and compiling a "wish list." Some time after this visit, a GOBI Development Agenda was submitted for consideration by librarians in Ohio. GE2 alpha and beta testing has since been conducted in the state. Ohio has been and continues to be a close partner to YBP as new components of GE2 are designed and implemented.

As OhioLINK libraries came onboard, their individual YBP approval plan profiles were posted to the OhioLINK website for the purpose of sharing and to promote cooperative collection management across the state. As the number of profiles multiplied, the task of comparison became very complicated. YBP and Ohio have been experimenting (in some of the initiatives discussed in the previous section) with a new profile format that allows the side-by-side comparison of multiple profiles.[18] This tool, developed for Ohio, has applications in any environment in which multiple profiles exist, even on a single campus.

Financial Resources: Renewable?

One can imagine the development cost of the technology described in the previous section as well as the costs to continuously maintain and update that technology. In the case of YBP, how can this development be sustained? YBP's investment in technology has enabled the company to offer innovative services to other customers, thereby providing it with a significant competitive edge in the marketplace. It has also positioned the company well as a prospective partner for innovative projects.

With current trends in state budget-cutting for education, where will OhioLINK find the funds to develop and maintain the technology that has served it so well? While the consortial discount was not the basis for selecting a vendor, the ability for all libraries, large, small, medium-sized, and specialized, to benefit is worth noting. Declining budgets and serial pricing issues stress purchasing power even more. Most OhioLINK libraries have been able to improve their buying clout as a result of the OhioLINK-YBP contract by adjusting workflows to incorporate continuations coverage with approval plans, and by increasing efficiency through electronic services such as GobiTween, GobiSelect (a process of downloading bibliographic records to the local system for duplication control and ordering), PromptCat, and physical processing.

Another issue in the coordination of approval plans is determining the financial burden each participating library must bear. For OhioLINK, the financial commitment rests most heavily with individual libraries who support the travel expenses and staff time to attend meetings to plan and learn about new initiatives. New OhioLINK procedures require that libraries plan, adjust and adapt workflows to take advantage of new services. Change always requires an investment in people and training; however, we feel strongly that the development of a system like OhioLINK *requires* that changes in individual member library procedures and workflows be made.

Currently, cooperative collection management initiatives are directed by committee or task force, a group of hardworking professionals who all have other full-time jobs. Although progress has been steady in working collaboratively on collection development, it has not always been as quick as we would have liked. Recognizing the need for a full-time person devoted to coordinating collection building across the state, the CBTF proposed the funding of a position of coordinator whose principal charge would be to advance two priorities stated in OhioLINK's strategic plan:

- Expand resource sharing of the collections
- Maximize the impact of cooperation on our purchasing power to expand information access.

Due to the state budget woes, however, the position has not been funded. The CONSORT libraries won a grant to hire a manager for their cooperative collecting project. This has made a clear difference in the ability of these libraries to move forward with experimental cooperative projects, some of which we have already mentioned. Perhaps this can be a model for future cooperative efforts.

From the vendor side, the Ohio experience has clearly demonstrated the importance of having a dedicated staff to develop and manage the unique complexities of cooperative ventures. Ohio is labor-intensive, however, it affords YBP the opportunity to work intimately with a very large academic library system, from which it draws enormous and incomparable experience with complex library systems and development initiatives.

Political Turf

G. Edward Evans[19] states that the biggest barrier to cooperative collection building is people and that the planners of a program must overcome a variety of psychological barriers:

- Fear of change
- Loss of autonomy
- Passive resistance, inertia and indifference
- Questioning the quality or reliability of one or more of the proposed partners.

There are two important issues here: "Who gets to buy and keep stuff?" and "We don't want OhioLINK to decide what we need." Knowing that the words "cooperative collection management" can carry a politically ticklish load, the task force was anxious to avoid misunderstandings surrounding the intent of a statewide approval program. The task force drafted two simple documents outlining what the intentions were of the consortial approval plan project, and what they were not (see Appendix 1). These documents, along with meetings and an open discussion via a listserv, were used with some success in preventing inevitable misperceptions.

"Selling" a consortial approval plan on campus can be a very difficult business, but it is a part of the mandate that OhioLINK has assigned itself. Strong leadership by librarians on the various campuses shows faculty and students the value of having a strong collection across the state. In the case of the CONSORT libraries, the fact that cooperation allows them to have a full representation of current publishing in playscripts, and greater depth in the Asian studies collection is a point that the library director can take to the college administration to seek more funds. It is also an attribute that will make the institution more attractive to prospective faculty, and will certainly please current faculty as well. The political difficulties destructive to the cooperative effort will creep in. For example, if a group of libraries were to decide that a single copy rather than 3 of the expensive and generally low-circulating *Lecture Notes in Mathematics* (Springer-Verlag) was sufficient among them, there might well be some unhappiness in the Math departments of the institutions that would cease purchasing this expensive series. However, by agreeing to buy just one copy of an expensive title in a prolific series with low circulation, the libraries are allowed to collect a greater number of unique titles and thereby enrich the breadth of the collection.

Similarly, there is sometimes a suspicion that since this effort is apparently counterproductive to the vendor, who would prefer to sell 3 copies of the Springer-Verlag title, YBP would not be anxious to support cooperative efforts. The truth requires us to understand that ultimately YBP's existence will depend not on selling 3 copies rather than 1 of an expensive title in Ohio, but rather on developing the ability to support the libraries in achieving their goals and, thereby earning a greater share of their business.

Education and Re-Education

Continuing education and communication of ideas, procedures and information is imperative to the success of the OhioLINK mission. Over time, with staff turnover and the foibles of human memory, the CBTF has found that continuous education and re-education is needed. It is enough to recall that some librarians, even in Ohio, believe that it is OhioLINK's goal to develop a supra-profile that will strip them of their collecting rights and duties. It is also important to keep pace with changes in technology, particularly the technology that the vendor is continuously developing to make all aspects of the vendor-library (-consortium) relationship(s) more effective. There are also a great many efficiencies that can be enjoyed in Ohio because all the libraries use Innovative Interfaces and many use YBP as their primary vendor. Efficiencies cannot be realized in the libraries and new services will be doomed to failure if the staff is resistant to change, and ultimately these individual failures affect achievements of the consortium. It is critical that OhioLINK and YBP keep people informed and educated.

We would conclude this section on cooperation and coordination with some deadly accurate "bullets" to consider when establishing a resource-sharing program:[20]

- Avoid thinking of the cooperative as "supplementary" and an "add-on"; instead, consider it as something it is impossible to do without.
- Have planners spend time working out operational details.
- Realize that the system *should* cause major operational changes in the member libraries.
- Avoid thinking of the system as providing the library with something for nothing.
- Have the cooperative's funding and operations handled by an independent agency.

- Realize that it takes time; careful, complete communication; and one or two persons who take on the leadership role with patient understanding for such a project to succeed.
- *Remember that above all else, forming a cooperative is a political process.*[21]

DEVELOPMENT OF THE NOT-BOUGHT-IN-OHIO REPORT

Since the inception of our partnership cooperative collection development has been one of a core group of projects.[22] As discussed, OhioLINK and YBP have explored many avenues in attempting to coordinate the acquisition of English language monographs across Ohio. The undertaking has been fraught with difficulties, and, as will be the case in exploration, many of the avenues have proven blind alleys. However, these experiences have served to inform successive efforts, providing an ever stronger platform from which to launch new initiatives. Generally speaking, our pursuits in cooperative collection development can be grouped under two rubrics: "approval plan coordination" and "post-approval plan coordination." Our purpose here is to discuss the second rubric, "post-approval plan coordination." We will point out that the fundamental difference between the two methods is that the first attempts to capture titles via approval plans *as they are published and become available*, while the second method is *retrospective* in nature. The "post-approval plan coordination" of collecting treats titles well after they were published and have been available, and, therefore, does not involve approval plan coordination in any way. We have come to call the form that this process has taken the *Not-Bought-In-Ohio Report (NBIO Report)* or simply the *Not-Bought* report.

The process of setting up individual approval plans at libraries across Ohio required much time and energy both for the libraries and for YBP. It was only after many of the approval plans had been set up and gone through an initial period of trial and revision that resources could be brought to bear, in a concentrated fashion, on the possibilities of cooperative collection development within the essentially monographic relationship established between OhioLINK and YBP. By this time, we had begun to accumulate a substantial quantity of data regarding purchasing from YBP in Ohio. An obvious first step in approaching cooperative collecting was to examine this purchasing history. Many data were collected and studied to answer questions such as: "How many copies of a title were purchased in Ohio?" "How many titles sold just one copy?" but the question that lies at the base of this paper was: "How many titles were not purchased at all in Ohio?" Rather than discuss how many duplicate copies of books were being purchased in Ohio, the CBTF felt that if collection managers in Ohio knew what was not being purchased–certainly a more positive approach–buying patterns and purchasing decisions could be altered. Since one of the mandates of OhioLINK is to enrich the availability of information in Ohio, the answer to our question also represents the "scope of the problem" identifying gaps in the web of monograph collecting across Ohio. The answer to this question has born fruit immediately in terms of expanding the number of unique titles available in Ohio. Some of the reasons for this success are obvious, while others are more subtle; all are worthy of discussion.

Owing to the success of the OhioLINK patron initiated resource-sharing option which quickly moves materials around the state to fill requests in 24-48 hours, traditional interlibrary loan (ILL) requests have dropped significantly. During the 2001-2002 fiscal year OhioLINK libraries requested over 650,000 items held by member libraries and the numbers continue to increase yearly (does not include periodical requests). To put this number in perspective, the University of Akron (UA) requested 28,558 items from other OhioLINK institutions during 2001-2002, and lent 41,463 items to other OhioLINK libraries making the UA a net lender. During that same period, UA's traditional ILL requests for books numbered only 816 items–meaning only 816 items were not available in the state, and therefore needed to be borrowed from out of state. Almost 3% of the total items not available in the state for UA library patrons could have been provided from within state had the *Not-Bought-In-Ohio* project been implemented. When this figure is multiplied by the number of academic libraries across the state one begins to see the scope of the problem.

Scope of the Problem

How many titles recognized in the YBP approval universe were going uncollected in Ohio? Before a routine profile revision visit, YBP will often compare YBP profiled titles with those actually purchased by a library. This comparison is often useful to see where an approval plan may suffer important lapses, and more generally, to use as a tool during the profile revision process. To collect and study this data for 70 or 80 libraries across the state, many of which have multiple approval plan accounts and still more firm order and standing order accounts, represents a gigantic leap in complexity both in terms of the simple mechanics of gathering data, as well as in the ability to uncover meaningful patterns in the results. And, of course, all this occurs well before beginning to consider how to act on the results, which presents us with yet another hurdle.

Lacking a clear idea of how the results might look, it was easy to gain agreement on the mechanics of the project.[23] We would simply gather a file of all approval titles profiled by YBP in the course of a single month, and match these against the Ohio order history in the YBP database. We left a 3-month gap between the time we ran our report gathering data on Ohio purchasing and the time the titles were actually profiled in order to allow adequate time for collection managers to have made decisions regarding titles for which they had received approval notification slips.

NBIO Reports: *Our Findings*

YBP typically profiled just over 1,000 unique titles per week for treatment on its approval plans at the time the project began. In the initial report, we discovered that Ohio was being *notified* of nearly every title that YBP profiled, that is, at least an approval notification slip or a book had been sent to some OhioLINK library. Of the 4,666 books (this number includes 452 alternate editions) profiled by YBP in January of 2000, the first month chosen for the *Not-Bought* report, Ohio libraries did not purchase 1,047 (including alternate editions; 1,028 titles were unique) from YBP. We will use this report as a case study.

In order to quickly separate the wheat from the chaff, we sorted the list of titles by the readership level. We suspected that the "popular" level titles ("POP," defined as "materials intended for casual reading or individual self-help or instruction as opposed to academic or professional study") would represent the largest portion of the un-purchased titles given the nature of OhioLINK. At first glance, the result did not seem to confirm our suspicions as the numbers of titles not purchased at each readership level were quite similar as can be seen in the table below. However, on closer inspection, it is evident that *as a percentage* of the total number of items profiled at that level, far fewer POP level materials were collected in Ohio (57% of these titles were not bought) than titles profiled at the other levels. The fact that far fewer titles are profiled at the POP level owes generally to the market that YBP serves. We suspected that the Professional level materials ("PROF," defined as "practical guidebooks written for working professionals in fields such as Education, Business, Law, Medicine, Nursing, or Social Work," and also "as works of extreme technical difficulty or treating such esoteric subjects as to interest only well-trained specialists in the field") might also be somewhat well represented among the materials not purchased for similar reasons. One reason for this is that many of the PROF level materials are collected by special and professional libraries (e.g., Law and Medicine), which often use specialized vendors. Once again the data supported our expectation: 35.4% of the profiled titles were not purchased.[24]

Readership Level	# Titles Profiled (including alternate editions)	% of Total	# Unique Titles Profiled	% Unique Titles	# Not Bought (Unique)	% of Not Bought	% of Unique Titles Profiled, Not Bought
POP	497	10.65	493	99.20	282	27.4	57
PROF	663	14.2	643	97	228	22.2	35.4
GEN-AC	1269	27.2	1163	91.65	219	21.3	18.8
ADV-AC	2237	47.9	1915	85.6	299	29.1	15.6
Total	4666		4214	Avg. 90.3	1028		24.4

The composition of the POP category included 33 *Complete Idiot's Guides*, 14 *Fodor's travel guides*, 13 *Karen Brown guides*, 12 *SAM'S Teach Yourself* books, and 10 *IDG Books for Dummies*. A full third of the POP books not purchased can be accounted for in these series or among the publishers of these types of guides (other examples of well represented publishers were QUE, Barron's, Frommers, CityPack). Many of these materials, and particularly the computer guidebooks, are best presented in electronic formats as they are often reference works to be consulted rather than read cover-to-cover. They also go out-of-date quickly (not to mention the problem of theft). POP level materials not purchased are also commonly found classed in GV (Recreation. Leisure), HQ (Family. Marriage. Women), and in PR and PS (English and American literature respectively, in which genre literature and first novels constitute a large body of material). These numbers reveal the generally shared underlying belief among collection managers that there is no need to spend additional funds, staff time, and space to collect these materials. Interestingly, there has been debate over the need to continue to include the POP level in the *NBIO Report*. One side has argued that the file best serves busy librarians by focusing as much as possible on materials likely to be of interest, which does not often include POP level titles that have not already found reason to be purchased. The other side, however, believes that the number of titles in the file is small enough, especially considering that collection managers need only consult their own subject areas of the *NBIO* file, that there is no harm in having a full showing of titles not bought. Owing to the diversity of opinion within the Collection Building Task Force (reflecting that among OhioLINK libraries), it has been agreed that the POP category will remain in the report.

At the Advanced Academic ("ADV-AC") level, more than half of the 299 un-purchased titles cost over $100. Just under half of the titles at the Professional level were over $100. None of the POP titles and just 21 of the 1,163 General Academic titles cost more than $100. Generally, libraries will set $100 as the approval plan price ceiling, meaning that for titles above this ceiling notification slips are sent in lieu of the book. The price ceiling can be–and often is–adjusted within a profile to reflect the relative costs of titles in specific subject areas. Our findings here have indicated that perhaps more use of this flexibility should be employed in approval plan profiles.

As for publishers, Routledge was well represented with 117 titles remaining un-purchased (almost all expensive Kegan Paul reprints in psychology). Prentice Hall had 87 unsold titles. There were 35 unsold titles from Springer-Verlag (often the *Lecture notes in . . .* series), 31 from Lippincott, Williams, & Wilkins, and 29 from McGraw-Hill. W. B. Saunders, the American Mathematical Society, Kluwer, and Zondervan were also well represented. Again, there are no real surprises here. The number of Routledge titles reflects the skepticism commonly expressed towards this publisher (particularly regarding the price differential between paper and cloth editions). The publishers of "PROF" materials are also well represented for reasons already discussed. Zondervan is a strong participant in the POP category.

At the beginning of this section, we noted that at least a notification slip had been sent to some library in Ohio for nearly every title that YBP profiled. There were just 16 titles for which no books or no notification slips were sent anywhere in Ohio, and for which YBP received no orders from any OhioLINK library. Of these, significantly, 12 were from the UK and had no U.S. editions. All 12 had been reviewed in the *Times Literary Supplement* and *each was an important book* (one was the Whitbread biography of the year). At that time, no Ohio library used YBP's UK approval services, nor did any use YBP's *Times Literary Supplement* approval plan service (available on U.S. approval plans). The CBTF has recognized that the integration of Lindsay & Howes (YBP's UK subsidiary) approval plans (as well as firm order and standing order accounts) is an important step in carrying forward their efforts in coordinating collection development.

A partial manual review of the first *NBIO* file by simple ISBN at the University of Cincinnati[25] revealed that at the POP level about 20% of the titles were in fact in the OhioLINK shared database; at the PROF level, 45% were in the database; 36% of the ADV-AC titles were present; and 25% percent of the GEN-AC titles were also accounted for. When these titles were further reviewed for alternate editions the percentages of titles available in Ohio increased as would be expected. It was clear that these numbers reflected purchases from other vendors, gifts, orders placed after the *NBIO Report* had been completed, and standing orders (with other vendors). Since this review was not comprehensive, these figures did not serve as an exact measure, but rather as a strong indication that (1) Ohio was in fact doing a better job of collecting than YBP's numbers demonstrate, and (2) that the data necessary for analysis was scattered and efforts needed to be made for its unification.

This review by the University of Cincinnati underlined the importance of finding a method of efficiently removing those titles already owned in Ohio from the *NBIO* file before releasing the file to collection managers for purchasing. OhioLINK has developed a method of matching the YBP *NBIO* file against the shared OhioLINK database in order to remove the duplicates. This process served to remove an average of 250-350 titles that had been acquired from sources other than YBP from the *NBIO* file. As would be expected, these duplicates were located principally among the ADV-AC level materials, followed by the GEN-AC level, and to a much lesser degree among PROF level materials. There were few if any duplicates ever found at the Popular level (supporting the findings from YBP purchase data discussed above, that POP materials not already purchased were unlikely to be purchased).

The number of duplicates found, however, in matching the *NBIO Report* against the OhioLINK shared catalogue was cause for an important decision regarding the design of data collection. The first report had allowed for a 3-month period between the time of YBP profiling and the time of the report. A significant number of titles that had appeared as "not ordered" at the time the report was generated, were in fact ordered shortly thereafter–but still before the report had been made available in Ohio. It was decided, therefore, to allow a 6-month lapse from the date of profiling to the running of the report. This would allow those selectors who held notification slips "in reserve" ample time to make decisions (and for review sources to exert their influence on ordering), and so reduce the number of *NBIO* titles. Allowing more time for titles ordered in Ohio to be accounted for in YBP's database would also serve to reduce the number of titles in the *NBIO Report* that would match holdings in the OhioLINK shared catalog.

The Next Hurdle: The Mechanics of Buying

The report itself has been a tremendous success from the outset, but the question of how to enable a process of selection and acquisition has presented a host of problems. The CBTF needed to insure that the *NBIO* titles would be reviewed, and that the desirable ones would be "adopted" by some Ohio library, and no longer "orphans" (as the task force liked to call them)–although it was clear that some of these books could remain orphans as far as they were concerned!

The mechanics of generating the *NBIO* file of titles became routine. Rather than immediately making the *NBIO* list available publicly to OhioLINK libraries, the CBTF assumed responsibility for experimenting with various review and purchasing processes. As in the case of other cooperative collecting efforts, there were the usual obstacles to be overcome. On a very basic level, there was the problem of facilitating the ordering process, while at the same time safeguarding against duplication. First, the idea of posting the list on the OhioLINK website was discussed, but no satisfactory method of interacting with the list could be found. Then there was the question of whether or not the book should be removed from the list once it was purchased? Could selectors do this at the point of purchase? Would duplication occur? Would it be undesirable? How would we encourage busy collection managers to visit the website regularly and review this lists considering all the other responsibilities with which they are burdened?

The CBTF decided that the *NBIO* list should be produced as a packet of standard YBP yellow notification slips (when all else fails, produce more paper!). The idea was to pass these from library to library, removing notification slips for ordering, solving the problem of duplication and allowing participating libraries to integrate purchasing into their regular workflow. This method also allowed the titles to be separated and sent to libraries in different ways (by subject, by price, by dollar amounts committed to the project, etc.). Even with a small group of libraries participating, this method bogged down and proved unreliable; the process was slow and the slips would inevitably lose their way (or lose steam along the way).

It was decided to post the list in GOBI, YBP's online acquisitions and collection development database. YBP created a single "OhioLINK" in GOBI; the intent was to assign each participating library a sub-account[26] on which to select and order. The idea offered clear advantages over earlier ideas (especially in that it allowed the full integration of this workflow into that used in individual libraries):

- It allowed libraries across the state to access the list simultaneously; titles could be searched by desired criteria (LC class, publisher, series, etc.);
- Titles could be ordered directly via GOBI or selected, downloaded to the local system (also in "batch mode"), and ordered via the Innovative Interfaces system;
- The library's regular technical service specifications such as book processing, cataloging and other outsourcing options with YBP could be observed for these purchases;
- Management reports available to all GOBI users would function fully for this special account, thereby enabling a wide variety of reports (including expenditure reports) to be used to analyze activity at any time by any participating library;
- Titles purchased would also become visible to all OhioLINK libraries in the consortial history screen ("GobiTween").

But best of all, as the titles were ordered, they would disappear automatically from the online list, thereby removing the issue of duplication.

This method also pushed the question of responsibility for purchasing a step further; if the list were opened up to all libraries in Ohio, many titles could simply be acquired as desired. After a period of "open purchasing," it would be a relatively small step to arrive at a design assigning responsibility for the "clean up" of titles that had still not been purchased. A report on this "relatively small step" will have to wait as, alas, we have not yet been able to take it.

A question developed regarding the security of each sub-account. What would protect one library from inadvertently placing orders on an incorrect account? Might a collection manager from the Bowling Green State University mistakenly purchase an *NBIO* title on Ohio University's sub-account? Some felt the risk would be too great and the potential consequences grave as the process was opened to libraries across the state. Here, one might recall G. Edward Evans indicating "Questioning the quality or reliability of one or more of the proposed partners" as psychological barrier to cooperative ventures; however, given the intended scale of this project, the possibility of error seems a reasonable cause for concern.

The original GOBI was unable to offer a solution to this concern as the assignment of passwords was fixed at the *general account* level rather than at the *sub-account* level. Even weighing all of the benefits of the GOBI method, the issue of security nevertheless brought the project to its knees. Fortunately, the cavalry is charging in from over the hill to save the day in the form of GOBI Edition 2 (GE2), which permits individual access to be controlled at the *sub-account* level, thereby providing the desired level of security. Beyond resolving the issue of security, GE2 will allow the *NBIO* to be run and managed directly and on-demand by the end users, i.e., the participating libraries.

CONCLUSION

Not long ago, a vendor who was visiting the University of Akron library mentioned that he had recently been in Louisiana and was asked by one librarian during a library visit if she could "have one of those OhioLINK things," meaning the consortial approval plan. Unfortunately, distressed at missing a possible sale, he had to tell the librarian he was fresh out of them! It wasn't a package deal he could pull off the shelf.

Thinking about his remark, after the vendor left my library, I mused to myself, wondering how would a vendor reconstruct an OhioLINK in another place? What would it take? The vendor would need to find a geographic area that was not more than a two hour drive for anyone to a shared meeting site, a city large enough to have good ethnic restaurants for catering working lunches at those meetings, and a firm policy that no meeting should last past three o'clock to beat the rush hour traffic out of town. After these tactical needs have been met, the OhioLINK package requires strong leadership, good vendor partnerships, excited and motivated staff, and a hardworking group of creative risk-takers. Once these requirements were met, then, and only then, would the package be for sale. After getting past these hurdles, having the vendor add the *NBIO Report* to the standard OhioLINK package should be a piece of cake!

The experiences of the Collection Building Task Force, some of which we have reviewed in the preceding paragraphs, confirm the accuracy of a warning issued by Richard J. Wood: "It should be apparent that the implementation of cooperative collection assessment and development projects is long, arduous, complex and time consuming, and that it requires considerable commitment in terms of planning, organization, time, and funds."[27] OhioLINK and YBP have broken much ground here, and their work serves to broaden the collection of academic monographs available within the state. In the process we hope to have created a model that can find use in libraries beyond the borders of Ohio. The lessons learned from working with YBP on the *Not Bought* initiative will serve the task force well in pursuing its agenda with other vendors (foreign approval plans, etc.). These lessons will enable YBP to offer these services to other consortia. Is it too early to be thinking about statewide consortia looking across state lines, or to peer institutions in collection building attempts? Can the *NBIO* initiative be expanded beyond Ohio, perhaps to Indiana and Pennsylvania, in cooperative collection building ventures? The technology is there, but are we?

NOTES

1. Shreeves, Edward. "Is There a Future for Cooperative Collection Development in the Digital Age?" *Library Trends* 45 (Winter 1997): 387.

2. Diedrichs, Carol Pitts. "Designing and Implementing a Consortial Approval Plan: The OhioLINK Experience." http://wwwcrl.uchicago.edu/info/awcconf/awpapersgenl.htm: 30. Subsequently published in *Collection Management* 24, 1/2 (2000): 15-44.

3. The importance of this distinction is nicely drawn by David Swords, Vice President of International Sales, YBP, in an unpublished paper, entitled "Cooperative Collection Through Interactive Profiles."

4. John Secor, founder of YBP, has long held "partnering" with libraries as a core value ("Partnering: A Powerful 'What to Do' Management Tool or Just Another Fad?" *Against the Grain* 10:1 (February 1998): 70-73). Partnerships have been achieved to varying degrees long before YBP's relationship with OhioLINK, however, the difference is that the OhioLINK mission *requires* partnership with the vendor while relationships between individual libraries and the vendor do not. Also see: Gammon, Julia A. "Partnering with Vendors for Increased Productivity in Technical Services or, Bleeding Edge Technology." *Library Acquisitions: Practice & Theory* 21:2 (Summer 1997): 229-235; Shirk, Gary. "Lee Tzu's Pit: Partnering in Dangerous and Chaotic Times." *Library Acquisitions: Practice and Theory* 22:4 (Winter 1998): 415-421.

5. Halloran, Daniel P. "1998 from a Book Vendor's Perspective." *Against the Grain* 11 (February 1999): 30. Mr. Halloran, currently President and CEO of Blackwell's Book Group, was President of Academic Book Center at the time his article was written.

6. We would like to remind readers of the very low profit margins within which monograph vendors operate (not to be confused with margins in other sectors of the book trade). Considering the exacting and extraordinary requirements of supporting a consortium on the scale of OhioLINK, and bearing in mind the substantial discount provided, it should come as no surprise that the greatest benefits to the vendor in this relationship lie in developments that represent a competitive advantage rather than in dollars earned. For interesting discussions, see: Shirk, Gary. "Understanding the Library Marketplace." *Against the Grain* 13:5 (November 2001): 24-33; Nauman, Matt. "Evolution of the Supply Chain in Academic Library Bookselling." *Against the Grain* 13:5 (November 2001): 36-39.

7. Perrault, Anna H. "The Shrinking National Collection: A Study of the Effects of the Diversion of Funds from Monographs to Serials on the Monograph Collec-

tions of Research Libraries." *Library Acquisitions: Practice and Theory* 18:1 (Spring 1994): 15-16. For other interesting comments on this report see also, Nardini, Robert F., Charles M. Getchell, Jr., Thomas E. Cheever, "Approval Plan Overlap: A Study of Four Libraries." *Acquisitions Librarian* 16 (1996): 77-78; Diedrichs, Ibid., 6-7.

    8. Sanville, Thomas. *Expectations Fulfilled, Expectations Yet to Keep.* Columbus, OH: OhioLINK, 1996; *Snapshot 1998: OhioLINK, Six Years of Serving Ohio Higher Education.* Columbus, OH: OhioLINK, 1998.

    9. Diedrichs, Ibid., 7-8.

    10. Armstrong, Kim and Robert F. Nardini. "Making the Common Uncommon? Examining Consortial Approval Plan Cooperation." *Collection Management* 25:3 (2001): 87-105.

    11. These figures are drawn from the correspondence of David Swords, Vice President of International Sales, YBP, with the Collection Building Task Force, OhioLINK.

    12. The authors of the already cited article "Approval Plan Overlap" make the following observation: "The 'core' idea can carry two meanings. It can refer to a core of books necessary to the mission of a particular library, without reference to any other library. Or, it can refer to a core of books so important that nearly every academic library should acquire them. In describing approval plans as a method for building core collections, librarians have seldom been clear about which meaning was intended. If the latter meaning is understood, these references to core collections stand in remarkable contrast to overall collection overlap, which consistently have found scanty common ground among libraries."

    . 13. http://www.ohiolink.edu.

    14. We will hasten to point out that "consortial approval plan" is a misnomer, leading one to believe that there is a master program busily churning far away as it makes decisions as to which titles will go to which libraries. No such monster exists–yet. We shall discuss this shortly.

    15. http://www.ybp.com.

    16. Psychologists' recent studies of cooperation in organizations support the view that effective cooperation is most readily achieved by forming small working teams. Workers should focus on sets of mutually desirable interdependencies and outcomes that link stakeholders, rather than emphasize the issues or problems of a single stakeholder. Such groups tend to foster cooperation rather than competition, and collaboration has been shown to strengthen such groups and encourage them to complete more challenging tasks. Mosher, Paul H. "Cooperative collection development equals collaborative interdependence" in *Collection Management: Current Issues* edited by Sarah Shoemaker. New York: NY, Neal Schulman, 1989. p. 31.

    17. It is a significant advantage to cooperative efforts to have the entire state running on the same integrated library system. To facilitate participation in the approval plan by member libraries and to provide help for staff, Innovative Approval Plan Loaders were purchased by OhioLINK and made available free of charge to individual libraries.

    18. David Swords, YBP, developed (and continues to develop) this format.

    19. Evans, G. Edward. *Developing Library and Information Center Collections.* 4th ed. Englewood, CO: Libraries Unlimited, 2000. p. 461.

    20. Evans, G. Edward. *Developing Library and Information Center Collections.* 4th ed. Englewood, CO: Libraries Unlimited, 2000. p. 475.

    21. Our thanks to David Swords, who is the author of this timeline.

22. See Appendix 2 for a timeline of the *NBIO* project.

23. One peril to consortial efforts is getting lost in the generation of endless reports and minutiae which devour the time and energy participants will typically have available. Strong leadership is required to navigate around this black hole.

24. As a humorous aside, among the 'professional' titles not bought was the *ALA Survey of Librarians' Salaries*! Also missing from the state's collection were *30 Days to a Smart Family*, and *Boundaries in Dating: Making Dating Work* (both from Zondervan), both, we would think, potentially useful in fostering future consortial development.

25. These numbers were supplied by Jerry Newman, Assistant Dean for Collection Development at the University of Cincinnati.

26. GOBI accounts allow the creation of up to 98 sub-accounts, more than sufficient to cover Ohio's needs, at least at this early stage.

27. Wood, Richard J. "The Axioms, Barriers, and Components of Cooperative Collection Development" in *Collection Management for the 21st Century; A Handbook for Librarians*. Ed. G. E. Gorman and Ruth H. Miller. Greenwood, 1997, p. 239.

APPENDIX 1

Vision Statement for OhioLINK Consortial Approval Plan: What it is and What it isn't.

What it is

- A single OhioLINK contract covering an English language approval plan for participating institutions
- A project to strengthen collection resources and cooperation among OhioLINK libraries by increasing diversity of collections by the most cost-effective means
- A library specific profile created, managed and maintained by each local library
- Access to a Web-based tool provided by the vendor which displays the approval selection activities of other participating OhioLINK institutions
- A contract which would allow for firm ordering and continuation ordering from the same vendor
- An alerting system to appraise collection managers of the number of copies already purchased within OhioLINK to inform selection choices
- An algorithm developed by consensus among the participating institutions which may provide an initial allocation of particular titles to particular institutions
- A voluntary project done in phases as libraries are able and willing to participate

- A plan to facilitate the purchase of material normally purchased on approval or via firm order regardless of the library's intent to circulate
- A plan including options for purchasing cataloging and shelf-ready materials by individual library choice
- A plan that operates with normal approval plan requirements for returns and vendor viability
- A contract that would address the quality of service provided as well as coverage and discount
- A plan with options for participation by 2 year and 4 year institutions

What it isn't

- A single centrally-controlled, statewide approval profile covering all institutions
- A contract which limits a local library's choices about where to place firm orders or continuation orders
- A system to limit the number of copies of any given title in the state or prevent the purchase of multiple copies statewide
- A process to limit the individual library's choices about which titles to purchase locally
- A mandatory process
- A mandate to make all titles purchased available for circulation
- A project to mandate the receipt of cataloging and processing from the vendor
- A process to limit the returns or require purchases within the state
- A contract awarded solely on the basis of discount

In summary, the approval plan would be a voluntary project to extend options and efficiencies for individual libraries and the state while not constricting choices available to any individual library to develop its local resources as deemed most appropriate.

APPENDIX 2

History of the *'Not-Bought-In-Ohio' Report*

January 1999: Establish GobiTween and preview it with Ohio University. Make appropriate changes and set-up GobiTween so that any OhioLINK library can see whatever action YBP takes on any title for each Ohio school.

February 1999: GobiTween implemented

May 1999: Meeting in Columbus between OhioLINK librarians and YBP. Develop the idea for a *"Not-Bought-in-Ohio Report."* Discuss possible cooperative collection experiments, including with the Five Colleges and the engineering work group.

June 1999: At YBP, M. Zeoli and Ruth Fischer collect data and prepare the first *NBIO Report*. The report becomes the model of a production means for OhioLINK libraries to share the responsibility for buying worthwhile academic titles not owned by any library in the State. Analysis of the data show that owning "too many" copies of a title is not a considerable problem.

November 1999: D. Swords meets with the Five Colleges to talk about cooperative profiling. YBP agrees to prepare (1) comparative list of publishers on the approval profiles of the colleges, (2) report of titles in philosophy owned and not owned by the colleges, and (3) a comparison of the philosophy profiles of the colleges.

December 1999: D. Swords meets with the engineering workgroup to plan a cooperative profile in engineering. YBP delivers the publisher lists, report of titles not owned, and comparison of philosophy profiles to the Five Colleges. YBP delivers approval profiles to OhioLINK for posting to the OhioLINK website for comparative purposes.

January 2000: D. Swords circulates report to CBTF on cooperative profiling. Deliver comparison of profiles to the engineering workgroup with suggestions for developing a cooperative profile.

March 2000: M. Zeoli and D. Swords produce second *NBIO Report*.

May 2000: YBP executives meet with the CBTF. Develop plan to move the *NBIO Reports* onto a production schedule.

June 2000: M. Zeoli and Swords work out schedule for *NBIO Reports*. Deliver report and analysis to Jerry Newman.

August 2000: YBP confirms the feasibility of putting *NBIO Reports* in GOBI so that selectors can review notification slips online and need not send slips from one university to another. With CBTF, work out possible workflow scenarios for the *NBIO Reports*.

Academic and Commercial Roles in Building "The Digital Library"

Mark Sandler

SUMMARY. The University of Michigan and the University of Oxford have encouraged the research library community to fund creation of structured SGML/XML text-files for a significant portion of the Early English Books Online (EEBO) corpus of digital images created by ProQuest Information and Learning Company. These full-text editions, linked to the corresponding digital facsimiles of the works, enable word or phrase searching across the corpus along with the display of the corrected modern texts for reading and editing. Creating thousands of these text editions will significantly extend intellectual access to this historically important content, making possible new avenues of research across a broad range of disciplines. The significance of the EEBO Text Creation Partnership is to be judged not only by the usefulness of resulting product but also by the success of the business plan under which the text editions have been created. These successful experiences have not yet sufficiently raised consciousness among libraries and consortia–even those participating in the EEBO-TCP–that would cause them to question lower quality production methods and less library- and user-friendly models still being promulgated by the vendor community. *[Article copies available for a fee from The Haworth Document Delivery Service: 1-800-HAWORTH. E-mail address: <docdelivery@haworthpress.com> Website: <http://www.HaworthPress.com> © 2003 by The Haworth Press, Inc. All rights reserved.]*

Mark Sandler is Collection Development Officer, University of Michigan, University Library, 205 Hatcher North, Ann Arbor, MI 48019 (E-mail: sandler@umich.edu).

[Haworth co-indexing entry note]: "Academic and Commercial Roles in Building 'The Digital Library.'" Sandler, Mark. Co-published simultaneously in *Collection Management* (The Haworth Information Press, an imprint of The Haworth Press, Inc.) Vol. 28, No. 1/2, 2003, pp. 107-119; and: *The New Dynamics and Economics of Cooperative Collection Development* (ed: Edward Shreeves) The Haworth Information Press, an imprint of The Haworth Press, Inc., 2003, pp. 107-119. Single or multiple copies of this article are available for a fee from The Haworth Document Delivery Service [1-800-HAWORTH, 9:00 a.m. - 5:00 p.m. (EST). E-mail address: docdelivery@haworthpress.com].

http://www.haworthpress.com/web/COL
© 2003 by The Haworth Press, Inc. All rights reserved.
Digital Object Identifier: 10.1300/J105v28n01_09

KEYWORDS. Digital libraries, Early English Books Online (EEBO), cooperative collection development, ProQuest, electronic publishing–cooperation

I find it interesting that so much of the talk in academic circles of *"building the digital library"* excludes the role of the commercial sector in the production of content to populate its virtual shelves. When we were all about building print libraries, it was understood that commercially motivated publishers supplied us with content. With the switch to electronic resources, however, it seems that many of our colleagues think that the digital library of the future will be the sum of small scale, high cost conversion efforts to capture the images of Wisconsin circuses, a few issues of an early bicycle magazine, a couple of volumes of Scottish or American verse, the work a 16th century Italian playwright (richly tagged) and many other odds and ends from hundreds of grant-funded projects. While we try to keep up with these myriad digital projects–and try with even less success to keep our readers abreast of what is available to them through elaborate schemes of metadata creation and harvesting and registries–we seem to be denying the point that the real digital library, like the print library before it, is being created by Elsevier, the scholarly societies, JSTOR, ISI, Gale, ProQuest (including Chadwyck Healey), netLibrary, etc. While there are exceptions, a sober assessment suggests that our federations, forums, and grant driven initiatives are simply nibbling at the margins of a larger digital library. The scaleable projects, the important content, the current publications–i.e., the resources with "legs"–are most likely being produced by commercial publishers with one eye on user needs and the other on the bottom line. So, if this is assessment is close to reality, what becomes the role of the research library community in shaping the digital library?

THE EEBO EXPERIENCE

Before attempting to answer the question of the role of research libraries, let me establish my credentials as someone who has had the opportunity to gaze upon the golden calf of commercially produced content. In 1998, ProQuest Company (then Bell & Howell) brought to market digital images of approximately 100,000 early English texts that many research libraries already held in microfilm (STC I, STC II and the Thomason Tracts). Titled Early English Books Online (EEBO), the corpus was significant both because of the formative place of the content in western heritage as well as for the critical mass of material involved. As measured in bytes (or terabytes) EEBO was the largest digital project ever brought to the library market. As such, the overall cost was high, and at a time when budgets were being squeezed by a slackening economy and heightened demands for access to current electronic journals in science, technology and medicine. How would the library market react to such a massive project as that undertaken by ProQuest?

To keep a long story short, we can summarize the reaction of the library market as three-fold: some libraries had money (including some surprisingly small libraries that had year-end or other special funds) and purchased EEBO early on with little fuss. More still thought the price tag was too steep to warrant consideration. And, a third group began pushing for enhancements to the product as a condition of purchase and to gain greater control of the content through participating in this process of enhancement. It's primarily this latter response that I want to discuss in this paper but it could be helpful to say a few words about the early adopters and early naysayers of new library content.

TO BUY OR NOT TO BUY

Large purchase decisions in libraries are not always a rational process of assessing the match between needs and resources. Rather, decisions are often driven by a single–and not always informed–advocate (faculty or librarian). Sometimes it is because support for early purchase can be the result of a relationship to content, a relationship to a company, or even an individual sales representative. Sometimes it is because of a desire to do something (read *anything*) for a particular discipline or department. Sometimes it is because someone else bought it, or maybe even because someone else didn't buy it. My point is that not *every* library–or perhaps it would be more correct to say *any* library for *every* purchase–completely and carefully evaluates both the content of a new collection (regardless of format) and the actual quality and effectiveness of the representation of that content. "Pre-pub" or early adoptions reflect (or should reflect) confidence in the publisher, and a reasonable expectation based on past performance, that projects underway have a high likelihood of success.

In the area of humanities text corpora, Chadwyck-Healey built numerous collections on pre-pub investments because customers knew more or less what they would be getting–or at least that they would be getting *something*. With some of the newer players in this market space–and that would have included ProQuest when EEBO was being developed–it is unclear that one could have a very clear sense of their capacity to deliver high quality digital images that could be called forth in real time by a sufficiently sensitive and user-friendly search engine. In any case, my larger point here is that some libraries on some days purchase resources–even those involving very large commitments–with little actual scrutiny.

Decisions *not* to purchase large collections can be equally casual. In many libraries, and among many consortia, it is simply easier to pursue smaller, bite-sized purchases. Often, it might seem a better use of limited resources to buy several small collections that would support myriad constituencies than to invest in one "super-sized" collection that provides a surfeit of resources to only one user community. In still other cases, it is difficult for librarians to get beyond sticker shock of a hefty price tag to assess the value of the collection in terms of unit costs or potential use. With more than 100,000 volumes, the EEBO collection was priced (list price) at less than one dollar per volume. How much further can we as consumers expect to beat down the unit costs of production for such work–especially when we look at the unit costs incurred by many academic libraries engaged in similar efforts? Cost effective or not, I realize that it is not easy to fund resources in the neighborhood of $100,000–even for the country's largest and best funded libraries. Purchases of the magnitude of EEBO invariably involve planning and coalition building–no individual bibliographer or collection manager can simply say "yes" and fund it out of pocket. So, a decision not to buy, or a non-decision that results in not buying, can also reflect a shortage of the time and team-building skills needed to bring together a group that could move such a purchase forward.

PRESSING FOR BETTER PRODUCTS
WITH MORE ADVANTAGEOUS TERMS

The notion of libraries organizing to make resources better as a condition of purchase is an offshoot of the digital library environment. In the print world, books–or even reels of microfilm–came to us complete, and while we had the option of rejecting these resources, it was generally not feasible to modify a resource once it was available for distribution. E-products, on the other hand, are dynamic, often released incrementally, and maintained and upgraded by the publisher over time. In the case of electronic resources, I would argue that the library community not only has an opportunity to shape a product, it has an obligation to present and future users to insist on desirable changes. Likewise, given the size of the required investments (and the corresponding risks) one would imagine that publishers and vendors would want to stay very close to market needs and perceptions, seeking input early and often. Midstream changes, and product rescue efforts after the fact, can be expensive and difficult to implement while in full-scale retreat. Better to encourage systems of collaboration at the early stages of development so that market expectations are clearly understood by the sellers, and so that the buyers, in turn, understand the cost and quality trade-offs underlying product decisions.

The EEBO Text Creation Partnership (EEBO-TCP) entered the scene in 1998 to offer an early response to the EEBO marketing effort. We believed then, and believe now, that making the EEBO content searchable was an enhancement that our users would demand and was a way to move beyond the limited access provided by cataloging records and accompanying microfilm images to take full advantage of the power of digital access. ProQuest never denied this, but simply and correctly felt that such an undertaking at their end would make the product unaffordable to all but a literal handful of institutions. When it was suggested that Michigan believed it could rally the community to bear some this cost if the funding libraries would be eventual owners of the text files, ProQuest began working to see if they could find a way to support such a joint venture. Over time, the details were worked out and this unusual partnership between a commercial vendor and the academic community was codified.

From the outset, the EEBO-TCP lead-institutions (the Universities of Michigan and Oxford) talked about the vision of creating a subset of 25,000 accurately keyed and tagged editions of works. This "product" however, was always less important than the principles and practical library truisms that dictated how and why the texts would be developed.

- Libraries, as a more or less unified market, need to establish realistic standards for digital products. Such standards should be cost effective, rather than an abstract ideal, and when producers meet these standards, libraries should be willing to pay. When products fail to conform to standards, libraries should withhold support regardless of the attractiveness of the content.
- Library staff have certain skill-sets, and access to campus users who have yet other skill-sets and expertise, neither of which can we routinely expect to find in the employ of commercial vendors.

This is an important basis for partnership that would make better information resources than either libraries or commercial vendors are likely to produce working on their own.

- When dealing with historic texts, or even current scientific journals, it seems axiomatic that users would benefit from greater uniformity of search and retrieval protocols. While publishers compete to produce ever better interfaces, and this competition undoubtedly does lead to improvements, the net effect for users is a level of complexity and jarring dissimilarity that works against successful retrieval across collections.

- Even if there were convergence of interface, it would in many instances be desirable to integrate collections behind a single interface rather than expecting users to move from one publisher's collection to the next to retrieve resources on a single search entry. Expecting users to understand the relationships between EEBO and the Eighteenth Century Short Title Catalogue, or Kluwer journals as opposed to Elsevier journals, is to burden them with market distinctions that bear no relationship to discipline or subject boundaries. While it is hard to imagine commercial vendors transcending their own branding, libraries could provide a neutral ground for bringing together content in aggregated files–as they always have on their bookshelves.

- Research libraries have an obligation to preserve content across generations, and have an excellent track record for meeting this responsibility.

- Finally, research libraries need to own and manage key resources for the long haul. Important collections with durable content should be part of the capital investment of the nation's research libraries and we shouldn't countenance the desire of commercial interests to move materials out of the public domain by virtue of converting them from one format to another. Commercial firms are entitled to a return on their investments in conversion but libraries need to own their collections and make them broadly available as is consistent with their educational mission. Rights to important cultural resources should ultimately revert to purchasing libraries with few if any fetters on their use beyond general conventions that regulate intellectual property rights.

These principles outlined above have been an underpinning of the EEBO Text Creation Partnership and are the basis for ongoing discussions with publishers other than ProQuest to extend their acceptance as the basis for creating text editions of other historic corpora.

The EEBO-TCP is at this point a successful cooperative effort supported by almost seventy academic libraries in the U.S. and abroad to fund the creation of full-text editions of works in the Early English Books Online Corpus. The text collection now stands at two thousand accurately keyed and tagged texts online and we've not abandoned the goal of converting 25,000 texts over the next five years. For partner libraries, the text files will be made available for local load and management and eventually (within the next twelve years) any library could make the texts available to any constituency that they choose to serve.

The unit costs of this effort are also an attractive endorsement for such collaboration. At this early stage of the project, ARL partner libraries have paid approximately $25.00 per converted EEBO-TCP text. With the cash on hand, and existing library commitments, the cost will be approximately $5 or $6 per TCP volume and this could drop to $2 per text if more partner libraries sign on. This is clearly a bargain rate for the permanent addition of quality resources to a library collection.

EEBO has likewise proven to be a very successful product for ProQuest. Approximately 150 institutions have purchased access to EEBO images–a number that in just three years surpassed the number of STC standing-order subscribers recruited over a sixty-year development and sales effort. All involved would say that at least some of this success should be attributed to the unusual partnership that ProQuest struck with the academic community. The partnership has allowed ProQuest to supplement its image product with the opportunities that full-text conversion offers for new kinds of research. Creating text editions allows discovery and innovation by opening up the corpus to truly granular retrieval of words and concepts, with links to the corresponding page images. The market appeal of this arrangement has not been lost on competitors as they seek to bring similar content online.

EEBO and EEBO-TCP (image and text) have developed as complementary representations of these historically significant works, and each approach adds value to the other. While the EEBO-TCP effort is independent of ProQuest–the work being done by staff at the Universities of Michigan and Oxford, with partnership fees collected by the Council on Library and Information Resources–we recognize that the project benefited greatly from the support offered by ProQuest. The company has been instrumental in marketing the text effort and is contributing far more money for the privileges of partnership than any single academic library. Nonetheless, our view of the EEBO Text Creation Partnership is that it is a project being led and financed by academic libraries, which must ultimately control the standards and production methods. Most important for the long-term, libraries will retain the rights to own and distribute the text collections in accord with the goals and mission of their institutions.

EXTENDING THE EEBO/EEBO-TCP MODEL

The commercial success of EEBO has caused other publishers to overcome risk-aversion and commit to moving forward with mega-conversion projects of their own. Most closely aligned to EEBO are Gale's Eighteenth Century Collection and Early American Imprints produced in microform by Readex. Both of these collections provide important extensions of EEBO content by time and place. The two publishers have been considering conversion of these collections for many years but are now moving forward, likely based on business plans justified by the market acceptance of EEBO.

In the case of the Eighteenth Century, Gale has already issued a press release indicating its intention to work with the library community along lines established by the EEBO-Text Creation Partnership. For users, this would mean that the EEBO text files extending from 1473-1700, could be combined with thousands of 18th century texts, and searched as a single corpus, with corresponding page images "grabbed" from the appropriate publisher server. This level of integration is a compelling vision for scholars. Early American Imprints (the Evans/Shaw-Shoemaker bibliographies) could likewise be incorporated into such a research environment if the publisher can come to grips with the benefits of this level of collaboration. From the perspective of partnering institutions, it would be a great service to our users if we could integrate the texts from all three of these cornerstone collections behind a single interface, allowing the user to choose if their search term should apply to one, two or all of the collections keyed to a single standard and tagged in conformance to a unified Document Type Definition (DTD). It is also the case that libraries that own these text-files in perpetuity will be able to use them in conjunction with other projects and collections.

While the publishers will have to decide if they can accommodate the principles underlying the Text Creation Partnership, their decision will largely be driven by the reaction from the marketplace. Will libraries accept page images and uncertain OCR searchability, or will they insist that some of the texts in these culturally significant corpora be accurately keyed and tagged to allow for more precise searching, browsing of section heads, retrieval of keywords in context, and displayable and printable text? Obviously, keyboarding and tagging adds cost so it is a significant collection decision to determine how much libraries can afford to invest in these collections. Assuming that the market expresses a desire to have some texts accurately produced, will our colleagues insist that they be granted ownership rights to these texts, including the right to integrate them with other collections, or would they be satisfied to pay a commercial vendor to produce, house, and control these texts along with the corresponding page images? In yet another possible outcome, would libraries and repositories settle for a royalty on commercial sales rather than claim ownership and control of the content? And finally, would users prefer to pay a commercial vendor for texts as product (even if the vendor subcontracts with an academic institution to actually produce the texts) or would they prefer to pay into a cooperative initiative to produce as many texts as possible depending on the rate of community participation–i.e., the number of paying partners?

While many libraries have approached the EEBO Text Creation Partnership output as a *product*, it was conceived by the initial advocates at Michigan, Oxford and even ProQuest, as a set of principles that could be applied in such a way as to support the goals of both commercial publishers and the academic library community. Because of the library-friendly aspects of this TCP arrangement, it is always disappointing to us when libraries compare EEBO/EEBO-TCP to traditional products and end up deciding in favor of the latter. In some cases, these decisions are program driven and sensibly reflect for the needs of a particular campus. For the library community as a whole, however, it is important that our collection librarians pay attention to principles that ultimately advance our relative standing in the marketplace.

Although EEBO-TCP can claim a measure of success, I'm not sure that the project has done enough to underscore the importance of liberal terms of use, and the benefits of ownership to research libraries. It would be disappointing if this were seen as an isolated opportunity specific to EEBO that can't or shouldn't be applied to other similar projects. We would not like to see libraries too willingly cede the gains that we feel were made in our relationship with ProQuest. There can be no argument that the terms of EEBO-TCP favor libraries and their users. But, they have also provided tremendous opportunities for ProQuest to realize a strong return on its investment. Others vendors that would attempt to circumvent the issues of standards, rights and ownership should be held to account.

THE BENEFITS OF PARTNERSHIP

While my greatest fear, post-EEBO, is that the library community will accept disadvantageous sales approaches and licensing terms for collections of core content and enduring value, there is also the possibility that the EEBO-TCP model could be undermined from a different direction. Some librarians, when presented with the TCP principles, seem emboldened to promote the idea that libraries could develop these collections totally independent of the commercial information providers. While I have some empathy for these views based on confidence in library skills, and can think of some significant successes, my own experience with EEBO and other projects makes me dubious that this level of coordination is feasible among libraries. To my mind, it is highly unlikely that repositories would cooperate to release their content to the larger library community without significant remuneration. It is further unlikely that the community could develop a viable funding model that would transfer considerable funds to one or several production sites. Finally, the kinds of investments required to market/sell an international project are considerable, and very unlikely to be carried out successfully by one or several libraries. While I don't think EEBO would have accomplished its excellent sales track record were it not for the Text Creation Partnership, I'm equally assured that the TCP would not have achieved anywhere near its present level of success were it not for its connection to the EEBO image product and the support of ProQuest.

ProQuest (or other commercial conversion vendors) brings to the table the following assets in support of partnerships with academic institutions:

- Image product with rights of distribution
- Production and business credibility
- Sales force and marketing staff–international market penetration
- Relationship with content providers
- Capital–both ongoing contributions to support conversion and front money in advance of revenues
- Drive to bring a product to market–time-bound goals
- Some content knowledge based on managing the collection in other formats.

EEBO-TCP could not have reached its current levels of success without early support and funding from ProQuest. It was also helpful that the EEBO image product was viable even without the searchable text, allowing TCP a protracted period in which to seek funds and ramp up production. Finally, the national and international sales effort would not have been carried out on an effective level if left to the devices of an academic library. It is unfortunate, but a fact nonetheless, that most institutions assessing a project like EEBO/EEBO-TCP require ongoing contacts over an extended period of time to make a purchase/partnership decision. Even as a library colleague, it frequently involves unabashed "sales" calls to actually bring a decision to closure. While we can quibble about the extent of value added by commercial sales and marketing efforts, it is naive to overlook the work involved in distribution and its relationship to funding creation.

Conversely, libraries offer vendors the opportunity to create far better products than they could build on their own, without having to assume all the risks of missing the mark on production schedules, quality standards, or other aspects of a project. When the TCP set out to convert EEBO texts, we announced an intention to do so at a minimum accuracy standard of one error in 20,000 characters (99.995). The fact was that, given the difficulty of the texts with which we were working, we didn't know for certain that the keyboarding vendor community could meet this standard, or do so in a cost effective manner. While happily this has worked out, we always believed that had it not we could come back to the community and say that it doesn't appear possible to meet this standard for the material in hand. We believed that a lower but achievable standard would still offer a tremendous resource for most users. I was confident that our "colleagues"–as opposed to "customers"–would accept such a change as a good faith decision by a peer, rather than as a contract breach or profit-driven effort to cut back on quality and service. *Trust* is a tremendous asset that libraries can bring to the process of resource creation.

In the case of EEBO-TCP, the lead libraries brought

- Production capability/credibility in dealing with humanities texts
- Content credibility–in the library and on campus
- Concept investment that translated into will to work and to commit resources
- Director/Collection Development Officer/bibliographer marketing connections
- A cooperative spirit reflected in trusting collaborative relationships.

This was not a project that could have been done by a commercial vendor because of the skill sets required, because of the need to draw feedback and direction from end users, and because of the untested expectations set for the conversion vendor community.

While ProQuest quickly recognized the value of adding searchable text to their records and page images, some vendors and some librarians might question the need for such a project to be done–at additional cost–when OCR searchable text is available. This will be the crux of the issue for future efforts at forging such commercial/academic partnerships. Does the full-text really add enough value to warrant the additional costs? For me, the answer is, "yes, for a limited subset of texts." Conducting a simple keyword search over a corpus of 100,000 texts, and then following "hits" when no structure is displayed (chapter heads and section heads) and no surrounding text can be viewed, seems an exercise fraught with danger and frustration. The corpora are huge, and the cues for tracing hits are all but non existent. By virtue of their significance and likely use, some texts deserve to be more fully represented; displayed and readable in modern fonts, browsable by virtue of rendering tagged chapter, section, and feature headings, and reproducible for incorporating the text into other work. With many new corpora on the horizon, it will be interesting, and I believe important, to see if the library marketplace affirms this judgment about the value of keyed and tagged editions of digital facsimiles. Then it remains to be seen if the marketplace will likewise affirm the value of full ownership of these texts–and the right to freely distribute them in support of the principle of public domain access–as opposed to accepting the limited rights of ownership supported by traditional product licenses.

CONCLUSION

We started by asking about the role of the research library in shaping a digital library that is being created first and foremost by commercial publishers. I think the answer is that libraries need to find a way to leverage their skills, resources, and most significantly, buying power, to work in partnership with commercial firms, giving clear messages as to the nature of the products they want and the terms under which they are willing to access them. In the instance of EEBO, it was argued that libraries could claim ownership of the text file because it was primarily their money that was used to create it. In a sense, library money (and library content) drives all commercially created resources. Accordingly, we should be mindful of our role in the creation process and advocate for arrangements that support our long-term interests and those of our users. The importance of the EEBO Text Creation Partnership will be reflected in how it influences other likely conversion efforts–e.g., the Eighteenth Century, the Nineteenth Century, Goldsmith-Kress, and Evans-Shaw/Shoemaker. Will the publishers of these collections adopt production/marketing/licensing models based on the EEBO experience or will they seek to adopt more insular approaches to production and restrictive licensing? If so, will the market accept such an approach given the expectations developed around the EEBO-TCP? If libraries are to remain true to their oft stated values, it is hard to see how they could accept licensing terms that restrict a reader's right to access culturally significant texts in the public domain.

The Case for Belts and Suspenders: Risk Management Aspects of Cooperative Collection Development

Bernard F. Reilly, Jr.

SUMMARY. Librarians have a responsibility to assess as precisely as possible the risks we take in cooperative collection development activity, and to put in place measures that will minimize that risk. As cooperative development programs are planned and designed, they should be supported with instruments that clearly define the nature and duration of the obligations and benefits of participation in those activities. Second, because of the stake that the larger community holds in the success of individual cooperative collection development efforts, the precise terms of those agreements should be published or made as widely known as possible, along with all referenced documents and specifications. Risk management is likely to become increasingly important in librarians' everyday work as managers of information and knowledge resources, and in their preservation role as well. Good practice in this realm of activity and the resultant transparency can reduce risk to the investments of the entire community by providing a basis for making informed decisions about development and preservation of every library's collections and resources. *[Article copies available for a fee from The Haworth Document Delivery Service: 1-800-HAWORTH. E-mail address: <docdelivery@haworthpress.com> Website: <http://www.HaworthPress.com> © 2003 by The Haworth Press, Inc. All rights reserved.]*

Bernard F. Reilly, Jr., is President, Center for Research Libraries, 6050 South Kenwood Avenue, Chicago, IL 60637-2804 (E-mail: reilly@crl.edu).

[Haworth co-indexing entry note]: "The Case for Belts and Suspenders: Risk Management Aspects of Cooperative Collection Development." Reilly, Bernard F., Jr. Co-published simultaneously in *Collection Management* (The Haworth Information Press, an imprint of The Haworth Press, Inc.) Vol. 28, No. 1/2, 2003, pp. 121-134; and: *The New Dynamics and Economics of Cooperative Collection Development* (ed: Edward Shreeves) The Haworth Information Press, an imprint of The Haworth Press, Inc., 2003, pp. 121-134. Single or multiple copies of this article are available for a fee from The Haworth Document Delivery Service [1-800-HAWORTH, 9:00 a.m. - 5:00 p.m. (EST). E-mail address: docdelivery@haworthpress.com].

Digital Object Identifier: 10.1300/J105v28n01_10

KEYWORDS. Cooperative collection development, risk management

Cooperative collection development involves partnerships among libraries, universities, publishers, and other organizations that join together to accomplish, through the acquisition or creation of source materials, the development of research collections. As in all cooperative endeavors the success of such activities relies upon the shared investment of resources, the allocation to the various participants of specific roles and responsibilities, and the timely fulfillment of those responsibilities. These roles and responsibilities may be short-term commitments, fulfilled during a specified, limited time period. Or they may be ongoing commitments, undertaken for long or even indefinite periods of time.

In addition, cooperative collection development activities normally involve a sharing of ownership in the resources collectively developed or acquired through those activities. More broadly this involves apportioning each participant's interest in the potential benefits of the project. This interest, at its most obvious, is the participant's share in ownership of, access to, or other benefits from, the resource acquired or developed. This could mean the use or even physical possession of the collection acquired, the right to modify a digital resource developed, or the ability to decide on continuation of an electronic subscription. This interest though might also go beyond the actual resources developed and include other returns on investment, such as compensatory payments arising from a vendor's breach of supply or license agreements, or royalties or fees derived from permissible "downstream" uses of the resource controlled by the group.

Conversely, risk is also shared among participants in cooperative collection development projects. Participating libraries can be exposed to losses that might arise from negative consequences and scenarios stemming from those activities. Such costs might include the loss of a party's investment due to procurement failure or fraud on the part of an agent or vendor, purchase or delivery cost overruns, substantial unforeseen price increases, or even monetary penalties and damages because of copyright infringement or breach of a vendor contract by another project participant. In collection development activity, however, the major cost incurred is usually the cost of long-term maintenance of the acquired resource.

Risk is generally defined as exposure to the chance of injury or loss. For our purposes here it is the likelihood of a library's suffering ill consequences as a result of participating in a cooperative collection development endeavor. This paper will suggest how risk enters into cooperative collection development activities, and indicate broadly some measures that can be taken in those activities to enable this risk to be more effectively minimized.

THE SCOPE OF THIS INQUIRY

Cooperative collection development activities take a wide range of forms. They can involve creating an online library of primary source materials in digital form contributed by multiple institutions. This was accomplished under the Library of Congress/Ameritech National Digital Library Competition project. They can also entail the sharing of responsibility for comprehensive collecting in a particular domain, such as the Research Library Cooperative Acquisition Program in Latin American Materials undertaken by the University of Texas, Stanford University and the University of California at Berkeley. Other cooperative collection development efforts include compacts among libraries to cooperate more broadly on collection development and preservation, as exemplified by the CONSORT Cooperative collection development Project created by the Five Colleges of Ohio.[1]

Cooperative projects come about in various ways: through the top-down initiative of a central organization; through the mutual self-interest of organizations that share a set of common goals and conditions; or through the concerted efforts of members of a particular community of interest, like area specialists or collection development officers in a particular field. Consequently cooperative projects can be configured differently and possess varying degrees of organizational integrity. On one end of this spectrum are informal, loose voluntary affiliations; on the other end are consortia that are actually incorporated as dedicated legal entities.

The purposes for which such affiliations are created can be memorialized in a number of ways. Ideally this is done by creation of governing documents of one kind or another, that specify the activities to be undertaken, the participating entities, and the terms of participation. These documents can be the bylaws of the corporation, contracts, licenses, or written agreements. Since most cooperative collection development activities are not specifically regulated by laws or statutes, controls that exist for such projects are only those that stem from these governing documents. Yet there is a surprising, even alarming, lack of formalization to some of these activities. To a large extent cooperative collection development programs and projects tend to be based on trust and only in part on formal compact.

In the commercial sector similar development activities tend to be supported contractually. A robust infrastructure consisting of written cooperative agreements, licenses, and the other documents underpin and specify the roles and commitments of contributors, vendors, beneficiaries, and other participants in joint ventures. This infrastructure rests upon a base of contract law and commercial code that govern transactions and trade in the larger economy. Such an apparatus is intended to provide a "safety net" of sorts that underwrites the processes of collaboration and exchange, and enables participants to limit and manage the various risks associated with these processes. Moreover, when the underlying agreements are open to public view or government regulation they also provide a measure of transparency for endeavors that may involve significant investment by participants as well as affecting the interests of third parties.[2]

In the non-profit knowledge sector, particularly in libraries, the contractual side of this apparatus is not well developed. Programs that are formalized through nonbinding instruments such as letters of intent, memoranda of understanding, and guidelines are the norm. Many cooperative projects are undertaken with the roles of officers and governing bodies imprecisely specified. In many ways these are high risk propositions, endeavors in which participants are likely to obtain a low return or even loss on the resources they invest. Moreover, the absence or inadequacy of contractual underpinning in such projects prevents libraries and participants from exploiting the large array of risk management tools and strategies that the world of commerce has developed over the course of several centuries.[3]

It is not the purpose of this study to identify the extant projects and programs that are deficient in this respect. Clearly there are exemplary, and less exemplary, cooperative efforts. Rather than find fault with particular cooperative efforts, it is more useful to identify those characteristics of cooperative projects that expose the participating organizations to greater hazard, and to suggest ways in which risk can be minimized.

This author does not presume, moreover, to render an assessment of the relative success of specific cooperative efforts. In fact more research is needed to determine whether there has been a direct correlation between the relative strength of the risk management architecture of projects and the success of those projects. It is clear, however, that the manner in which projects address participant risk in their planning and organization will have a real impact on the longevity of the resources acquired and developed.

It is worth highlighting some very good practices adopted in individual cooperative efforts. These have yielded a corpus of documents, models, and tools that can help libraries engaging in these activities mitigate the risks. Through the judicious construction of licenses and agreements, some recent print, microfilm, and digital collection development projects have been able to underwrite fulfillment of roles and the continued "ownership" of cooperatively developed resources by investors and other stakeholders.

ALLOCATING RISK

Cooperative collection development endeavors involve sharing of the costs of the endeavor among multiple parties, whether those costs are the purchase price for library materials or the expenses involved in creating an electronic resource. Risk management takes that strategy to a second level, by distributing the costs of potential losses from the endeavor to abate risk. This involves apportioning among the investing or interested parties the potential costs and liabilities that might accrue from the endeavor. This is done so that in the event of a loss no single party bears an unduly large share of the total damages. This second step is often not fully accomplished in most cooperative collection development projects.

As noted above, in cooperative endeavors the participants join together under some form of compact, stated or implied, with mutually agreed-upon terms, obligations and interests. Success depends upon the cohesion of the compact. Ideally the compact is memorialized, and the cohesion guaranteed, by a signed instrument like a cooperative agreement assigning roles and responsibilities of the parties and providing a basis for enforcement of same. Examples include the standard cooperative agreement executed between the Library of Congress and recipients of LC/Ameritech National Digital Library Competition grants, and the comprehensive license agreement used by the Research Libraries Group (RLG) and participants in its Cultural Materials Alliance.[4] Both documents set forth the respective responsibilities of the participants. The RLG instrument, for instance, clearly assigns responsibility for preventing unauthorized use of the digital resource to RLG. It also designates the owner of the copyright in the materials themselves and in the composite resource as the contributors of the source materials and RLG respectively.

Essential to this cohesion is the identification of legally eligible parties and their respective rights and liabilities. Unfortunately these are areas left ambiguous in many cooperative collection development ventures. Rarely determined in such agreements, for example, is the nature of each party's ownership of, or equity in, materials that are jointly acquired. Such equity could constitute a percentage interest in the total body of material, or title to a portion of the body of material. Such ambiguity affects the individual participants' access to the full menu of possible rights of ownership, such as the right to long-term possession or custody, or to derive revenue from secondary uses of the materials through exhibition or licensing for commercial use.

Parties identified in the agreements, moreover, should be legal entities, i.e., specifically identified individuals or legally vested corporations. In the eyes of the law liability cannot accrue to, nor can obligations be enforced of, an ad hoc or arbitrarily designated entity such as a "project" or a team. When the parties to an agreement are either not clearly identified, or are not specifically empowered to enter into a contract as representatives of a legal entity, the value of the contract and the usual protections of the law can be compromised.

The Cooperative collection development Program of the CONSORT Colleges clearly designates the parties involved. The documents governing this program, while not binding legal agreements, clearly indicate the authorities that stand behind them. The memorandum of understanding on the sharing of library materials among CONSORT libraries specifies the dates of approval by the colleges' Library Committee and chief financial officers.[5] The level of confidence in the project and its persistence is further increased by the high level of the signatories to the agreement and the amplitude of published documentation about the program's governance.

Attention to the identity of the parties, though important, is often overlooked, in rights agreements. Permissions obtained under cooperative projects to microfilm or digitize archives or collections and distribute copies thereof can be neutralized unless that party is a true entity. In the eyes of the law a project, committee, or task force normally has no legal standing. Acquisition of such title by an ad hoc organization will bring with it the requirement that title be formally assigned to a legal entity at some point, certainly before that organization goes out of existence. In most cases the rights or permissions conferred are nontransferable. The Center for Research Libraries Area Studies Microform Projects (AMPs), for instance, operate semiautonomously under the Center's administrative and fiscal umbrella but are not per se incorporated organizations. Hence the rights acquired to microfilm materials under those projects must be held in the Center's name on behalf of the project participants.

Third parties designated or referenced in cooperative agreements should also have this kind of specificity and standing. In lieu of such designation the party can be characterized in a way that reserves to the library the right to name such a party at a later date. The Joint Information Systems Committee (JISC) model license agreement, for instance, stipulates that with termination of the agreement the subscription content from the subscribed-to period will be delivered to a client or to a "central archiving facility operating on behalf of the UK Higher Education community without charge."[6] This allows room for the licensees to appoint an agent friendly to their interests at the critical moment.

The JISC model also provides another advantage, which is to assign certain important rights and responsibilities to a party that is accountable to all of the interested parties, and not to just one or two. When exclusive benefits or responsibilities for a resource are vested in only one of the parties, risk to the other participants increases.

LICENSING AGREEMENTS

The instrument most commonly relied upon to govern and control risk in electronic collection development activities is the licensing agreement. Normally executed between a publisher and a consortium or group of participating libraries, the licensing agreement sets forth terms intended to clearly assign the respective responsibilities of vendor and client. There has been much good work done in the field on specifying the best language for these kinds of electronic licensing agreements. Leading examples are the aforementioned JISC model agreement and the Council on Library and Information Resources/Digital Library Federation (CLIR/DLF) model licensing agreement, developed by Ann Okerson of Yale University.[7]

These models go a long way to minimize the risk of loss, or of curtailments on the use, of resources acquired cooperatively. For single publisher-library arrangements these kinds of agreements adequately allocate the specific collective risks and benefits inherent in the contract. But in instances where the client is a group or consortium of parties they should be augmented to specifically address the apportionment of obligations or liabilities and benefits *among* those parties.

Obligations might include legal costs arising from disputes over terms, or the negative consequences of unauthorized, ineligible, or infringing uses of the electronic materials by the licensee or by those whom the licensee allows to use the materials. (The JISC model license agreement, for instance, specifies that costs might be incurred for use of an expert to resolve disputes arising from the license and agreement.) Should bad things happen, liability might be judged to be shared evenly among the participants or allocated proportionately to the relative investment of a participating library absent an operative agreement addressing the distribution of responsibilities.

The individual library is exposed to other risks as well. With the demise of a publisher, or suspension of an access agreement, maintenance of the electronic resource might become the collective responsibility of the subscribers. Individual libraries might incur costs for same, which even if not explicitly stipulated in an agreement with a vendor or with the umbrella organization, might be mandated by established user dependence upon the resource. Similarly individual libraries incur preservation responsibilities and costs with respect to traditional library materials acquired under cooperative programs as well.

Likewise the participating library's share of benefits, or equity, should be specified as well. Under most content agreements if the vendor were to violate the agreement or to include in the resource materials that were infringing, offensive or libelous, there would be payments due the client. (In the CLIR/DLF agreement, for instance, the licensor is required to reimburse the licensee for withdrawal of content from the resource.) Absent other formal arrangements or extenuating factors, the respective share of participating libraries in the damages and benefits would be assumed to be equal. Where formal consortia or other standing umbrella organizations act as the agent of the individual libraries the client's share of both benefits and risks must be defined by membership documents or participation agreements.

Aside from defining the specific roles and interests of the parties, another way to contain risk is by strengthening the likelihood of continued compliance with a cooperative program. One method, employed by the Research Library Cooperative Acquisition Program in Latin American Materials undertaken by the University of Texas, Stanford University and UC Berkeley, is to create a reserve or fail-safe fund which can be drawn upon in the event of financial duress. This is a way of hedging against the sudden breach of a party's obligations brought about by an economic downturn or other unforeseen events. The published statement of principles governing the program contains a provision whereby each of the three participating libraries agrees to build up over time an escrow account in its own budget, large enough to cover the library's spending on the program for a twelve month period should fiscal cuts impair its ability to maintain its share of the program costs.[8]

OTHER SAFEGUARDS

Some cooperative efforts are held together in other ways. They involve participants bound together as part of a larger legal entity, such as a state university system, or under the jurisdiction of a federal agency. The integrity of programs undertaken by these participants is often secured, at least in part, by obligations enforced by laws, agency regulations, and other statutory requirements. In these laws and regulations such federations have a ready-made framework for assessment and abatement of individual risk that is not typical of most cooperative programs.

Under the Library of Congress/Ameritech digital library project, the obligations of the Library of Congress and the contributing libraries were underwritten by a relatively simple contract.[9] But appended to that contract were a set of "certifications" that specifically bound the participating library to a number of practices (regarding such things as nondiscrimination in hiring and contracting, federal debt status, and maintaining a drug-free workplace) which by extension governed the behavior of the parties. In a similar way the National Endowment for the Humanities, in its requirements on "Intangible Property" developed under NEH grants, incorporated by reference accessibility provisions of the Freedom of Information Act and certain government-wide regulations.[10] Thus "hard wired" to federal law the cooperative agreement, though brief, had some powerful incentives for compliance.

In fact, most contract documents and formal instruments are not stand-alone agreements. When tested they reach out by reference into a larger universe of legally discoverable documents that includes position descriptions, organizational by-laws and policies, and so forth. While these other documents may not have the force of a legal instrument they are often used in arbitration or litigation to shed light upon terms and parties named but not adequately defined in those instruments. For instance, in the absence of a specific formal authorization of an individual to represent a party to a contract, such authority is often formally delegated through a position description or employment contract.

Often an agreement itself is unimposing, but mentions other documents that by reference might govern the activities. The National Library of Australia's *Pandora* project, for example, a cooperative effort to archive all Australian-produced networked resources, is based upon a relatively general agreement among participating libraries and universities. That agreement incorporates by reference "a set of collection agreements which delineate the areas in which each participating library will take responsibility for archiving Australian online titles."

In collection development efforts undertaken under grant funds the obligations governing participants may also be embodied in an implied contract, whereby a grantee assumes certain obligations stated in the published terms of the grant competition by virtue of applying for and accepting funding. This approach is taken in the guidelines established by the National Endowment for the Humanities for its grant programs.

Conditions are also imposed on grant-funded collection development activities through cooperative agreements executed between funders and grantees. The Andrew W. Mellon Foundation and other philanthropic organizations, for instance, use such instruments to impose conditions on the commercial exploitation of digital resources and other intellectual property developed under certain of their grant programs.[11] While these conditions themselves do not pose risks to participants (unless violated) they may ultimately affect potential benefits to be accrued from efforts looking toward secondary uses of the resources developed.

RISK HORIZONS

Another strategy for controlling risk is to minimize the risk "horizon," or the period of time during which the parties are exposed to losses. In cooperative agreements, as in politics, term limits are desirable but infrequently imposed. Agreements of indeterminate duration signal a greater degree of risk. The likelihood of any party or organization fulfilling an obligation in perpetuity is doubtful at least. More precisely, open-ended obligations make those participants responsible for fulfilling obligations liable for costs that cannot be calculated and hence cannot be provided for in advance. The recent agreement made between Elsevier Science and the National Library of the Netherlands regarding the archiving of electronic journal titles, publicized as assuring "perpetual accessibility of scientific heritage" is evidently an open-ended one.[12]

The risk horizon can be limited by writing into the instrument a specified duration for which the agreement is to be in effect or, within the agreement, by limiting the duration for a specific responsibility. The former approach is taken in the cooperative agreement between the National Library of Australia and Australian National University for Chinese materials, which clearly establishes three years as its period in force. The Washington Research Library Consortium sets the length of time for which a participant is required to retain a "protected title" at five years.[13]

OTHER INTERESTED PARTIES

Even when the terms of a partnership are formalized to a high degree there can still be risk to other interested parties. American research libraries form a community whose members' fortunes are interlinked. Informal, voluntary cooperation among libraries is manifest in the efforts of libraries to avoid the unnecessary development of redundant resources. Interlibrary loan and Web dissemination enable unique collection resources developed by one library to be shared by others.

Because of this inter-reliance, the collecting decisions of one library or consortium often influence the behavior of others active in the same area. In this way libraries not directly participating in a cooperative collection development effort can have a real interest or stake in that effort's success. A library might rely upon another to collect or preserve unique materials or materials only available by virtue of a temporary window of opportunity. It can then make a great deal of difference to this larger community, for instance, how securely or for how long a party is bound to fulfill its obligations to a cooperative effort. The consequences of "courses not taken" can be dire.

When the specific terms of a cooperative endeavor are unclear, or are altogether unknown, the other actors and, to a lesser extent, even the participating parties are deprived of useful knowledge on which to base important acquisition or preservation decisions. In the absence of information all stakeholders then operate at a higher level of risk.

In a published report "Preservation Risk Management for Web Resource: Virtual Remote Control in Cornell's Project Prism," Cornell University digital preservation librarians underscore the dependence of the larger community on one cooperatively developed resource, the *Making of America* digital library developed by Cornell University and the University of Michigan:

> A spring 2001 survey of Cornell's and Michigan's *Making of America* collections revealed that nearly 250 academic institutions link directly to the MOA collections, although neither university has committed to provide other entities with long-term access. Similarly, a review of the holdings of several research library gateways over the past few years indicates growth in the number of links to open-access Web resources that are managed with varying degrees of control.[14]

Risk to other interested parties can be mitigated somewhat by transparency. Currently our collection development activities, particularly the development of electronic resources, are not very transparent. Few cooperative agreements that underwrite projects and programs, even major ones, are published. Hence we are often unable to calculate the risk of relying on others' performance of manifest responsibilities in a program or project.[15]

SOME CONCLUSIONS

Clearly there are limits to the application of the metrics and tools of risk management, developed in the world of commerce, to collection building and preservation. There is no standard or formula, for instance, for calculating the amount of risk that a library can tolerate under any given cooperative activity. The cost of missed collecting opportunities, the value of collections, and the useful "lifespan" of a particular holding or resource are all difficult to express in quantitative terms, while in the commercial sector financial return provides a universal absolute. Moreover, the degree of risk tolerance or risk aversion, the extent of the risk a university or library can or is willing to take, varies from institution to institution.

Like managers in the commercial sector, however, librarians are obliged to manage carefully the financial and human resources at their disposal. And the prudent management of knowledge resources is also a fiduciary responsibility. In a sense the collections and scholarly resources we develop and preserve are a form of wealth over which we exercise stewardship. This makes it necessary for us to assess as precisely as possible the risks we take in cooperative collection development activity, and to put in place measures that will minimize that risk. How, then, can this be accomplished?

First, as we plan and design cooperative development programs we should support them with instruments that clearly define the nature and duration of the obligations and benefits of participation in those activities. Such instruments should specifically identify the parties to whom those obligations and benefits accrue. This has a cost: the administrative burden of managing such agreements, of dotting the I's and crossing the T's, is significant. This cost might be alleviated somewhat by the sharing of best practices in this area, and publication of boilerplate text for cooperative collection development agreements like the electronic licensing agreement models provided by CLIR/DLF and JISC.

On a more basic level, we can also control risk when we create documents like position descriptions and permission agreements for digitization and microfilming, by addressing delegation of responsibilities and authority with regard to contracting to individuals in our organizations. Such practices would contribute to building a sturdy infrastructure on which to base solid and cohesive cooperative relationships.

Second, because of the stake that the larger community holds in the success of individual cooperative collection development efforts, the precise terms of those agreements should be published or made as widely known as possible, along with all referenced documents and specifications. This is now economically feasible with the World Wide Web as a publishing medium. But the effort to publicize these agreements will encounter resistance where for-profit partners or content providers are involved. These partners often prefer, even require, that the terms of their agreements with individual clients be kept confidential. The resultant lack of transparency permits commercial actors to operate more nimbly and advantageously in this market, but it undermines our ability to accomplish our mission and to accommodate the collective good as well. It is likely that risk management will not only become increasingly important in librarians' everyday work as managers of information and knowledge resources. It will also become inseparable from our preservation role as well. In general, good practice in this realm of activity and the resultant transparency can reduce risk to the investments of the entire community by providing a basis for making informed decisions about development and preservation of every library's collections and resources.

NOTES

1. The CONSORT (Colleges of Ohio Networked System Online for Research and Teaching) members are the libraries of Denison University, Kenyon College, Ohio Wesleyan University, and The College of Wooster.

2. The role of trust and self-regulation within particular communities of interest is now seen as an important force mitigating the negative effects of unbridled self-interest in the marketplace. Francis Fukuyama's book *Trust: The Social Virtues and the Creation of Prosperity* (New York: The Free Press, 1995) is a useful introduction to this view of trust and its role in market economies.

3. A very readable chronicle of the development of the science of risk management in the world of trade is Peter L. Bernstein's *Against the Gods: The Remarkable Story of Risk* (New York: John Wiley & Sons, 1996).

4. The Library of Congress *Sample Cooperative Agreement* form is posted on the Web at http://lcweb2.loc.gov/ammem/award/html/sample.html. A copy of the *RLG Cultural Materials Alliance License Agreement*, version 20010402c2, was made available to the author for this paper through the courtesy of RLG.

5. CONSORT Colleges, *Five Colleges of Ohio Memorandum of Understanding Regarding Sharing of Library Materials*, is published on the Web at http://www.wooster.edu/library/OH5/CCCD/CCCD_MOU.html.

6. Joint Information Systems Committee. *Model License for E-Journals*, approved 1999, on the Web at http://www.nesli.ac.uk/model.htm.

7. The CLIR/DLF model electronic licensing agreement, April 1, 2001, is at http://www.library.yale.edu/~llicense/modlic.shtml.

8. "Research Library Cooperative Program: Latin American Collections Statement of Principles" at http://www-sul.stanford.edu/depts/hasrg/latinam/rlcp/lascooperative.html.

9. The boilerplate text for the agreements for contributing libraries in the LC/Ameritech competition is included in Library of Congress National Digital Library. *Sample Cooperative Agreement* http://lcweb2.loc.gov/ammem/award/html/sample.html.

10. The National Endowment for the Humanities *General Grant Provisions for Organizations* (revised July 2002) cites "government-wide regulations issued by the Department of Commerce at 37 CFR part 401, 'Rights to Inventions made by Non-

profit Organizations and Small Business Firms Under Government Grants, Contracts and Cooperative Agreements.' " Available at http://www.neh.gov/manage/ggps.html#.

11. See *Explanatory Statement on The Andrew W. Mellon Foundation's Intellectual Property Policy For Digital Products Developed With Foundation Funds* at http://www.mellon.org/ip.policy.2.pdf.

12. "National Library of the Netherlands and Elsevier Science Make Digital Preservation History" press release issued by the Koninklijke Bibliotheek, August 20, 2002, at http://www.kb.nl/kb/resources/frameset_kb.html?/kb/menu/ken-arch-en.html.

13. National Library of Australia, *ANU-NLA Collection Cooperation Agreement on Chinese Provincial and Provincial Capital City Statistical Yearbooks*, adopted August 1998, updated November 30, 1998, available at http://www.nla.gov.au/policy/chinaanunla.html; and Washington Research Libraries Consortium *WRLC Policy Cooperative Holding of Journal Titles*, adopted March 1992, updated August 2002, available at http://www.wrlc.org/poljour.html.

14. *D-Lib Magazine*, vol 8, no.1 (January 2002) at http://www.dlib.org/dlib/january02/kenney/01kenney.html.

15. The Elsevier Science–National Library of the Netherlands electronic journals archiving agreement, cited above, potentially has a significant bearing on the security of a large and valuable shared resource and on the print archiving decisions of many libraries invested in the resource. The text of the agreement was not readily available for inspection as of this writing.

The AAU/ARL Global Resources Program: The View from a Crossroads

Deborah Jakubs

SUMMARY. The Global Resources Program was created in 1996 to address problems of access to international research materials, the "crisis in foreign acquisitions." A joint endeavor of the Association of Research Libraries (ARL) and the Association of American Universities (AAU), the program capitalizes on technological advances to expand the array of resources available to scholars. The paper reviews the program's accomplishments, evaluates progress on the original goals, and speculates on areas of future emphasis, within the context of cooperative collection development strategies. *[Article copies available for a fee from The Haworth Document Delivery Service: 1-800-HAWORTH. E-mail address: <docdelivery@haworthpress.com> Website: <http://www.HaworthPress.com> © 2003 by The Haworth Press, Inc. All rights reserved.]*

KEYWORDS. Global resources, foreign acquisitions, cooperation, collection development, Association of Research Libraries

The Global Resources Program (GRP) was created in 1996 to address serious problems of access to international research resources, the

---

Deborah Jakubs is Director, Collections Services, Duke University Libraries and former Director (1996-2002), Global Resources Program, a joint endeavor of the Association of American Universities (AAU) and the Association of Research Libraries (ARL).

Address correspondence to: Deborah Jakubs, 220 Perkins Library, Box 90193, Duke University, Durham, NC 27708 (E-mail: deborah.jakubs@duke.edu).

[Haworth co-indexing entry note]: "The AAU/ARL Global Resources Program: The View from a Crossroads." Jakubs, Deborah. Co-published simultaneously in *Collection Management* (The Haworth Information Press, an imprint of The Haworth Press, Inc.) Vol. 28, No. 1/2, 2003, pp. 135-145; and: *The New Dynamics and Economics of Cooperative Collection Development* (ed: Edward Shreeves) The Haworth Information Press, an imprint of The Haworth Press, Inc., 2003, pp. 135-145. Single or multiple copies of this article are available for a fee from The Haworth Document Delivery Service [1-800-HAWORTH, 9:00 a.m. - 5:00 p.m. (EST). E-mail address: docdelivery@haworthpress.com].

http://www.haworthpress.com/web/COL
© 2003 by The Haworth Press, Inc. All rights reserved.
Digital Object Identifier: 10.1300/J105v28n01_11

135

"crisis in foreign acquisitions," which had been identified in a set of detailed studies that provided the rationale and momentum for the GRP. The program, a joint endeavor of the Association of Research Libraries (ARL) and the Association of American Universities (AAU), has now reached a crossroads: the funding that supported its first six years has been expended, and it is not yet clear what direction the program will take in its next phase. This paper will address the best practices of the GRP's "regional projects" and explore how and why the program's orientation shifted dramatically, from a focus on cooperative collection building at its inception to an emphasis on access within just a few years. Everyone is well aware of the difficulties of creating, coordinating, and maintaining truly effective cooperative collection development programs–if we pooled the years dedicated to this cause by those who attended the Aberdeen Woods II meeting, supposing the average in the group is ten years, we would discover that we have spent a total of over thirteen centuries trying to establish viable cooperative programs, and/or to sustain them. The Global Resources Program offers a look at the "new dynamics" of cooperative collection development, and raises questions about old models and their relevance and applicability today.

A brief history, for orientation: In December 1996, the Andrew W. Mellon Foundation awarded $450,000 to ARL to create the AAU/ARL Global Resources Program (GRP). The endorsement of the AAU was especially important, because it signaled that university presidents and provosts were engaged with the issues that led to the GRP, namely, problems research libraries faced in the acquisition and distribution of foreign-language resources. An AAU Task Force on this topic, a precursor to the GRP, concluded in its lengthy final report in 1994 that there was, in fact, a critical need to focus efforts on this area, and produced a set of recommendations:

> The major North American research universities and libraries should organize a distributed program for access to foreign acquisitions. This program should include the Library of Congress and foreign national and research libraries working together in sharing responsibility for acquiring, organizing, and facilitating access to foreign acquisitions.

> The major North American research universities and libraries should implement the program through three demonstration projects.

Universities should plan and fund the electronic infrastructure necessary to support the new avenues of access and delivery crucial to the success of a distributed North American collection.

University leaders and their research librarians should articulate incentives to scholars and faculty for moving away from local and toward remote access, so that an individual institution's library may develop in-depth collections in a few selected areas, but provide remote access to many more in-depth collections.[1]

Germany, Japan, and Latin America became the focus of the demonstration projects, and a 1996 ARL publication, Jutta Reed-Scott's *Scholarship, Research Libraries, and Global Publishing* provided further impetus to launch the GRP. Originally intended to support three years of activity, the Mellon funding stimulated over five years of work focused on improving access to international research materials through cooperative structures and the use of new technologies. A related objective was to generate increased communication with the scholarly community regarding future information needs involving international research materials.

The goals for the GRP were based on a "tactical plan" devised by ARL, which suggested:

- The creation of a Global Resources Program with a federated management structure, hosted by ARL in cooperation with AAU.
- The appointment of a full-time coordinator for an initial three-year term with responsibilities for continued development and improvement of the program.
- An educational effort to inform faculty about the Global Resources Program and to build consensus on the proposed strategies for addressing needs.
- Working with the research library community to strengthen and advance area librarianship.
- Establishment of an Advisory Council that would include chief academic officers from AAU and ARL institutions to guide the development of the program.

Goals outlined in the proposal focus primarily on program expansion and outreach to faculty and scholarly associations:

- Identify "lead institutions" for each region, to collect and make accessible a range of materials;

- Encourage those institutions to pursue relationships with foreign publishers of newspapers, journals and books to enable them to make these materials available in digital form;
- Inventory relationships between individual libraries and research institutes and/or libraries abroad;
- Mount information about the commitments and linkages on the Web;
- Conduct on-campus symposia and make presentations at meetings of scholarly associations;
- Collaborate with scholarly and library organizations to set national policy on issues of importance to the global resources arena;
- Develop fully the Web-based protocol of library strengths, collecting policies and responsibilities of participating institutions;
- Conduct a survey of area specialists, in cooperation with the Council of National Resource Center Directors (CNRC) of Title VI;
- Conduct a survey to determine the new roles for and future supply of area librarians.

Of the goals proposed for program expansion, several were achieved, although not necessarily as originally anticipated. "Lead institutions," rather than being formally named, emerged within each of the projects. This was determined by the size/strength of the particular area collections at a given library and/or the energy, enthusiasm, and initiative of the area specialist librarian. Some institutions have been acknowledged as lead institutions for many years. Relationships with foreign publishers have been pursued within the regional projects rather than by individual institutions, and have selectively led to consortial product licenses as well as digitization projects, although perhaps not on the scale originally envisioned. One of the earliest Global Resources activities was to conduct an inventory of linkages between North American libraries and other institutions abroad. At that time, such information did not prove to be very useful, but it has now resurfaced as a priority for Phase II of the GRP.

The outreach goals were, for the most part, also achieved. Presentations about the challenges and goals of the GRP were made at numerous scholarly meetings. A survey of area studies center directors was completed in April 1998, and largely confirmed that faculty prefer that materials be available locally, because their experience has been that document delivery/interlibrary loan services are not able to supply materials quickly and efficiently. The AAU Task Force recommendation that we "articulate incentives" to faculty and scholars for "moving away from local and toward remote access" was proving, not surprisingly, to be difficult to address.

The web-based listing of collecting strengths and policies has not been implemented, in large part because of the labor- and time-intensive nature of the project. In addition, current metadata harvesting projects underway under the Open Archives Initiative (OAI) will make this function moot. Participants in the regional projects believe that they have a good sense of "what's where" in terms of library collections. Users may not know where special library strengths can be found, but they now have access to Internet searches that reveal local websites, lists of resources, and access to local OPACs. It is not clear whether faculty and student use of such a separate, conspectus-like online listing of library strengths, which would be duplicative of other sources, would be worth the investment of time and effort. In the brief five years since the Global Resources Program was initiated, online access to information about library collections has increased dramatically and this goal no longer seems relevant.

REGIONAL PROJECTS

The GRP includes seven regional projects, each offering a different model for expanding access to scholarly resources. Six of them–on Africa, Germany, Japan, Latin America, South Asia, and Southeast Asia–have become well established. Another, the Slavic Document Delivery Project, was proposed toward the end of the initial grant and has not yet become fully operational. Brief descriptions of the projects are provided below; for more information, see the cited websites.

The African Newspaper Union List Project (AFRINUL)
http://www.crl.uchicago.edu/info/camp/afrinul.htm

The Center for Research Libraries (CRL) is host to AFRINUL, a multi-institutional project to produce and maintain an electronic union list of sub-Saharan African newspapers. A joint initiative of the Africana Librarians Council (ALC) of the African Studies Association (ASA) and the Cooperative Africana Microform Project (CAMP) of CRL, AFRINUL also complements the ICON project. The database will consolidate holdings information for collections in North America and will later expand to include holdings in Africa, Europe, and elsewhere. The project also has a preservation component, to be carried out at Northwestern University, and plans to digitize the content of newspapers as well, to facilitate research on African political, economic, and cultural events. The project has fifteen participating libraries.

The German Resources Project
http://grp.lib.msu.edu/

The German Resources Project is the sole North American/German library initiative for cooperation in bibliographic control, collection development, digital projects, and document delivery. The project's website provides full information on the four working groups that are active in these areas. The numerous achievements of the German Resources Projects include: the establishment of the German Resources Partnerships Project, in which North American library selectors for 27 subjects (German studies and beyond) are matched with counterparts in Germany; consortial access to xipolis.net, a set of major German reference databases; the expansion of exchange relationships to include more materials and more players; development of digital projects; an active document delivery system between North America and Germany; and the translation of AACR2 into German. Especially noteworthy is the project's unique model of peer-to-peer relationships, collaboration between North American research libraries and European libraries with very strong historical collections. The project has 47 members.

The Japan Journal Access Project
http://pears.lib.ohio-state.edu/NCC/jpnpjct.html

The Japan Journal Access Project's foremost emphasis is on international document delivery. After an initial focus on cooperative collection development and scientific/technical publications (during its pilot phase), the project turned attention to rapid access to materials held only in Japan. A major achievement was the commitment by the National Institute for Informatics (NII) to implement the ISO ILL Protocol in their interlibrary loan system. This international standard will permit ILL requests and responses to be exchanged between and among Protocol-compliant systems such as OCLC and RLIN. The Union List of Japanese Serials and Newspapers reflects the continuation of early cooperative collection development efforts. The project has 38 participating members.

The Latin Americanist Research Resources Project (LARRP)
http://lanic.utexas.edu/project/arl

The Latin Americanist Research Resources Project was launched as a pilot and, at an early stage, secured an additional 1:1 matching grant of $60,000 from the Mellon Foundation. Each participating library was to contribute a one-time fee of $3,000. Early expectations were that the project would have 20 participants; current membership stands at 46, so the matching funds have totaled $138,000. This additional funding has enabled the project to develop a multi-faceted array of project components, and to attract additional funding from the U.S. Department of Education. The project includes:

- LAPTOC Database (Latin American Periodical Table of Contents)
- Distributed Resources
- Presidential Messages
- Case Study on Cooperation
- Latin American Partnerships
- Latin American Open Archives Portal

The Slavic Document Delivery Project
http://www.ku.edu/~slavlib/arlproject.htm

This project is in its formative stage. The goal is to create a document delivery system between libraries in Slavic countries and in North America. Initially, six libraries in East Central Europe and the countries of the former Soviet Union were expected to participate, with a core group of North American libraries as their counterparts.

The Digital South Asia Library (DSAL)
http://dsal.uchicago.edu

The Digital South Asia Library and the closely related Digital Dictionaries of South Asia project both originated with seed money from the Global Resources Program. Both have attracted significant additional funds from the U.S. Department of Education. DSAL is expanding access, through digitization, to numerous categories of research material:

- Books and Journals
- Dictionaries
- Bibliographies
- Images
- Statistics
- Maps

The Southeast Asia Indexing Project/Thai Journal Index
http://content-dev.lib.washington.edu/thai/index.html

The Project is composed of two parts: a project based at Cornell University Library to enhance the range of materials represented in the *Bib-*

liography of Asian Studies and a project based at the University of Washington to provide access to Thai journals, using scanned images of part of the original text and transliterated metadata. Both are projects sponsored by the Committee on Research Materials on Southeast Asia (CORMOSEA), a subcommittee of the Association of Asian Studies.

WHATEVER BECAME OF COOPERATIVE COLLECTION DEVELOPMENT?

Of the seven regional projects within the Global Resources Program, only two have a stated focus on "cooperative collection development." The overwhelming emphasis is on *access*: two union lists; four document delivery structures; a nearly pervasive digital focus throughout. This is a far cry from the "distributed program for access to foreign acquisitions" recommended by the AAU Task Force–or is it?

When we think of cooperative collection development, we think books. We think print. We think Farmington Plan. We think assignments. We think central coordination. The Global Resources Program has approached cooperative collection development from a different perspective, staying in sync with the ubiquitous dynamic of digital access. The GRP's regional projects are cooperative, and they involve multiple institutions. They are bringing users what they need and want, be it the latest article from a Mexican journal, a German document, a historical map of India, or a Japanese working paper. What they are not doing (with one notable exception) is centrally managing distributed responsibility among a large number of institutions for the cooperative acquisition and cataloging of books and journals published abroad, those materials whose fate was the concern of Jutta Reed-Scott and the authors of the many studies that make up her book.

The exception is the "Distributed Resources" component of the Latin Americanist Research Resources Project, which depends on voluntary specialization among 28 libraries. It is a cooperative collection development effort in the "classic" sense. Twenty-eight of the nearly fifty project members have agreed to reallocate at least 7% of their collection funds to deepen their collections in established areas of local emphasis. The result has been enhanced coverage of non-core materials, expedited cataloging, and expansion of "the commons" of materials available to all. All Latin American countries and many subject areas (e.g., labor) are covered. It has worked well for reasons that everyone attending this conference will understand: participation is voluntary; the area of collecting focus is locally determined, based on local strengths and needs (i.e., not a centralized assignment to collect in an area that is not of particular local interest); and it is blissfully free of bureaucratic complexity, loosely coordinated by a single individual in a participating institution.

Why did the GRP not create a distributed model? Each project developed according to specialists' assessments of the scholarly needs of the field or region. For example, the projects on Africa and Japan stressed that cooperative collection development would be more easily accomplished if a union list were created first. Other projects focused on the "chicken and egg" issue, seeking to put in place well functioning structures for expedited international document delivery and interlibrary loan, since faculty were likely to be more accepting of "remote" collections if they could have rapid access to them.

The evolution of the GRP from its original goal of centralized coordination, a "federation" of institutions all embracing a very rationally designed and distributed set of responsibilities for collecting and cataloging print materials occurred rapidly. Projects were proposed that sidestepped the idea of assigning such responsibilities, focusing instead on using technology to bring about rapid access to resources needed for scholarship and teaching. The rapidity with which the technology advanced, making available approaches to access that were not "on the radar" at the time the proposal was written and funded, refocused the GRP more on this area and less on the challenges of "classic" cooperative collection building. The memories and baggage of the Farmington Plan, the reluctance within individual libraries to dedicate funds and efforts to collecting materials for anyone other than their own faculty, the inability to take the more daring steps of canceling journals and relying on the holdings of other institutions, or adjusting collecting policies to focus more intensely on an area that would support national needs rather than only local needs–all these came into play, along with the sheer excitement of trying out new digital technologies and designing new means of electronic access. A new approach was more intriguing than an old one. Thus the GRP took a detour toward access.

I remain concerned about the "crisis in foreign acquisitions," and, to some degree, with the constant refrain of inadequate collections budgets when true cooperation and a greater degree of interdependence could help to make our collective spending go farther. Is it fear of local faculty dissatisfaction? Probably. Is it concern about the complexity of coordination and the burden of bureaucracy? Perhaps. Do we need to continue to worry about whether we are collecting "the universe" of all appropriate research materials from abroad? I think so, but maybe it's time to be realistic about what we can and can't do within North America and with our own budgets. The pressures of providing expanded access to electronic resources (most duplicated many times throughout our libraries) have further curtailed our ability to acquire a broad range of international materials.

If we can build international alliances, as the German project has done, and focus on document delivery, as the Japan, German, and Latin American projects have done, we will provide access to more resources. If we draw more international partners into our arena, as the South Asia and other projects have done, we can move to a new model of resource sharing that does "expand the commons." At the same time we can promote the development of capacities–such as the digitizing being undertaken in India–elsewhere in the world. If we pursue consortial deals, such as the *xipolis* package that the German project was able to craft, we will save money. I do not believe that the projects of the GRP have failed to create a viable model of cooperative collection development; the program has adapted the model to take advantage of the available technologies and branched out creatively with efforts that could not have been foreseen or predicted in 1995.

In retrospect, the past five years–the first five years–of the GRP have offered many lessons, some unanticipated, some not so surprising. Changing collecting behavior is notoriously difficult. This has been borne out in the GRP, especially in the Latin American project, whose cornerstone is the LAPTOC table-of-contents database to which all participating libraries, as well as several Latin American partners, contribute. LAPTOC now offers open access to the tables-of-contents for over 700 journals, approximately 140,000 articles and delivery of articles to users at participating institutions. Originally intended not only to facilitate direct, unmediated user access to non- or little-indexed journal articles, but also to encourage cancellation of some commonly held titles (in order to redirect those funds to other titles), LAPTOC has led to minimal, if any, cancellations. I am reminded of the early years of the RLG Conspectus (back in the Stone Age of cooperative collection development) and the reluctance of some well-known libraries to rely on others even when those fellow institutions had committed formally to a PCR, or "Primary Collecting Responsibility." Times have not changed much in this area. In that case it was a trust issue: how do I know that Library X's level 4 is the same as MY level 4? Just as PCRs never really took root beyond fairly marginal areas–Icelandic Studies, for example–our ability to orchestrate a federated and interconnected system of collecting remains out of reach. Or perhaps it is still within the reach of regional consortia.

This is a transition year for the Global Resources Program. A new director, my colleague and friend Dan Hazen, is already at work developing the next phase. The achievements and lessons of the first five years will provide, to some extent, a map for the next five. A closer relationship with researchers and faculty will be of critical importance. For example, the Council of National Resource Center Directors of Title VI is planning, post-September 11, to create a website that will provide information on language skills and area/disciplinary knowledge available throughout the United States. Preliminary conversations about including information on library collections have been very positive. More publicity for the program's goals and achievements is a must. Building on the strong relationships already in place with the Center for Research Libraries, and finding a larger role for the Library of Congress and other national libraries, will also be important. A cross-regional and cross-disciplinary focus will benefit those scholars whose work is not limited to one field or part of the world. Perhaps an expanded role for publishers and booksellers, already developed to some extent in the Latin American project, will emerge. Links to cataloging (access too, of course) have already been constructed in the German project, and could easily develop for other areas. More sharing among projects of "best practices" will advance the larger goals of the Global Resources Program and result in stronger new projects. The Program should not lose track of its roots in the "crisis in foreign acquisitions." I hope that the new, exciting models of cooperation that characterize the GRP can also incorporate a means to collect and preserve print resources from around the world. Who knows where the next five years will take us?

NOTE

1. Association of American Universities Research Libraries Project, *Reports of the AAU Task Forces* (Washington, DC: ARL, May 1994), pp. 13-14.

International Information
and the Postmodern Academy

Dan Hazen

SUMMARY. The international collections in North American research libraries are at a crossroads. While no library can continue to pursue comprehensive collections, our research libraries have become interdependent to the extent that even the most localized initiatives serve scholars anywhere within the country. The ever easier communications of today's globalized world suggest that national boundaries may be less and less relevant as well. Measures to improve bibliographic description and access, refine systems for delivery, cultivate and then more rationally allocate specialized staff resources, and consolidate international partnerships comprise a full and pressing agenda. However, these measures may not be sufficient to provide our users with enduring access to all of the resources that they require, or to ensure equitable library support across the full range of world areas and scholarly disciplines. This paper addresses these issues by exploring five loosely related questions concerning the conceptual underpinnings for our international efforts. Clearer understandings of current possibilities and limitations are essential. New models for our work may also facilitate more adequate responses. *[Article copies available for a fee from The Haworth Document Delivery Service: 1-800-HAWORTH. E-mail address: <docdelivery@haworthpress. com> Website: <http://www.HaworthPress.com> © 2003 by The Haworth Press, Inc. All rights reserved.]*

Dan Hazen is Director, Global Resources Program and Librarian for Latin America, Spain and Portugal, Harvard College Library, 197 Widener, Cambridge, MA 02138 (E-mail: dchazen@fas.harvard.edu).

[Haworth co-indexing entry note]: "International Information and the Postmodern Academy." Hazen, Dan. Co-published simultaneously in *Collection Management* (The Haworth Information Press, an imprint of The Haworth Press, Inc.) Vol. 28, No. 1/2, 2003, pp. 147-180; and: *The New Dynamics and Economics of Cooperative Collection Development* (ed: Edward Shreeves) The Haworth Information Press, an imprint of The Haworth Press, Inc., 2003, pp. 147-180. Single or multiple copies of this article are available for a fee from The Haworth Document Delivery Service [1-800-HAWORTH, 9:00 a.m. - 5:00 p.m. (EST). E-mail address: docdelivery@haworthpress.com].

Digital Object Identifier: 10.1300/J105v28n01_12

KEYWORDS. Global resources, foreign acquisitions, cooperation, collection development

INTRODUCTION

The international collections in North American research libraries are unequalled anywhere else. Local holdings at some foreign libraries certainly surpass those in the United States, as do the printed colonial (and in some cases post-colonial) materials available in some former imperial powers. Overall, however, U.S. holdings are unique in their breadth and depth. Intense scholarly interest, ample funding, aggressive acquisitions programs, and repositories safe from war and civil strife have all played a role.

Today, however, our international collections are at a crossroads.[1] No library can continue to pursue comprehensive collections. On the other hand, North American research libraries have become interdependent to the extent that even the most localized initiatives serve scholars anywhere within the country. The ever easier communications of today's globalized world suggest that national boundaries may be less and less relevant as well; and, of course, libraries in other countries can often pursue their local materials more effectively than we can from here. Efforts to devise better means to identify and then gain access to remote resources therefore make perfect sense. Arrangements to share specialized staff may likewise permit cost-effective local operations that both rely upon and reinforce our interdependence.

Measures to improve bibliographic description and access, refine systems for document delivery, cultivate and then more rationally allocate specialized staff resources, and consolidate international partnerships comprise a full and pressing agenda. These measures are essential as we look toward research libraries' overall future, and also as we more specifically consider scholarship that draws on materials from other parts of the world. But are they sufficient to ensure that our users enjoy enduring access to all of the resources they require? Furthermore, do today's emphases on electronics, access, specialization, and cooperation adequately and equitably serve all disciplines and world areas? Other issues, though they may seem narrow, have substantial practical implications as well. For instance, how do our ever more democratic (or populist) visions of a "shared commons" of information resources square with the reality of weak and strong institutions that are investing in this "commons" at very different levels and with very different goals?

This paper explores some of these issues from a North American perspective. It opens by summarizing our many accomplishments in international acquisitions and our promising future of intensifying interdependence. But the picture begins to cloud as we more closely examine "international information" as an analytical category, and dims even more as we consider what we aren't now covering. Patterns of collecting strength and weakness, emphasis and neglect, may in some cases both reflect and affect our more general response to contemporary scholarship. Does our practice favor materials that are primarily relevant to only one ideological and methodological camp? Are we adequately addressing the interests of emerging professional programs as well as longstanding area studies constituencies? Different clusters of research resources, broadly associated with specific academic disciplines, seem to behave in predictable ways. Analyzing these behaviors may suggest both the areas most urgently requiring our action and the most appropriate responses. The essay concludes with reflections on the potential scope, as well as limitations, of this alternate approach.

SOME STORIES OF SUCCESS

The library community can point with pride to many international collecting successes. Our everyday operations are built around an acronym soup of cooperative agreements and consortial commitments. Moreover, our institutions are by now so fully immersed in an organizational context of mutual reliance that individual efforts to meet local or even personal ends inevitably serve the community as a whole. Formal cooperative activities often deliver extra benefits and added value, but almost any initiative related to acquisitions or access has a positive effect.

A number of examples, drawn primarily from the Latin American arena with which I'm most familiar, can suggest the current range of both cooperative programs and individual initiatives. Latin America, like any other region, is of course unique in its information output, structures for publishing and distribution, and scholarly agendas, and also in the nature and limitations of its cultural institutions.[2] External efforts that are both welcome and sensible in this area might thus prove unworkable, redundant, or obtrusive in other parts of the world.

The Latin Americanist Research Resources Project (LARRP) is one of several regional ventures subsumed within the Global Resources Program, which is in turn a joint initiative of the Association of American Universities and the Association of Research Libraries.[3] LARRP's growing membership consists of forty-seven North American libraries (not all of them ARL members), plus five foreign partners. Many LARRP activities have been funded by external grants and participant contributions. These include a project to digitize printed source materials, another effort to create a major table-of-contents database for sparsely-held Latin American journals, and partnerships with Latin American institutions to index additional journals and to capture and preserve websites and web publications. LARRP's "distributed resources" component, by contrast, is voluntary and entails no overhead costs. This effort also builds upon a long history of cooperative collection development. Specialized and separately negotiated acquisitions assignments are fulfilled through each library's commitment to redirect at least seven percent of its Latin American monographs' budget to the target area. Overall redundancy is thereby reduced while the group as a whole acquires more unique titles. LARRP, by providing a renewed sense of purpose and achievement, has also carried the unexpected side benefit of reenergizing many participant libraries and librarians.

The Latin American Microform Project (LAMP) has taken a different approach.[4] LAMP is a voluntary and self-sustaining consortium of forty-two libraries, administered through the Center for Research Libraries, whose activities are funded by member dues and occasional external grants. LAMP's members together determine the filming projects it will pursue, often in Latin America and typically in partnership with local repositories. Negative and positive microfilm are almost invariably deposited with the host institution, and the projects whenever possible seek to strengthen local microfilming capacity. LAMP's activities are based on pooled funds and shared decision-making. New LAMP acquisitions are deposited at CRL to ensure that they are freely available for loan.

LARRP and LAMP differ in finances, governance, and goals. On the other hand, both are cooperative efforts that are open to all. Both initiatives have necessarily accommodated the varying priorities of large and small institutions, and of libraries with broad-based acquisitions as well as narrow specializations. The collections consequences are not always clear. For example, LARRP's "distributed resources" assignments enhance targeted areas of local acquisitions for all participants. At small libraries, however, the resulting intake may fall well beneath the level already sustained by some larger members, resulting in an only nominal contribution to the community. A similar and recurring conversation within LAMP contrasts the merits of acquiring expensive microfilm sets already held by some libraries with projects to film more esoteric materials that are new to all. (This particular debate has lost some of its intensity as more fluid arrangements for interlibrary loan have reduced the need to hold separate, "community" copies of expensive sets at loan-oriented repositories like CRL.)

It can take time and energy to reconcile the interests of disparate consortial partners. Another approach therefore builds cooperation around libraries that consider themselves peers from the start. The University of California at Berkeley and Stanford University, for instance, have for twenty years sustained formal arrangements, ratified by the library directors, to share their Latin American collecting responsibilities. The program from the first has also emphasized the fluid movement of both books and users between these close-by campuses. The arrangement ratcheted to a new level in 1998 by adding the Nettie Lee Benson Collection at the University of Texas, Austin.[5] While the distances are suddenly large, the anticipated benefits will still in the first instance reflect intensive cooperation among plausible peers.

Other emerging consortia are based on geographic proximity. Voluntary regional groupings within the Latin Americanist library community cover the Northeast (LANE), South and Southeast (LASER), Midwest (MOLLAS), and California (Calafia). Calafia is more or less typical in maintaining its own website to provide general background as well as links to participant librarians, libraries, catalogs, and collections.[6] The members normally meet twice a year, once within the region and again at a national conference. A great deal of business is conducted via e-mail. Collections cooperation is encouraged as well, in Calafia's case through special plans that divide responsibilities for current acquisitions from northern and southern Mexico.

Some cooperative efforts are even less structured. ICCG, the Intensive Cuban Collecting Group, was an informal, voluntary effort of the late 1980s and early 1990s, particularly championed by Princeton's Peter Johnson, among North American libraries with significant Cuban holdings. (Strained international relations precluded Cuban participation.) These participants together generated lists of important journals and then confirmed North American holdings in both hardcopy and microfilm. Many participants also lent their holdings for filming, thereby enabling microfilm sets that were as complete as possible. The group declared success and disbanded after about five years of work.

ICCG was spontaneous, informal, and agile. Its sole purpose was to enhance overall access to critical research materials. Some narrower efforts, at times designed to support local programs–though typically with an eye to the broader community–have been similarly effective. Four examples suggest some of the possibilities:

- The Library of Congress Office in Rio de Janeiro was established in order to support LC's acquisitions from Brazil and neighboring countries. Additional services, now available to paying participants, include subscription programs for Brazilian journals and for music CD-ROMs. The Rio office has also broken new institutional ground through its program to seek out Brazilian ephemera, organize and film these materials, and then offer the "Brazil's Popular Groups" (BPG) microfilm for outside purchase. BPG holdings are by and large produced outside of the commercial publishing sphere by grassroots groups such as social movements, non-governmental organizations, political parties, and labor unions. The microfilm thus affords a unique means of capturing primary source materials from Latin America's largest country. Heavy demand for the film, broad support from the research library community, and secure sponsorship within LC all testify to its impact.
- The "Brazil's Popular Groups" initiative owes a great deal to the energy and imagination of staff at the Rio office. A somewhat similar project, which provided much of the model for BPG, is based at Princeton. Peter Johnson, Princeton's longtime Bibliographer for Latin America, Spain, and Portugal, had by the early 1980s cultivated collecting agents in many of the Latin American nations then under military rule. These agents, who were chosen for their understanding of events, personal connections, and productivity, ferreted out opposition and clandestine materials that were shipped to Princeton to be organized, cataloged (at a collection level), and microfilmed. Many of the originals were retained, and the film was made available for purchase. (Peter Johnson himself initially served as Princeton's sales agent, though a commercial distributor later took over this chore.[7]) Sales revenues have been returned to the program. Latin America's redemocratization, while shifting the focus of grassroots activism, has also enlarged the scope of both debate and publication. The Princeton University Latin American Pamphlet Collection, like BPG, has become a mainstay for libraries seeking primary documentation on popular movements and social change. The Princeton example further shows how visionary individual efforts can expand the universe of research materials available to the community as a whole.
- Another individual effort, again based within a single institution, centers on Chilean acquisitions at the University of California at Berkeley. Berkeley's Latin American bibliographer, Carlos Delgado, has devised a unique exchange relationship with Chile's

National Library which capitalizes on legal deposit provisions that require printers to provide multiple copies of their publications. While compliance is far from complete, the National Library is inundated with extra copies of the materials that printers do provide, among them many titles that never enter the commercial marketplace. Berkeley has therefore engineered an arrangement through which it purchases non-Chilean materials, selected by and for the National Library, in exchange for free access to the depository duplicates. This program has enabled Berkeley to obtain more than 4,000 titles, of which about 1,900 are new to OCLC.[8] A similar effort is also in place with Cuba's National Library. Not all North American libraries have acquisitions funds that can be used to purchase materials for other collections, and only a few Latin American repositories have so much to offer. These examples nonetheless exemplify the potential impact of efforts by a single bibliographer at a single institution.

• A final example of an individual's project with a broad general impact mixes new and old technologies. Karen Lindvall-Larson, Latin American Studies Librarian at the University of California, San Diego, has constructed a website on Latin American elections that provides chronologies, links to official election and campaign websites, reports, and voting results for an expanding group of countries.[9] UCSD's collections cover the same ground as exhaustively as possible, and both the website and the hard copy acquisitions are tied to the "distributed resources" initiative of the Latin Americanist Research Resources Project. Scholars and librarians from all over the world now rely on this resource.

While the list could go on and on, these examples are sufficient to demonstrate the general benefits of efforts ranging from formal, fee-based consortia to informal cooperative initiatives, and to individual projects as well.[10] None of these initiatives, however, emerged in a vacuum. All have rather been enabled by broad contexts of support in which four elements particularly stand out: an accommodating institutional structure; shared standards and procedures; sufficient resources; and energetic champions. Each element merits additional comment.

Institutions. Latin Americanist librarians have, over the years, built up a reputation for effective cooperation. Most would agree that the field's premier professional organization, the Seminar on the Acquisition of Latin American Library Materials (SALALM) has played a critical role.[11] SALALM has for about fifty years served as a vehicle for librarians, scholars, and booksellers to analyze and then address trends and needs in both research and publishing. Changing scholarly and instructional agendas, an evolving information marketplace subsuming ever more media and formats, shifts in library budgets and priorities, and dramatic transformations within the region itself have all been tracked through SALALM. The body likewise provides a channel both to propose and to publicize new initiatives. The Latin Americanist Research Resources Project, the Latin American Microform Project, and regional groups of Latin Americanist librarians all function in close organizational proximity to SALALM. Perhaps most important, SALALM has fostered the working relationships, friendships, and close collegiality that are indispensable in efforts that require interdependence and trust.

Other cooperative efforts rely on distinct institutional bases. SALALM has been important for the Latin Americanist Research Resources Project and the Latin American Microform Project, but the Association of Research Libraries and the Center for Research Libraries have respectively provided sponsorship and administrative support. The willingness and ability of the entire research library community to underwrite these central agencies, through separate fee assessments or general dues, is crucial. Similarly supportive institutional structures are associated with almost all enduring cooperative efforts, and also with individual efforts at the local level. Even such spontaneous initiatives as the Intensive Cuban Collecting Group relied on SALALM as the locus for its meetings and communications.

Standards. Most North American librarians take for granted that new cooperative efforts will conform to accepted standards and procedures. Bibliographic descriptions for hard copy materials, for example, are expected to follow AACR-2 and the MARC format; standard protocols for interlibrary loan will be employed in initiatives to share resources. Cooperation tends to remain more hesitant in areas where common standards or "best practices" have not yet emerged. Thus, for instance, distributed digital projects combining materials from different libraries still tend to be scarce.

Libraries within Latin America, with some notable exceptions, have lagged in embracing common standards. Formats for bibliographic records are frequently idiosyncratic, microfilming procedures are often ad hoc, and interlibrary loan relies on personal connections. In other world areas, perhaps particularly those in which non-Roman scripts come into play, the challenges are even greater. Increased standardization is in many cases a precondition for cooperation. Achieving common standards, however, requires leadership, organizational coherence, trust, and community resources. The process is seldom straightforward, and almost never merely mechanical.

Resources. Any effort to strengthen library collections or improve access to remote resources requires extra support. Even such low over-head activities as the "distributed resources" component of LARRP require central coordination and local tracking. And even such seemingly unobtrusive projects, if successful, will increase the number of unique titles that require original cataloging. Increased interlibrary loan traffic is likely as well. The costs, while delayed and to some extent hidden, are nonetheless quite real. Many cooperative efforts, of course, are based on direct cash outlays. Even "free" personal initiatives entail opportunity costs as specialists pursue one activity rather than something else.

Not all individuals, or institutions, will control sufficient resources to participate in cooperative efforts. In some very active fields, the array of projects and their associated demands may also be too broad to sustain a critical mass of participants in each and every one. Setting priorities is essential as consortia, participant institutions, and individual specialists make their choices.

Champions. All successful initiatives require champions with the energy, vision, autonomy, and means to develop and implement an agenda. Finding these individuals entails much more than casting about for knowledgeable specialists. Institutions must respond with support, or at least forbearance, if would-be leaders are to devote time and energy to co-operative activities. Provisions for travel and office expenses are essential. It's equally important to ensure that those engaged in off-site projects aren't penalized when it comes to promotion and review. Innovation and initiative require champions. Champions, in turn, only emerge from flexible and supportive institutions.

This section began with descriptions of Latin Americanist information initiatives that illustrate some of our options in the international sphere. Many other efforts could be added to the list, from Latin America and also from other parts of the world. These examples, however, don't explain how, or why, international collecting is different from mainstream acquisitions. It's easy to obtain trade imprints from places like England or Germany. It's at the same time difficult to collect, say, ethnic publications from the United States. Are we justified in lumping our international efforts into a special conceptual category?

Responses to this question can follow several different lines.

1. One approach focuses on the regional peculiarities of the information marketplace. Areas with highly developed booktrades typically produce timely and fairly complete national bibliographies, and also boast

efficient distribution systems for their books and journals. Some materials will always escape the net, but most publications are easy to find. Generally speaking, this kind of accessibility characterizes market-based societies, such as the United States and Western Europe, in which cultural goods are treated as commodities. Both publication and distribution are centrally controlled in most command economies, like the old Soviet Bloc or Cuba. Political and security mandates, however, can limit the availability of specific items even when the information universe is easy to apprehend. On the other hand, many countries with weaker markets, typically those labeled as "developing," either can't, don't want, or don't need to organize their cultural and knowledge output. The extraordinary acquisitions efforts that are only occasionally required in sophisticated publishing markets here become the norm. "International" collecting, when viewed from a marketplace perspective, particularly entails the labor- and skill-intensive efforts needed to build collections in areas with spontaneous booktrades and incipient systems of bibliographic control.

2. This response, while easy to grasp, is not entirely satisfying. For instance, the AAU-ARL "Global Resources Program" includes projects for Germany as well as South Asia, and for Japan as well as Latin America. What do we make of the developed world cases? Today's fluid communications and often permeable national frontiers here come into play. Converging legal provisions, scholarly expectations, marketplace mechanics, and communications capabilities have created environments conducive to resource sharing. Many developed world "collecting" initiatives therefore focus on shared resources and document delivery. The underlying expectation, of course, is that each affiliated library holds materials that are unique. In this case, international cooperation differs from domestic agreements primarily in the need for arrangements that reflect a range of languages, legal structures, and cultural norms. One end point imagines international library connections that are tantamount to cross-cultural mergers.

3. The interpretations suggested so far view "international resources" in terms of their availability to and accessibility among libraries. These materials can also be described in terms of academic disciplines and scholarly communication. Some scholarly fields prescribe rigorous research methodologies, the results of which are conveyed through highly normalized reports. Some of these fields are also effectively trans- (or non-) national: their practitioners participate in what amounts to a global conversation, often conducted in English, and typically mediated by individuals and institutions in the developed world. Scholarship in astronomy or mathematics, for instance, has little to do with a researcher's location.

The disciplines themselves track and organize the information resources upon which they rely. Libraries may need to pursue foreign as well as domestic publications, but the materials are fairly easy to identify and obtain. The situation is dramatically different in many other fields, including some sciences. Research in botany or geology, for instance, is often local, even though these disciplines also support laboratory studies and theoretical work. And scholarship in many fields of the social sciences and humanities is entirely diverse and dispersed. Discipline-based bibliographies and indexes may not effectively represent these materials, some of which will also fall outside of geographically-based publication registers. Scholarship that originates in the developed world is likely to be fairly well represented in compilations based on either geography or discipline, but both kinds of coverage are much spottier for items produced in more peripheral locations. And, of course, poorly tracked materials–'zines, small-label records and CDs, niche newsletters, and so on–pop up in even the tidiest milieux. The omnivorous scholarly appetite for all such expressions reinforces an expansive view that would find "international" resources in every corner of the world.

Professional programs in fields like law, business, public health, and public policy, are integral parts of North American universities. Many institutions, however, have traditionally supported these schools through library branches that focus almost exclusively on English-language materials from the United States. But these programs also require ever more international information. The associated efforts, including provisions to recruit or prepare knowledgeable staff, are still getting off the ground. "International," once again, is an almost ubiquitous concept.

4. A final approach to understanding "international" information within a globalized academy focuses on the validity of "globalism" as an analytical construct. Placid predictions of hybridity or even homogenization stand in vivid contrast to depictions of an enduring conflict among distinct and often hostile civilizations.[12] Mutually exclusive groupings, each characterized by a particular blend of ethnicity, religion, and culture, are in this view permanently vying for position. The West, while but one of several such civilizations, now boasts overarching economic and military power. All nations and societies, in consequence, participate to some degree in structures and processes that originated in the West, and also produce scholarship and other expressions that reflect Western disciplines, values, and concerns. These resources are by and large accessible to our libraries and scholars. Many other materials, however, reflect very different impulses. From a "civilizational" perspective, "international"

collecting particularly focuses on often-elusive indigenous expressions from outside the West.

We began this section by describing some cooperative collecting successes from Latin America. The discussion moved on to a quick exploration of the elements necessary for success, and a longer reflection on exactly what we mean by "international" collections. Different responses reveal a variety of starting points and perspectives, which in turn suggest a range of practical consequences and alternatives. We now look more closely at these interrelated circumstances and challenges.

FOR EVERY SILVER LINING A CLOUD

Despite our collecting achievements, we're still missing a great many international research resources. Perhaps most obvious, materials budgets are limited and the world's information output continues to grow. Locally, but also together, we're acquiring a shrinking proportion of new publications.[13] Other reasons trace back to libraries' overextended mandates and ever-expanding priorities. Shifts in local and remote demand also play a role, as do cost considerations, uncertain needs for duplicate copies, and the impact of preservation. Some cooperative responses seek to improve overall access to the resources that we already hold. This stance, however, often sidesteps questions of whether we have previously collected or now acquire the international materials required by all of our users. The relationship between academic agendas and resource accessibility poses some particularly sticky challenges.

The collecting mandates of academic libraries have evolved over time. All these repositories support instruction. Libraries in institutions concerned with research as well as teaching also pursue the scholarly record, though this goal has become more elusive with expanding output and increasing prices. The cost of scholarly journals, particularly in the sciences and technology, continues to rise more rapidly than either general inflation or monograph prices.[14] Electronic products, many quite expensive, also convey new scholarship. Libraries, universities, and scholars themselves have responded by forming buyers' consortia and by sponsoring (still somewhat fitful) non-profit alternatives to commercial publications.[15] In the end, however, library acquisitions often seem something of a zero-sum game. Despite often substantial infusions of new funds, there's rarely enough to go around. Keeping current with the scholarly record–just in English–typically squeezes other collecting areas, including international acquisitions.

More and more academic libraries are also expected to hold primary research resources. Scientists talk of huge sets of raw digital data. Humanists and social scientists often demand more traditional materials from categories that were formerly dismissed as "popular" or "non-scholarly." We thus pursue comic books, dime novels, and popular music, as well as "serious" literature and dense analytical tomes. The demand is eclectic, intense, and immense.

The dynamics of higher education have added to the pressure. Fully credentialed scholars are dispersed among small as well as large institutions, and the need for library materials is correspondingly broad. Almost every college and university also offers courses that challenge learners to wrestle with primary sources, which are therefore sought by students as well as professors. We're hard-pressed to respond.

Finally, our internationalized academies by their very nature affect library roles. International students and faculty seek materials that reflect their backgrounds and experiences. Professional programs ranging from business to law, public health to architecture, journalism to urban planning, require foreign materials as they prepare their students for a changing world. Our audience for global resources has become more and more diverse.

International collecting is also affected by expectations and procedures within our libraries. Costs, redundancy, staff support, and preservation are important both for individual institutions and for consortia:

- *Cost.* Materials from other countries vary wildly in price. Production costs, dealer mark-ups, and exchange rate fluctuations all enter in. Even seemingly inexpensive materials can lose some of their price appeal when the costs of specialized procedures (which still include transliteration for some non-Roman scripts) and staffs are factored in. These investments only make sense when there's strong local demand. The popularity of pre-packaged microfilm sets like "Brazil's Popular Groups" or Princeton's Latin American pamphlets may hint at the unfulfillable collecting aspirations of many nonspecialized libraries. Foreign acquisitions require special infrastructures that only a few libraries can sustain.
- *Redundancy.* Readily accessible information is a central library goal; Instantaneously accessible digital resources are increasingly common in the sciences, technology, and some professional fields.

Contracts for access rarely accommodate resource sharing, so specific constituencies typically have to decide between paying for a subscription (sometimes as part of a consortium) or simply doing without. For their part, hard copy materials remain central to a great deal of scholarship. These resources must be physically retrieved from library stacks or borrowed through interlibrary loan, and then consulted by one user at a time. We can't anticipate how many copies of a particular work will be needed in order to satisfy a nation's (or even a campus's) demand. Some titles may never be consulted, so a single and secure copy of record might suffice. In other cases, greater demand will warrant multiple holdings.[16] Detailed analyses of interlibrary loan logs, including failed requests as well as successful transactions, might expand our understanding.

- *Staff support.* Libraries have gradually learned to acquire mainstream books and journals with smaller and smaller staffs, even though the same efficiencies rarely apply to more marginal materials. On the other hand, substantial specialized support is still essential in order to identify, contract for, mount, and maintain electronic resources. Maturing markets, better products, more refined pricing and service models, and our general movement toward an ubiquitous digital future suggest that things will eventually become easier. In the short term, staff support for all hard copy acquisitions has tended to dwindle relative to that associated with the electronic arena.

- *Preservation.* Libraries are on fairly solid ground when it comes to reformatting or otherwise preserving printed materials. But nonprint media pose greater challenges, and long-term prospects for the digital products whose acquisition and everyday use now absorb disproportionate staff energy are still rather bleak. (One proposed solution somewhat paradoxically calls for multiple, multi-institutional acquisitions of electronic resources as the basis for long-term preservation.) The hard copy acquisitions that are often simple to acquire and preserve are losing ground relative to electronic materials which, perhaps, may not endure.[17]

For all our collecting triumphs, we're missing a great many research resources. Finite budgets and competing priorities limit our chances for substantially greater acquisitions. We therefore need to carefully examine our current solutions to make sure that they work well for all of our collections, students, and scholars.

Academic libraries have grappled with limited purchasing power and intensifying scholarly demand in several different ways. One approach focuses on better access to the materials we already hold. Persistent pockets of uncataloged materials, as well as cataloged books and serials not yet represented with online records, are now being processed.[18] Libraries are also integrating descriptions of photograph collections, sound recordings, and other nonprint resources within their catalogs. Emerging plans to describe Internet resources pursue much the same goal. OCLC and RLIN, our most comprehensive union catalogs, represent holdings at an expanding set of local and international repositories. Collection-rich institutions formerly on the fringes of cooperative networks are being encouraged to join.[19] The universe of materials to which we enjoy bibliographic access has grown apace.

New protocols for interlibrary loan, including user-initiated procedures that minimize expensive staff interventions, are for their part facilitating document delivery. ARIEL and related technologies allow very rapid transfers of articles and other relatively brief documents. Groupings like the Berkeley-Stanford-Texas partnership mentioned above, or the "Borrow Direct" consortium in the Northeast, offer expedited delivery services to their participants.[20] An "information commons" is only plausible if all holdings are easy to consult both intellectually and physically, and we're devoting a great deal of energy to this goal. Nonetheless, we still need to identify and acquire new materials. Better bibliographic and physical access to the research resources already in our collections, while essential, won't meet all our needs.

The universe of source materials required to support today's scholars, in other words, exceeds any repository's (or consortium's) collecting capacity. But our discussions of international resources and library dynamics have so far implied that scholarly demand is essentially undifferentiated both within fields and across the academic landscape. In fact, however, research agendas are sharply divergent. We therefore need to explore whether our collecting gaps are distributed equitably, or at least defensibly. Uncomfortably enough, it appears that certain areas of scholarship are routinely shortchanged.

Some academic fields are effectively global or transnational. While researchers in certain scientific and technological disciplines, for instance, may be scattered throughout the world, the sources for and products of their studies are easy to identify and acquire. The most urgent collections issues instead center on costs.

Collecting efforts in some other fields, most notably within the social sciences and humanities, interact more profoundly with diverging methodologies, ideologies, and agendas. One stream of international inquiry, variously characterized as developmentalist, hegemonic, or imperial, focuses on the projection of Western technologies, economic structures, and political and social values to other parts of the world. Individual scholars may favor or oppose the process, or simply avoid direct judgment as they assess its impacts and consequences. But all these researchers in the first instance address the West's institutions and imprint. Professional programs in fields like business, law, or public policy, as they prepare students for "global" careers, embody a particularly instrumental perspective within this general stream.

A different academic perspective instead focuses on "otherness" in all its manifestations. Much traditional research in disciplines like history, anthropology, and literary criticism falls within this realm. More polemical analyses, often with strong political overtones, combine theory with empirical evidence in explorations that can be highly controversial. Some of these research projects, subsumed under such exotic labels as "subaltern studies" or "queer theory," seek to challenge supposedly stable categories like gender, race, ethnicity, and class–or geography and language, in order to expose the presumptions of power embedded in our everyday culture and institutions. The emphasis on the marginal, which includes non-Western societies and civilizations, particularly encourages international sources and perspectives. Scholarship that presumes to reinterpret Western culture and consciousness, of course, is as fully rooted within a Western ethos as more traditional studies. Both research sources and analytical processes nonetheless tend to differ from those of scholars more fully enmeshed in "Western" instrumentalism.

This broad-stroke characterization of diverging scholarly agendas only begins to suggest their political and ethical overtones. Tensions roil between the camps, and also within each one. The scholars here grouped under the "developmentalist" label, for instance, argue over priorities, methods, and goals. Can or should economic progress be distinguished from political freedom and social equality? Does development necessarily exacerbate inequalities among and within nations, or strengthen Western hegemony?[21] Are the abstract economistic analyses associated with "rational choice theory" on one hand, or rigid ideological programs on the other, at all useful in the real world?

Controversy abounds within the other camp as well, again emphasizing the political implications of different approaches. Some, for instance, argue that those who would celebrate–or even simply describe–the "other" are inadvertently smoothing the way for homogenization and control.[22] Greater understanding may enable us to better appreciate our common humanity, but does that understanding also portend a new round of domestication and subordination? Or does it rather create a basis for different groups, whatever their origin, to rally for self-determination and self-defense? Reducing the world to familiar terms may be simplistic, presumptuous, and morally wrong. Or not . . .

Academic libraries, like the academy itself, find themselves in the sometimes awkward position of supporting these opposed streams of study and discourse from institutions whose foundations are firmly within the "global" or "imperial" camp. The North American university, while certainly a vital source of inquiry, is also a center of power. Our libraries are parts of the package–though parts whose particular salvation may eventually lie in the physical and digital projection of holdings to audiences whose interpretive frameworks and ideological expectations are very different from our own.

Our immense international collections reflect the capabilities as well as the appetites of North America's academic enterprise. But expanding output and increasingly diverse demand consistently outpace our resources: our coverage remains incomplete. It's no surprise that we focus most successfully on formats to which we are accustomed and on the scholarly record that has traditionally comprised our collecting core. Newer scholarship, which deliberately emphasizes the marginal, creates vastly broader demands. Partial responses can certainly be parsed as the kind of catch-up, heads-above-water effort typical of all acquisitions work. But the shortcomings particularly impinge upon the off-center and de-centering research agendas that challenge traditional scholarship. Our somewhat facile explanations can therefore sound simply like excuses for the status quo. A closer look at the needs may suggest some additional possibilities.

SCHOLARLY INFORMATION
AND THE INSTITUTIONAL RESPONSE:
A MOSAIC IN THE MAKING

Our discussion has highlighted strengths as well as shortcomings in our international collections. We have also alluded to some of the disciplinary and geographic variations in how information resources are produced and then made available. Libraries have been inventive in efforts to make their holdings fully known and readily accessible. Nonetheless, our collections are incomplete. Diverging scholarly agendas, academic ideologies, and collecting routines, moreover, may in some instances foster imbalances in the coverage that we do provide.

In order to enhance this information base, we first must look closely at what our collections are all about and how they behave. This section begins by delving into collections from a library perspective. It then assesses them from the viewpoint of scholarly needs, as aggregations of information resources associated with specific disciplines and fields. New analytical models may help us to more fully understand our current situation and also our best options for action.

Every academic library is embedded within and dependent upon its parent college or university. Local priorities necessarily frame each library's goals. Local aspirations, in the aggregate, also delineate the resources that we together provide. Characteristics common to all libraries and library holdings inform our possibilities as well. The nature, browsability, and integrity of library collections; the costs and benefits of cooperation; and the elements that drive interlibrary loan all have an effect. Each of these considerations will become more salient as collecting consortia expand.

Library collections and their use. Library collections are conscious constructions of information resources in which the interplay among thematically related books, journals, and media materials invokes and activates a whole whose value is greater than the sum of the parts. Collections are most readily apprehended and exploited in the aggregate, even as their component titles are also accessible one at a time. Browsing has been a crucial element in enabling users to take full advantage of library collections. But traditional browsing becomes ever less feasible as local collections are fractured among on- and off-site repositories, and as virtual collections are assembled from dispersed resources. The utility and integrity of collections as meaningful constructions are thereby reduced. The impact can be particularly significant in fields for which current bibliographies, reviews, and citations are not readily available.

Finding a way to represent widely scattered materials as coherent collections is particularly daunting in cooperative contexts. We currently rely upon massive, undifferentiated bibliographic databases like OCLC and RLIN for intellectual access to our collective holdings. These files are now being further enriched (and complicated) as nonprint and electronic resources join the mix. This expanding coverage of individual resources may, paradoxically, be obscuring our ability to discern collections. Discipline- or subject-specific bibliographies, guides, and conceptual maps might help, though matters of content, presentation, currency, and maintenance all demand attention. Electronic enhancements to existing bibliographic records, for example, by combining limited page scans of each work with provisions for very flexible subject retrieval, might more directly restore a capacity similar to browsing in the stacks.

The costs and benefits of cooperation. Our understanding of collections and how they are used needs to stretch as we move toward local, and cooperative, holdings that are linked but dispersed. Cooperative efforts also raise issues of governance, funding, and sustainability. Fully participatory programs ensure that all voices are heard, but questions of process can crowd out substantive progress. Some institutions therefore prefer tightly efficient arrangements among a very few peers. Viable cooperative programs also require every participant to perceive advantages that at the very least offset the associated costs. The relevant actors are institutions, but also individuals. The rewards, advantages, and expenses can be intangible as well as explicit. And all these quantities may be differently valued by different actors. A part-time selector at a smaller institution, for instance, might more enthusiastically welcome the opportunity to participate–even modestly–in a new cooperative program than full-time colleagues already swamped with assignments. Any continuing endeavor, finally, will ebb and flow. Sustainability implies the capacity to adjust to shifting levels of energy and participation, as well as to changing political and technological frameworks.

Interlibrary loan. Academic libraries differ in terms of their missions, resources, and size. Their parent institutions likewise vary in their means and aspirations. Relatively few libraries have the mandate and the capacity to sustain substantial international collections. Our "international" scholars, however, are ever more numerous and dispersed. The demand for foreign materials therefore extends far beyond the collecting institutions. Online union catalogs and improved arrangements for interlibrary loan, while essential, also have crosscutting effects. On one hand, isolated scholars can more and more effectively draw upon the country's collective resource base as we enlarge our "commons" of information resources. Meanwhile, universities compete for students and scholars, with easy access to information one element in the draw. Libraries that have assembled strong collections need, at the least, to ensure that the holdings they acquire for their own students and scholars remain locally available.

The operations of interlibrary loan also have an effect. Most collecting consortia worry about acquiring and processing specific sets of material, but then take interlibrary loan for granted. Local ILL procedures, however, often mandate predetermined sequences for polling and requests. Disjunctures between the rosters of collecting consortia and preferred partners for interlibrary loan can make it difficult to evaluate cooperative programs. The wear and tear of interlibrary loan, finally, carries preservation consequences that are rarely recognized.

Libraries' collecting and collections, both local and cooperative, are conditioned by each repository's internal routines. Successful cooperation further involves the institutional contexts, standards, resources, and champions that were reviewed early in this essay. All these elements, however, are only activated as scholars go about their work. Different clusters of disciplines require different kinds of research resources. The scholarly record for different groups of fields likewise varies in terms of its production and dissemination. These characteristics help determine what libraries can do and also what they might attempt.

Librarians' analyses of scholarship and research resources have typically differentiated between the humanities, the social sciences, and science and technology, with the fine arts and professional fields like law or business shunted off to the side.[23] Each disciplinary grouping is customarily described in terms of its distinctive research methodologies and information sources:

- The humanities encompass the disciplines–literature, the classics, philosophy, sometimes history, sometimes the arts–that focus on the particularities of human experience, expression, and creativity. Research tends to be specific, models and methodologies rather diffuse, and the role of synthesis and theory often secondary. Research sources include both the fruits of previous scholarship and the overall record of human expression.
- Scholarship in the social sciences, by contrast, seeks models that can be applied across the board. Methodologies are tight, and empirical research often complements the written record. Datasets and statistical compilations supplement more discursive forms of information.
- In many scientific fields, finally, laboratory work–whether the "laboratory" be the natural world or an experimental research facility–provides the data with which scholars attempt to establish laws, principles, and theories. Information moves quickly, and libraries are perhaps most useful as custodians for the scholarly record.

This depiction of the academic firmament is plausible and easy to understand. It's also fairly simple to apply to library functions like acquisitions or reference. However, it may no longer reflect reality. Three fundamental shifts are changing the picture:

- Scholarship in almost all fields has become more interdisciplinary. Not only are specific sources consulted by unexpected users, but research models and methodologies are routinely borrowed as well. The lines between fields are ever less distinct, and once-simple assumptions concerning research issues and methodologies have come into question. Traditional disciplines and their boundaries are by no means irrelevant, but "postmodern scholarship" adds more fluid approaches and concerns.

- Research resources are themselves ever less the exclusive province of discipline-based cliques. Many older academic libraries–Harvard is an example–still provide vestigial reading rooms for scholars in fields like philosophy, Sanskrit, or the classics.[24] Such fine-grained differentiation makes less and less sense, partly because separately staffed facilities are so expensive, but much more because even very specialized resources are now consulted by researchers from many fields. This cross-fertilization is not limited to areas within, say, the humanities alone, in which classics scholars review archeological reports or literary analysts investigate musical forms. Classical scholars today also work with climatological data, and literary critics ponder psychoanalytic theory. Broad correlations between scholarly fields and specific sets of research resources certainly persist. Again, though, the lines have blurred.
- Scholars require information in a growing variety of formats. Librarians, among others, are struggling to understand and then bridge the chasms between print and nonprint media, and between analog and digital information. Scholarly uses of artifacts produced and held outside of libraries–museum collections are a good example–are also provoking more inclusive efforts to provide intellectual access across formats and institutions. As all these challenges command our attention, however, our earlier preoccupation with academic disciplines may be giving way.[25]

The simple distinction between the humanities, social sciences, and sciences is losing some of its force. Different conceptual approaches to our collections and services may also allow new frameworks for thinking about how and where we should act. One possibility looks from a different angle at how academic fields utilize information and produce new scholarship. These patterns reflect each field's sociology of knowledge and ecology of information, as further informed by the information marketplace's role in mediating access to its research sources and products. The following exercise, heuristic rather than prescriptive, and tentative rather than assured, seeks to illustrate and also incite the close-grained discussions that might lead to nuanced practical plans.

Scholars and scholarly fields interact with information resources in different ways. One interpretive approach looks for clusters of disciplines whose information needs are in some ways similar. A provisional analysis suggests three broad categories.

1. *"Transnational" disciplines that rely on readily accessible and well-controlled information.* Fields like physics, mathematics, computer science, medicine, and (especially in times past) classics or papyrology, are characterized by globalized or transnational scholarship.[26] Information resources are consumed within well-defined but geographically diffuse academic communities. Scholarly societies are often important in organizing these fields, whose tightly defined methodologies by and large correspond to well-ordered research agendas. Research in some areas requires only modest support, though the equipment costs in fields like astronomy or high energy physics can be staggering.

Transnational disciplines, through their professional associations and other proxies, often track their own scholarly sources and research results. The information marketplace, however, is in some fields (though by no means all) commercially inspired, and narrow circles of publishers and distributors can unilaterally impose excessive prices. Concerns related to national or commercial security also keep some material out of reach. The cost and strategic value of information, rather than the geography of scholarship, the dispersion of sources, or the availability of bibliographic data, pose the greatest obstacles to access.

This panorama is nonetheless in flux. Scholars themselves are sponsoring low-cost communication channels like Paul Ginsparg's "arXiv e-Print archive" for preprints in some scientific fields. Emerging alliances like SPARC are similarly attempting to counter profit-driven oligopolies, this time through noncommercial communitarian alternatives.[27] The potential impact is global, not least because students and scholars from less developed areas have simply been priced out of some fields. The prevalence of digital information especially encourages efforts that deploy new technologies along with alternative models for dissemination. And, to repeat, the commercial ethos has never taken root in some transnational fields.

2. *"Internationalized" disciplines that rely upon both accessible and elusive information resources.* Some scientific fields, for instance biology or geology, draw in part upon field reports that may be produced by local agencies or even individual scholars. Inquiries in the social sciences, for example in economics or political science, may likewise rely on local data. The ensuing analyses and models sometimes result in new analytical schools or theoretical perspectives.[28] Researchers in fields like business or law may similarly utilize information initially produced for

local practitioners. The studies based on these eclectic source materials can bear on matters of policy, politics, and commerce. Such inquiries, whether theoretical or practical, are thus tied to specific countries or regions despite their origins in "internationalized" academic disciplines.

Universities as well as research institutes, think tanks, advocacy groups, and corporations account for many of these studies. Geographic, methodological, and ideological divides sometimes undermine disciplinary coherence. Scholarly output is not necessarily under complete control, and research results are scattered among a multiplicity of sources.

Research materials generated off the beaten track in some cases offer new data and divergent interpretations. However, these materials can easily elude both bibliographic guides and library collections. Sources like legal compendia, trade directories, risk assessment newsletters, and polling data, by contrast, are issued for commercial ends and are therefore simple to find. The prices are often quite high, and the academic market emphatically peripheral.

Improved access to this variety of material hinges on several separate efforts. Consortia, whether based within disciplines or built around libraries, can play two roles. The first is to ensure better bibliographic control and fuller access for all relevant resources. The second looks toward new or alternative access to commercial resources in a realm where communitarian and noncommercial initiatives have by and large not taken hold.

3. "Particularistic" disciplines that rely upon diffuse resources. Research in many fields in the humanities and the arts, and also in some social sciences (some kinds of anthropology, for instance), is moving away from predictable methodologies and canonical sources. These often imaginative inquiries instead draw from the unruly torrent of human expression in all formats and media, in an extravagant diversity that is almost impossible to delineate or describe. Scholars in these disciplines are every bit as far-flung as their sources, approaches, and concerns. They tend to associate through large umbrella organizations, and also small and sometimes sectarian groups.

The huge range of potentially relevant information resources defies characterization. Two problematic segments nonetheless stand out. A vast array of research materials, while sometimes inexpensive, are difficult to identify and frequently hard to acquire. International resources figure prominently within this category, which also includes "unfamiliar" materials from the developed world. The arts, particularly as represented by the entertainment industry, are by contrast notorious for products that fuse creative expression with commercial ambition. Aggressive pricing and rigid controls on use are often the norm. Music and movies provide scholars with unique windows into aesthetic styles and social concerns, among many other topics, but access is mediated through a marketplace motivated by profit.

The ever-expanding demand for diffuse resources may most fruitfully be addressed through coordinated acquisitions. Figuring out what exists, and then either acquiring these resources or ensuring access from reliable peer repositories, pose significant challenges. Improved access to expensive and commercially controlled materials, by contrast, may require high-level lobbying and legal action in areas including fair use, piracy, and intellectual property.

This breakneck survey focuses on researchers' utilization of and access to different sorts of information. Its division between "transnational," "internationalized," and "particularistic" fields moves away from the traditional "humanities," "social science," "science" typology. Three elements seem particularly important in characterizing the interactions between researchers and information: research resources, or scholarly inputs; the scholarly record, or research results; and the process of identifying and then ensuring access to particular groupings of information.

Research resources. Academic fields can be categorized in terms of the ease with which their sources can be identified and then used. The disciplines we've characterized as "transnational" by and large utilize resources that are easy to find. "Internationalized" fields, whose inquiries have a stronger geographic dimension, rely on both common and less accessible materials. The latter are frequently produced within and reflective of specific localities. Scholars in "particularistic" disciplines, finally, depend almost entirely upon local materials. Mathematics might serve as a "type discipline" for the transnational category, petroleum geology as an "internationalized" discipline, and art history as a "particularistic" endeavor.

The scholarly record. It's tempting to assume that the products of research, the fruits of discipline-based scholarly inquiry, will conform to established patterns of scholarly communication and therefore be accessible in predictable ways. But many of these materials behave more like research sources themselves, fluctuating widely in cohesiveness, cost, and availability. While only some academic libraries aspire to capture strong arrays of basic research sources, many more pursue the scholarly record. The associated complexities deserve particular attention.

Even in well-organized disciplines like astronomy or mathematics, research that's produced outside the developed world or disseminated in a non-European language may be pretty much lost. Scientific core publications, most commonly refereed journals or online sources, are presumed to represent all significant scholarship through an orderly and self-validating process. Those arguing that research from the margins never gets a fair hearing are only beginning to mount a response.[29] Research results that carry commercial or security value, including some doctoral dissertations, may also be deliberately suppressed.

The scholarly record in slower moving disciplines, while often favoring refereed journals, manifests itself in monographs as well. Research results are widely dispersed in both "particularistic" and "internationalized" fields. Local scholars and institutions are often central, especially in disciplines whose entry costs for exotic equipment or large research teams are low. Literary commentaries, public policy analyses, legal essays, and the like thus appear in a huge variety of outlets.[30] Nonmetropolitan scholars frequently hold unconventional or dissident positions. Identifying and providing access to their research is especially critical to ensure collections that represent a complete range of ideological and methodological perspectives.

The information marketplace. Identifying and acquiring different sets of information resources requires flexible infrastructures that can support may different approaches. The main obstacles are likely to vary from field to field.

High prices pose obvious barriers to access. Some resources, whatever the discipline, are intrinsically expensive to produce. The average cost of information resources also varies between fields. Systems of scholarly review and validation, publishing technologies, and institutional underpinnings (commercial publishers versus nonprofit scholarly societies, for instance) all have an impact. The effects of monopolistic or oligopolistic distribution systems are particularly acute.

The information marketplace, however, entails much more than price. The manner in which resources are described and made available is also crucial. The fields that we have labeled "transnational" tend to draw upon and also produce information that is easy to identify and retrieve, whatever its price. The more idiosyncratic resources that underpin our "internationalized" and "particularistic" disciplines, by contrast, are often poorly described and difficult to obtain. Neither scholarly associations nor centralized bibliographic agencies can control all these materials. Where cultural products are not yet regarded as commodities, specialized vendors and other intermediaries are usually in short supply. Responsive marketing infrastructures may simply not exist.

All these elements, considered together for each discipline, will suggest both the general characteristics of its information resources and any significant obstacles to access. A few examples may illustrate the point. Computer science is a "transnational" field in which researchers are widely dispersed. Some research is based in results-oriented commercial firms and military labs, while other efforts instead reflect the more libertarian culture of many independent programmers and academics. Research results, at least those made public, tend to circulate quickly. Libraries can perhaps most effectively promote the flow of information by lobbying against punitive or overly restrictive legislation, such as prohibitions on certain kinds of reverse engineering and source code analysis.

International law, by contrast, is a professional discipline in which researchers rely on general texts, and also legal codes, cases, and commentaries. This "internationalized" field draws upon materials prepared for practicing lawyers, and most resources are priced and distributed for local legal constituencies. New scholarship appears in a known universe of professional journals. The greatest challenges facing libraries may center on identifying foreign materials and on devising acquisitions strategies for sources designed, priced, and marketed for a very different clientele.

The classics is a different kind of field that by now seems to straddle the line between our "transnational" and "internationalized" categories. Not so long ago, however, one would have envisioned a close-knit academic community devoted to working and reworking a known and readily available corpus of sources which had survived since antiquity. The products of these inquiries were likewise finite, easily identified, and modestly priced. The field itself sponsored the bibliographies and guides that defined its sources, products, and frontiers. This quintessentially "transnational" endeavor has evolved toward broader inquiries that are informed by the archeological record and other kinds of recorded sources. Even though these materials are more diverse and more difficult to acquire, the classics still retains a good bit of its traditional "transnational" flavor. The challenges facing libraries also remain fairly mild.

Ethnomusicology, by contrast, lies at our spectrum's "particularistic" extreme. Research is intensely local and draws upon myriad sources that include commentaries and printed works, but above all the music itself. These materials are often difficult to identify and acquire. Informed enthusiasts, as well as academics, produce research reports that frequently mix sociology, anthropology, history, and biography with explorations of musical form and style. The products of research, as well as the sources, are eclectic, poorly controlled, and difficult to track. Library-scholar partnerships in both research institutions and producing areas seem essential in order to describe and then ensure access to these materials.[31]

These four examples, albeit depicted with a schematicism bordering on caricature, suggest some of the much greater variety displayed by all academic fields as they use, produce, and exchange information. Sources for scholarship range from the thoroughly controlled traditional universe of the classics; to computer scientists' research reports, programs, and data files; to ethnomusicology's dizzying local repertories of performance and print. The behavior of the scholarly record likewise shifts from field to field. Legal studies, here and abroad, typically appear in a limited range of professional publications. Research results in the classics, until recently, were largely confined to readily accessible outlets that were well described by the field itself. And ethnomusicological studies once again crop up all over the place. The nature of the information marketplace–open or closed, expensive or affordable, efficient or incipient–likewise varies. The most promising library strategies to improve research and scholarly communication therefore diverge as well.

A complete matrix of discipline-specific collections and needs will reveal a smorgasbord of possibilities for action. Intensified collecting, whether local or cooperative, may in some cases merit pride of place. Measures to improve bibliographic description, expand document delivery, or explore other means of remote access will at other times prove central. Support for more organized information marketplaces, defined by either discipline or geography, may sometimes make sense. Buyers clubs, political activism, legal challenges, and grassroots initiatives may be options as well. While some measures might seem to apply across the board, "lowest common denominator" solutions carry the risk of displacing the narrower responses that might be most effective within particular areas.

We've up to now considered the intellectual firmament one scholarly field at a time. This approach suggests both the range of potential responses and the policies that make sense for each field on its own. Establishing priorities among all areas of inquiry, however, requires different analytical tools. Risk analysis may draw attention to situations in which the academic community faces permanent information loss. Cost-benefit assessments, by contrast, can indicate interventions that will accomplish a lot at minimal expense. Neither of these approaches, however, will necessarily alert us to the redistributive effects of new activities, or their implications for areas that may have been marginalized for academic, ideological, or commercial reasons. New kinds of information resources and services, for instance digital products, are often funded by reallocations of funds from more traditional activities. While neither intended nor expected, the results can further distort our already skewed patterns of disciplinary support.

The information objectives of libraries, whether taken individually or in concert, provide another lens through which to examine needs and evaluate responses. While every academic library engages with local instruction, the issues of curricular support are pretty much irrelevant to this essay. Many repositories also aspire to represent the scholarly record insofar as it corresponds to local teaching and research. Identifying these materials, and then finding the means to acquire them, can stretch even those libraries that limit their reach to scholarly monographs and English-language journals. The efforts that would guarantee collection balance by comprehensively covering scholarly output may in some areas lie beyond the grasp of any single institution. When it comes to the full range of research sources, partnerships and consortia are in most fields the only hope. These can be informal or even implicit, as when individual institutions build unique collections that then serve the community as a whole. (Princeton's Latin American pamphlets here come to mind.) Alliances can also include museums and other cultural agencies, scholarly associations, and foundations, among other groups and entities.

This essay has examined international resources in terms of library collections, scholarly information, and academic disciplines. In many fields, particularly those that we've labeled "internationalized" and "particularistic," both research sources and the scholarly record include a strong international component. These resources can be difficult to identify and acquire. However, strong collections of printed works, media materials, manuscripts, and archives do exist in many foreign countries. Our interests are well-served when these remote sources become more accessible.

International partnerships presume reciprocal responsibilities and benefits. While the payoffs from international cooperation may seem obvious to us, the incentives for potential partners demand attention as well. Many foreign libraries have no hope of keeping current with information produced in other parts of the world, even when it concerns their own country or region. Paying for the expensive publications and databases essential for research in many "transnational" and "internationalized" fields is likewise out of the question. Overseas alliances can begin to lower the barriers.

While the mutual benefits of international cooperation may seem irresistible, the complications are legion.[32] Cultural differences; disparities in size, resources, and ambitions; peculiarities of policymaking structures and programmatic continuity; and issues of dominance and dependence, all enter in. Divergent technical standards can further complicate cooperative initiatives.[33]

Even familiar obstacles can take on different dimensions in the international arena. Any repository can be damaged by war, disaster, political intrusions, budget cuts, or inept leadership. The effects are particularly devastating where infrastructure is weak and resources are thin. The willful destruction of Sarajevo's national library comes to mind, as does the major earthquake in El Salvador that almost destroyed the country's most important local collection. International boycotts of apartheid-era South Africa affected library programs as well as everything else; different groups now propose the same scenario for Israel (and Cuba, and Iraq, and . . .). Labor actions and political disputes can have crippling effects: for example, student protests shut down Mexico's massive National University (UNAM), along with its flagship libraries, for the better part of a year during 1999/2000.

International cooperation, in other words, is desirable, unavoidable, and risky. Each member of a partnership or consortium brings specific strengths, possibilities, and weaknesses to the table. Preparations for a globalized information future need to assess the risks as well as the costs and benefits. Planned redundancy, where feasible, may suggest a solution. Reformatting programs, probably based on digital technologies as these processes become more manageable, may ultimately afford the best response.

CONCLUSION

This essay announced itself as an exploration of the nature, role, and adequacy of the international information resources now available through North American research libraries. Our inquiry has in turn highlighted five loosely related questions.

1. What does "cooperation" mean in our current context of connected collections and interdependent repositories? Formal consortia and structured groupings certainly remain both viable and important. But more casual efforts, among them those reflecting the enthusiasms of individual scholars and librarians, likewise serve the community. Our understandings of possibility and accomplishment need to stretch. So do our measures to support and reward these initiatives.

2. What are "global" or "international" resources? Today's information marketplace makes it easy to identify and acquire at least some materials from every corner of the globe. At the same time, even affluent countries with fully developed bibliographic and marketing structures generate resources that remain beyond our reach. "International" mate-

rials may simply be those produced somewhere else, though we at times use the term to imply resources that are created and then circulate outside of the marketplace. These materials appear to be especially associated with non-Western civilizations.

3. How and where do our international collections fall short? Academic libraries have always supported instruction. Many are also pursuing the record of scholarship. And some are gathering the primary sources upon which new studies can be based. Our scholars and their academic disciplines have become increasingly omnivorous, demanding all manner of resources in every imaginable format. The production of information resources likewise continues to grow, leaving our materials budgets ever further behind. No single library can hope to satisfy these expectations, and even collective responses may not be enough.

Nonetheless, we do better for some fields than for others. Academic fields in which the scholarly record and research sources are well-controlled, particularly disciplines that are "global" in nature, tend to be well served. Our coverage is weaker for disciplines characterized by eclectic scholarly demand for scattered and sometimes obscure source materials. Some of these apparently underserved fields, as they focus on the "other," evince dissident ideologies and dissonant methodologies. Our collections imbalances are therefore fraught with political and ethical overtones: we can't simply talk them away. On a less contentious level, our libraries are also only now awakening to the need for international resources to support professional programs.

4. Is the "collection" still a relevant concept? We've traditionally perceived library collections as coherent assemblages of carefully selected materials that reflect and address the information requirements of specific disciplines. Researchers, as they browse these holdings, can at once apprehend the whole and choose what they need. By now, however, on-site browsing is pretty much a thing of the past, due both to dispersed local holdings and to online union catalogs that describe a wealth of remote resources. Once-cohesive patterns of use, moreover, are giving way to cross- and interdisciplinary materials and methodologies. In the postmodern academy, cut-and-dried associations among scholarly disciplines, research methodologies, and information resources are no longer the norm. Today's researchers in effect create their own collections as they identify and explore highly individualized arrays of materials that are both local and remote, concrete and virtual, and based in print, images, and sound.

5. How might we most usefully characterize today's scholarship and information resources? Libraries base their operations and services on

mental models of their own mission and goals, and also of users and their needs. Our traditional map of the scholarly universe divides academic fields among the humanities, social sciences, and sciences, with the fine arts and professional programs pushed off to the side. This venerable model, however, appears ever less useful as postmodern scholarship and new information formats blur lines that once seemed clear.

Another approach instead focuses on the behavior of the information used by and produced within scholarly disciplines, and also the nature of the associated information marketplaces. "Transnational" disciplines transcend geography in their utilization and production of information which is generally easy to identify and (price permitting) obtain. "Internationalized" fields, among them some sciences, some social sciences, and some professional disciplines, rely on universal or abstract information but also localized data and reports. Many "particularistic" disciplines, finally, draw first and foremost from concrete expressions of localized creativity and concern. Both research resources and the scholarly record tend to be widely dispersed.

For libraries, the characteristics and capacities of different information markets are as important as the particularities of each field's research sources and scholarly record. In some fields and some countries, for example, the commodification of knowledge mandates library initiatives that specifically focus on markets and marketplace constraints. Consortial acquisitions and group licenses play the existing system for all it's worth. Unreasonable restrictions on use are another target for action. And efforts like SPARC aspire to create a new structure for scholarly communication. In other fields, however, scholars both rely upon and produce information that is scattered, poorly represented in bibliographies or guides, and often difficult to acquire. Cooperative programs for distributed acquisitions and international alliances may here comprise the most effective response.

Close, field-specific analyses are essential in determining information strategies for single institutions and also for the community as a whole. Joint programs also need to include risk assesssments, cost-benefit analyses, and close attention to any unintended redistributive effects resulting from measures that in isolation make sense. The goal, after all, is to ensure broader access to information across all disciplines and fields.

This discussion has focused on scholarly fields and their needs for information resources. Many cooperative efforts for library collections, however, are based in geography. The connections should be kept clear. For its part, the typology of fields here suggested responds to shifting disciplinary boundaries and changing patterns of information production and use. Scholarly agendas will continue to evolve, and new information will continue to emerge. Our models must likewise continue to change.

Libraries play a critical role in determining which texts, and images and sounds, our scholars are able to consult as they exercise and expand their models, methodologies, and visions. We will most adequately support these agendas by ensuring access to the full scholarly record and to a wide range of research sources. Accomplishing these goals requires resources and will. It also requires a clear understanding of the dynamics of our work.

NOTES

1. The "crossroads" terminology particularly resonates with recent reports on the AAU/ARL "Global Resources Program." See Deborah Jakubs, "The AAU/ARL Global Resources Program at a Crossroads: Achievements, Best Practices, New Challenges, and Next Steps" (prepared for the AAU/ARL Global Resources Program Advisory Board meeting of 14 January 2002, revised 26 September 2002), and Deborah Jakubs, "The AAU/ARL Global Resources Program: The View from a Crossroads," presented at "The New Dynamics & Economics of Cooperative Collection Development" conference, Aberdeen Woods Conference Center, Atlanta, Georgia, Nov. 8-10, 2002.

2. National variations in publishing patterns and bibliographic control are readily apparent. The similarly wide range of library capabilities may be less familiar. Within Latin America, for instance, national libraries in most instances are the beneficiaries of legal deposit and are also responsible for preparing national bibliographies. Both functions are carried out with varying degrees of thoroughness, timeliness, and success. See William Vernon Jackson, "Latin American National Libraries," in David H. Stam, ed., *International Dictionary of Library Histories* (Chicago: Fitzroy Dearborn, 2001), pp. 91-94, plus the entries for specific national libraries.

3. See http://lanic.utexas.edu/project/arl. (This and all subsequent URLs are valid as of 20 December, 2002.) Also see Dan Hazen, "The Latin Americanist Research Resources Project: A New Direction for Monographic Cooperation?" *ARL: A Bimonthly Newsletter of Research Library Issues and Actions* #191 (April, 1997), pp. 1-6.

4. See the Latin American Microform Project website: <http://wwwcrl.uchicago.edu/info/lamp.htm>.

5. The text of both agreements is available on the "Calafia" website, under "Agreements": http://www-sul.stanford.edu/depts/hasrg/latinam/calafia/.

6. See the Calafia website (cited immediately above).

7. This distributor is Scholarly Resources, Inc.

8. Some of these acquisitions simply have not yet become available through commercial channels. The final tally of unique titles is likely to be lower.

9. See http://dodgson.ucsd.edu/las/index.html.

10. Other examples of what might be labeled "implicit" cooperation include in-house microfilming, where bibliographic records in OCLC or RLIN alert other institutions preparing to reformat deteriorated materials to work that has already been

done. The Harvard-based "Program for Latin American Libraries and Archives," which provides small grants for preservation or access projects in research collections located within Latin America, is another example of an effort to improve the community's access to scholarly resources. See Dan Hazen, "Archival Research and the Program for Latin American Libraries and Archives," forthcoming in *Hispanic American Historical Review*.

11. See the SALALM website http://www.library.cornell.edu/colldev/salalmhome. html. SALALM's published record includes its annual *Working Papers* and its *Newsletter*.

12. See, for example, Samuel P. Huntington, *The Clash of Civilizations and the Remaking of World Order* (New York: Simon and Schuster, 1996).

13. The decline is documented in Jutta Reed-Scott, *Scholarship, Research Libraries, and Global Publishing: The Result of a Study Funded by The Andrew W. Mellon Foundation* (Washington, DC: Association of Research Libraries, 1996). Also see figures in the *UNESCO Statistical Yearbook* (Paris: UNESCO, 1964-99) and successor compilations.

14. See especially the yearly updates on "Monograph and Serial Costs in ARL Libraries" in the annual *ARL Statistics*: http://www.arl.org/stats/.

15. For library consortia, see the ICOLC (International Coalition of Library Consortia) website: http://www.library.yale.edu/consortia/. For cooperative initiatives to develop new models for scholarly publishing, see http://www.arl.org/sparc/, http://www.sparceurope.org/, and http://www.figaro-europe.net.

16. A classic and controversial study that suggested that [too] many acquisitions are never consulted is: Allen Kent et al., *Use of Library Materials: The University of Pittsburgh Study* (New York: M. Dekker, 1979).

17. The challenges of digital preservation are gradually becoming clear. See, for instance, *The State of Digital Preservation: An International Perspective* (Conference Proceedings: Documentation Abstracts, Inc., Institutes for Information Science, Washington, DC, April 24-25, 2002) (Washington, DC: Council on Library and Information Resources, July, 2002). Harvard's "Library Digital Initiative" website: <http://hul.harvard.edu/ldi>, particularly in its "Technical Development" section, describes practical development measures that include a "digital repository service." LOCKSS ("Lots of Copies Keeps Stuff Safe"), an approach pioneered at Stanford, relies on multiple, reciprocally validating copies for digital preservation.

18. The Andrew W. Mellon Foundation, for instance, recently awarded $830,000 for retrospective conversion work at Cornell University.

19. Cooperative initiatives are often harder to launch in difficult financial times, when institutions focus in upon themselves, than when budgets are strong.

20. "Borrow Direct" is an innovative cooperative effort based on user-initiated transactions and rapid turnaround times. See http://www.library.upenn.edu/services/borrowing/borrowdirect.html.

21. See, for example, Joseph E. Stiglitz, *Globalization and Its Discontents* (New York: W.W. Norton, 2002).

22. See Néstor García Canclini, *Hybrid Cultures: Strategies for Entering and Leaving Modernity* (translated by Christopher L. Chiappari and Silvia L. López, foreword by Renato Rosaldo) (Minneapolis, MN: University of Minnesota Press, 1995). Anouar Majid, "The Failure of Postcolonial Theory after 9/11," *The Chronicle of Higher Education* (November 1, 2002), pp. B11-12, is a brief recent contribution to the continuing debate over the limits of "hybridization" and essentialism.

23. See, for example, the three studies prepared for the Research Libraries Group beginning in the late 1980s: *Information Needs in the Humanities: An Assessment* (Stanford, CA: The Research Libraries Group, 1988); *Information Needs in the Social Sciences: An Assessment* (Mountain View, CA: The Research Libraries Group, 1989); *Information Needs in the Sciences: An Assessment* (Mountain View, CA: The Research Libraries Group, 1991). Reference courses in library schools typically assume the same kind of division.

24. Current acquisitions are processed for the general collections, and the once-exclusive special facilities by and large serve as departmental reading rooms.

25. The tension between formats and disciplines is in some respects echoed in current discussions concerning institutional repositories. See Raym Crow, "The Case for Institutional Repositories: A SPARC Position Paper," *ARL: A Bimonthly Report on Research Library Issues and Actions from ARL, CNI, and* SPARC #223 (August, 2002), pp. 1-4. The full version is available at http://www.arl.org/sparc/.

26. The results are sometimes biased in geographic terms, for instance, as medical research emphasizes ailments afflicting affluent populations over those endemic in poorer, often tropical, parts of the world.

27. For the "arXiv.org–e-Print archive" see http://arxiv.org. Also see Yale's "Liblicense" site, http://www.library.yale.edu/~llicense/index.shtml, especially "National Site License Initiatives" and "Developing Nations Initiatives." These responses, of course, all function within what many consider an untenable system of scholarly communication. Also see SPARC and the initiatives listed in footnote 14. "Institutional repositories" reflect a somewhat different model whose applicability across the full range of disciplines is not yet clear.

28. For instance, dependency theory, bureaucratic patrimonialism, liberation theology–and magical realism and salsa–are some of Latin America's theoretical and expressive contributions.

. 29. See the "Scientific Electronic Library Online" (SciELO) website: <http://www. scielo.org> for one effort to capture and promote "southern" science. Juris Dilevko and Esther Atkinson, "Evaluating Academic Journals without Impact Factors for Collection Management Decisions," *College & Research Libraries*, 63-6 (November, 2002), pp. 562-577, suggests another approach.

30. The "LAPTOC" component of the Latin Americanist Research Resources Project is for the first time providing table-of-contents access to a large number of hitherto neglected Latin American scholarly journals.

31. Another mechanism may be relevant as well. Some of our strongest research collections have been assembled by private collectors and then sold or donated to libraries. Florida International University, for example, has recently acquired a near-definitive collection of Cuban music, including sound recordings, from the 20th century. Few if any libraries could sustain this kind of comprehensive effort.

32. Dan Hazen, "Dancing with Elephants: International Cooperation in an Interdependent (But Unequal) World," in *Creating New Strategies for Cooperative Collection Development: Papers from the Aberdeen Woods Conference* (ed., Milton T. Wolf and Marjorie E. Bloss) (New York: The Haworth Information Press, 2000), pp. 185-213 (published simultaneously as *Collection Management* v. 24, nos. 1-2 and 3-4 [2000]).

33. The German Resources Project, another effort affiliated with the Global Resources Program, has translated AACR-2 in order to ensure that German bibliographic records are completely compatible with those produced in the United States.

PART II:
REPORTS
OF ABERDEEN WOODS I
WORKING GROUPS

Assessing the State
of Cooperative Collection Development:
Report of the Working Group
to Map Current Cooperative
Collection Development Projects

John Haar

SUMMARY. The working group developed its map through a web-based survey distributed internationally via listservs. Eighty-nine preponderantly North American cooperative projects responded. Almost three-quarters of them were born in the 1990s. State-based projects are prevalent, and most projects operate in compact regions. Academic libraries appear to participate much more frequently than other types. Not surprisingly, 75 percent of the projects feature the shared purchase or archiving of electronic resources. One-third engage in selection or management of

John Haar is Associate University Librarian and Director of the Central Library at Vanderbilt University (E-mail: john.haar@vanderbilt.edu).

The author would like to recognize the members of the working group for their many contributions to this report. Over more than a year, they developed a conceptual framework for the mapping project, designed and tested the survey instrument, created a plan for its dissemination, and encouraged consortia to respond. The members include: Margo Warner Curl (College of Wooster), Ginny Gilbert (Duke University), Erika Linke (Carnegie-Mellon University), Jane Treadwell (University of Illinois at Springfield), and James Simon at CRL, who created the website.

[Haworth co-indexing entry note]: "Assessing the State of Cooperative Collection Development: Report of the Working Group to Map Current Cooperative Collection Development Projects." Haar, John. Co-published simultaneously in *Collection Management* (The Haworth Information Press, an imprint of The Haworth Press, Inc.) Vol. 28, No. 3, 2003, pp. 183-190; and: *The New Dynamics and Economics of Cooperative Collection Development* (ed: Edward Shreeves) The Haworth Information Press, an imprint of The Haworth Press, Inc., 2003, pp. 183-190. Single or multiple copies of this article are available for a fee from The Haworth Document Delivery Service [1-800-HAWORTH, 9:00 a.m. - 5:00 p.m. (EST). E-mail address: docdelivery@haworthpress.com].

http://www.haworthpress.com/web/COL
Digital Object Identifier: 10.1300/J105v28n03_01

print materials, most often in area studies. Collaborative electronic purchasing has generated a boom in cooperative collection development, but traditional print-based cooperation remains rare and narrowly focused. *[Article copies available for a fee from The Haworth Document Delivery Service: 1-800-HAWORTH. E-mail address: <docdelivery@haworthpress.com> Website: <http://www.HaworthPress.com> © 2003 by The Haworth Press, Inc. All rights reserved.]*

KEYWORDS. Cooperative collection development, surveys, library cooperation, Aberdeen Woods Conference

The Center for Research Libraries (CRL) charged our working group to develop a "map" of current cooperative collection development projects and present prospective collaborators with a "tree of possibilities." The map (http://www.crl.edu/awcc2002/ccdsurveyresults.htm), the product of a survey process described below, incorporates data submitted by 89 active projects throughout the world. We believe it fulfills our charge through illustrating the span and variety of collaborative endeavors currently underway and offering a view of the potential of cooperative collection development. Though it represents an unscientific sample of cooperative collection development projects, it offers an opportunity to assess the state of cooperative collection development at the beginning of the twenty-first century.

In 1987 Joe Hewitt and John Shipman conducted a landmark study of cooperative programs in ARL libraries (Hewitt 1987, 191). They reported that cooperative collection development programs were widespread among ARL members. Collaboration occurred in multiple settings, including national, regional, and local consortia, state university systems, and bilateral agreements. Programs most often took the form of general agreements to purchase expensive materials and the selection and deselection of serials. Further, they found that "cooperative collection development programs involving formal, structured assignment of areas of concentration based on subject, language, or country are rare. Such programs, when they occur, are typically narrow in scope."[1] Our map and the Hewitt-Shipman report are not directly comparable. They surveyed ARL libraries; we solicited information from projects including all types of libraries. Yet we can, in a broad sense, examine how cooperative collection development has evolved in the fifteen years since the earlier study and whether there is reason to revise our perceptions of the extent and penetration of cooperative collection development programs.

The working group developed a web-based survey as the instrument for building the map. After testing a draft survey form on a small group of respondents, we disseminated a revised form (http://www.crl.edu/awcc2002/ccdsurvey.htm) internationally through over thirty library listservs and distribution lists, including a list of all those who attended the first Aberdeen Woods conference, in the fall of 2001. After the initial return date we contacted known consortia that had not responded and encouraged them to participate.

The survey form requested information about cooperative collection development projects, not consortia. Thus a single consortium could–and some did–submit separate responses for multiple projects. The group felt this approach was best suited to eliciting useful data about discrete cooperative collection development activities that might offer guidance to librarians considering collaborative projects or seeking to join active projects. We asked respondents to describe their projects briefly, answer questions about subjects and formats covered, and note types of cooperation incorporated in the projects. We also asked about types of working agreements and funding arrangements, and the form included fields for contact information about project directors or coordinators. We mounted the survey responses on a web database at CRL that permits users to browse by project names, subjects, formats, types of cooperation, geographical descriptors (assigned by the group), director/coordinator/contact persons, and sponsoring consortia.

The 89 submitted projects are preponderantly North American, but 20% of them feature participation by overseas libraries, particularly in Australia and the United Kingdom. How closely the international distribution of the responses mirrors the distribution of cooperative collection development projects is, unfortunately, a matter for conjecture since we lack reliable information about the extent of worldwide collection development collaboration.

Likewise we can only speculate about whether the 89 projects embody a clear majority or unrepresentative minority of American cooperative collection development ventures. It may be instructive that only 26 of the 151 members of the International Coalition of Library Consortia responded even though we explicitly included database-purchasing consortia in our description of cooperative collection development and solicited participation from ICOLC affiliates. Their return rate could be evidence that the survey data is a disproportionately small sample. It could, however, illustrate the lack of a broadly accepted definition of cooperative collection development. Most ICOLC members may not think of themselves as practicing cooperative collection development.

While 60% of our respondents reported that the shared purchase of electronic products was among their activities, only 15% reported electronic purchasing as their sole cooperative endeavor. Consortia whose only collection development function is acquiring electronic resources might have considered themselves so far outside the conventional rubric of cooperative collection development that responding would be inappropriate.

At a minimum the database offers an informative snapshot of the current state of collaborative collection development and management. The survey responses indicate, for example, that for most participating libraries cooperative collection development is a relatively recent undertaking. Fully 72% of the reported projects were born in the 1990s, confirmation of the emergence of database-purchasing consortia during the decade. Those projects where print-based activities are major components tend to have been in operation longer. While 52% of them began in the '90s, 33% date their origin before 1980.

If our virtual map of U.S.-based cooperative collection development projects overlaid a real map, it would reveal a geographic distribution inconsistent with the distribution of population. When we assign regional identifiers to each project based on the locations of the critical mass of its participating libraries, the Midwest is home to the most (36%), the Southeast the second most (22%). Only 13% are located in the Northeast, 3% in the Southwest, and 7% in the West. Nineteen percent of the projects can be classified as multi-regional or national.

State-based projects, many initiated through government funding, are prevalent among the U.S. respondents. Fifty-six percent of the projects report all their participants located in one state. Even where state mandates are not at issue, libraries are inclined to seek partners in fairly compact geographic zones. In 75% of the projects all participants are located in no more than two states, in almost all cases contiguous states. Where print-based activities are paramount, it appears that mutual interest is somewhat more determinative than proximity. Only 45% of these projects are based in a single state.

The database suggests that cooperative collection development is primarily an endeavor of academic libraries, though the response set may be weighted toward academics because we publicized the survey in venues that reach more academic than public or special librarians. In only one project do public libraries comprise all the members, and very few multitype projects responded. Large academic libraries participate more frequently than smaller academics. Many state-based consortia include both large and medium-to-small academic libraries, but few cooperative ventures consist exclusively of medium-to-small academics.

Responses to survey questions about the subject focus of collaborative enterprises are not enlightening. Because consortia typically acquire electronic products across the range of disciplines, no subjects can be said to hold preferred status. The subject area with the lowest level of reported activity is "language" (43% of the projects); the highest is "social sciences/law" (57%). Unsurprisingly, 69% of the respondents cite multidisciplinary projects. Many print-based projects collaborate on area studies (as revealed in their survey descriptions and websites), which also tend to be multidisciplinary in nature.

Format preferences are clear. Seventy-five percent of the projects engage in activities related to electronic resources, while 54% incorporate one or more print-related endeavors. Other formats attract considerably less consortial attention: microform 33%, video 21%, audio 18%.

Reports of type of cooperation serve to underscore the degree to which the acquisition of digital resources has become a powerful generator of library collaboration. Sixty percent of the projects broker the shared purchase of electronic products. A comparatively small 33% participate in the coordinated selection or purchase of monographs (print or electronic), 38% the coordinated selection or purchase of serials, and 30% the coordinated selection or purchase of other materials. Ten percent are building joint print serial archives; 16% are working toward the joint storage of print materials, and 12% on the joint storage of nonprint materials. Of the approximately one-third of the projects that include active print-related cooperative programs (more on this below), 71% coordinate monograph selection, and 65% serial selection.

Over half the projects (54%) operate through formal working agreements, including charters or instruments of incorporation. Thirty-five percent consider themselves the product of informal arrangements among participating libraries. Whether consortia are chartered or not, collaboration is a heavily self-supported endeavor. While many groups report multiple funding arrangements, 75% of all projects receive funding from member institutions. Twenty-eight percent receive government funding, and 23% have obtained grant funding.

Though the selection and management of electronic materials is the dominant mode of contemporary cooperative collection development, cooperative collection development was born as a strategy for coordinating the acquisition and retention of print resources. A careful analysis of the survey responses enables us to measure how successfully consortia have negotiated this traditional and still very challenging form of collaboration. No one would describe consortial electronic purchasing as problem-free, but initiating and sustaining print-based cooperation demands far more intensive planning and consultation among participants. The relatively small number of projects reporting significant print programs testifies to the degree of difficulty inherent in pursuing collaborative print collection building. While over half the projects indicate some print-based interest or activity, a close review of project descriptions and follow-up interviews reveals that far fewer incorporate a viable print component. Slightly over one-third of the 89 projects engage in the cooperative selection of print resources or the cooperative storage of print materials.

Print-focused cooperative collection development is often defined as a tripartite operation consisting of coordinated multi-library selection, bibliographic access to group holdings, and expedited document delivery. Many consortia that have put the second and third parts of this triad in place find that implementing the first part remains elusive. Survey responses, particularly project descriptions and comments, document that coordinated selection is a widely shared goal, but the same data frequently illustrates the complexities of closing the gap between intentions and results. For many projects reporting print activities, comments or websites frame accounts of coordinated selection in cautious phrases:

- explore the coordination of acquisitions
- conducting research into collaborative collection development
- under consideration as outcomes
- cooperative book purchasing is under investigation
- to be discussed and formulated
- has established a committee to explore collaborative collection development

The survey provides sobering evidence (as if more were needed) that those contemplating cooperative print collection building have taken on a formidable task.

Yet there is also much to remind us that print collaboration is not impossible. The map illustrates that print-based cooperative collection development is, if not exactly thriving, certainly alive, well, and even rich with opportunities for those able to stay the course and build sustainable programs.

- The University of Michigan (UM) and Michigan State University (MSU) cooperate in building eastern European resources in the humanities and social sciences. UM is responsible for the Balkans, while MSU collects materials on the Baltic states.

- Michigan and Indiana University have joined for almost twenty years in a similar project in Slavic collection development. Indiana focuses on Georgia and Slovenia, while Michigan concentrates on Armenia and Bosnia-Herzegovina.
- Duke, North Carolina State, and North Carolina-Chapel Hill (UNC-CH) are building cooperative monographic collections in Bengali, Farsi/Persian, Hindi, Urdu, and Tamil. They also collaborate in acquiring serials, nonprint materials, and microforms.
- Duke and UNC-CH share in developing research level collections on Latin America; each acquires specialized resources from assigned countries.
- The Minnesota State College and University System, supported by state funding, has organized a program that enables each member institution to designate collecting areas in which it will specialize. Other libraries can choose to reduce acquisitions in these areas.
- The Research Library Cooperative Program unites California-Berkeley, Stanford, and Texas-Austin in an ambitious venture to jointly build and share collections. They have reached formal agreement on distributing responsibility for building research collections in carefully defined focus areas of Latin American studies.
- The Tri-College Consortium, a project of Byrn Mawr, Haverford, and Swarthmore, features a shared approval plan (for two of the libraries). The members have also reduced duplication in their government documents collections.
- The Tri-College University Libraries (Concordia College, Minnesota State University, and North Dakota State University) divide responsibility for collecting items reviewed in *Choice*.

Area studies appear to form the surest path to success in collaborative print collection development, at least among large academic libraries. Incentives for cooperation may be stronger in these fields since building intensive multidisciplinary collections covering all of Latin America, Eastern Europe, or South Asia is beyond the means of even the most well financed libraries. Prospects for reaching agreement on collecting responsibilities are doubtlessly strengthened in focus areas that lend themselves to organization by country, language, or material type.

Several responses demonstrate that even where establishing a matrix for shared collection building is politically or organizationally unattainable, there are still avenues for cooperation. They are instructive of the scope of collaborative possibilities.

- The Brittle program, founded at the University of Kansas, includes over 60 member libraries. Members intending to make preservation photocopies submit their selected titles to a listserv. Other members have the option of requesting copies for themselves at reduced prices.
- PANDORA, a consortium of Australian libraries, is establishing a shared archive of Australian online publications.
- The Washington Research Library Consortium operates a shared offsite storage facility that serves seven libraries.
- The Southwest Regional Depository provides a storage facility serving Miami University, the University of Cincinnati, Wright State University, and Central State University.
- The University of Arizona and Arizona State University shared the services of a Slavic studies bibliographer.

What does the survey tell us about the state of contemporary cooperative collection development? Thanks to the proliferation of shared electronic purchasing, collaboration is flourishing. But if we assess only the traditional forms of cooperative collection development, principally joint print selection and storage, the picture is considerably less sanguine. In fact, there is little to convince us that much has changed in the fifteen years since Hewitt and Shipman conducted their study. Cooperative collection development characterized by formal, distributed assignment of areas of concentration is still rare and, for the most part, narrowly focused on area studies.

There is, however, reason to assume that cooperative collection development in all its forms still has the capacity for growth. The economic pressures that first caused it to appear as an attractive strategy have certainly not relented. Electronic resources promote cooperative collection development not only as products for consortial purchase, but also as enhanced tools of bibliographic access and document delivery. Response to the first CRL cooperative collection development conference signifies libraries' continuing interest in the topic. And though they may be relatively few in number, those projects that have overcome the barriers to shared collection building show us that progress is possible.

REFERENCE

Hewitt, Joe A. and John S. Shipman (1987). "Cooperative Collection Development Among Research Libraries in the Age of Networking: Report of a Survey of ARL Libraries," in *Advances in Library Automation and Networking*. Greenwich, CT: JAI Press.

Best Practices
in Cooperative Collection Development:
A Report Prepared
by the Center for Research Libraries
Working Group on Best Practices
in Cooperative Collection Development

Cynthia Shelton

SUMMARY. Best practices in cooperative collection development are based on interviews with 18 successful programs, which fall into three categories of cooperative effort: selection of print; electronic acquisition; and access, storage, and preservation. Questions probe opportunities, barriers, best practices, and lessons learned. Findings are collapsed into three areas of analysis: formation and founding; decision making, organization and administration; and funding and infrastructure. The successful coopera-

Cynthia Shelton, PhD, is Associate University Librarian, Collections and Technical Services, UCLA Library, 11334 Young Research Library, Box 951575, Los Angeles, CA 90095-1575 (E-mail: cshelton@library.ucla.edu).

The author would like to acknowledge members of the CRL Working Group on Best Practices in Cooperative Collection Development who conducted interviews, compiled entries for the bibliography, and read and commented on drafts of the report: Kim Armstrong, Carol Diedrichs, David Magier, Kent Mulliner, Mary Wilke, and Kit Wilson.

[Haworth co-indexing entry note]: "Best Practices in Cooperative Collection Development: A Report Prepared by the Center for Research Libraries Working Group on Best Practices in Cooperative Collection Development." Shelton, Cynthia. Co-published simultaneously in *Collection Management* (The Haworth Information Press, an imprint of The Haworth Press, Inc.) Vol. 28, No. 3, 2003, pp. 191-222; and: *The New Dynamics and Economics of Cooperative Collection Development* (ed: Edward Shreeves) The Haworth Information Press, an imprint of The Haworth Press, Inc., 2003, pp. 191-222. Single or multiple copies of this article are available for a fee from The Haworth Document Delivery Service [1-800-HAWORTH, 9:00 a.m. - 5:00 p.m. (EST). E-mail address: docdelivery@haworthpress.com].

tives displayed best practices in four important areas: communication and consultation, goals and focus, flexibility and adaptability, and technological infrastructure. *[Article copies available for a fee from The Haworth Document Delivery Service: 1-800-HAWORTH. E-mail address: <docdelivery@haworth press.com> Website: <http://www.HaworthPress.com> © 2003 by The Haworth Press, Inc. All rights reserved.]*

KEYWORDS. Collection development, cooperative collection development, best practices, library consortia, electronic resources, Aberdeen Woods Conference

MISSION AND METHODOLOGY

The mission of the Center for Research Libraries (CRL) "Best Practices" Working Group is to identify the circumstances or elements that either facilitate or work against the success of cooperative efforts in collection development and management and to distinguish the practices that sustain a viable and relevant cooperative project or program.

The Working Group adopted as its working definition of a cooperative collection development project that of the CRL Working Group that mapped current projects–"any collaborative activity characterized by planned, coordinated collection development and/or management. All collaborative enterprises, even informal working arrangements, are eligible for inclusion as long as they are active and viable." In order to develop a set of elements and best practices, the committee decided to conduct in-depth interviews with a sample number of projects whose viability, track record, and longevity indicated they were carrying out what could be called "best practices."

We used the 82 respondents to the Mapping Survey as an initial pool of potential interviewees, with the goal to identify around 20 respondents to interview. We wanted to obtain a representative sample of different categories of cooperative activities by size, focus, and makeup of participants. We also strove to have a representation of foreign cooperative projects. Projects from the Mapping Survey were evaluated in terms of the following variables: description of mission and activities, type of cooperation, subject and format, area of cooperation, and longevity. The committee members also weighed what we had learned from the published literature on cooperative collection development and considered projects that simply had earned a reputation as successful in the arena of cooperation.

THE PROJECTS

The committee conducted interviews with representatives from 18 projects, 16 of which had participated in the Mapping Survey. In the process of analyzing the projects for inclusion in our study, the committee found that the projects could be assigned to one of three categories:

- Type 1: Selection of Non-Electronic Monographs and/or Serials
- Type 2: Shared Electronic Purchase or Licensing
- Type 3: Access, Storage, and Preservation.

While some of the cooperatives surveyed were engaged in more than one of these types of cooperative activity, we chose to focus the interview on practices in a single category. While a listing and short description of each of the projects can be found in Appendix 1, it is useful to highlight some distinctive aspects of the projects and groupings.

Type 1: Selection of Non-Electronic Monographs and/or Serials. Five of the six cooperatives in this category are composed of academic libraries. Three of these are devoted to cooperative collection development in the arena of area studies. The Triangle Research Libraries Network (TRLN) has been a model of building cooperative collections among state institutions of higher education for years. CRL's Purchase Proposal Program represents a long-standing successful membership-run consortium of research libraries. The one multi-type library cooperative in this category is the Illinois Cooperative Collection Management Program (ICCMP).

Type 2: Shared Electronic Purchase or Licensing. Five of the cooperatives can be characterized as academic library consortia. The California Digital Library (CDL) and Florida's College Center for Library Automation (CCLA) are representative of large multi-campus public institutions of higher education. Louisiana's Academic Library Information Network Consortium (LALINC) crosses institutional lines in representing all public and private academic libraries. The Statewide California Electronic Library Consortium (SCELC) forms a consortium of small privates in a single state. Northeast Research Libraries (NERL) crosses state boundaries to bring regional academic libraries together. The remaining project in the category, OhioLINK is a true multi-type library consortium and has been on the forefront of building shared collections in electronic resources for years.

Type 3: Access, Storage, and Preservation. This category contains the three foreign projects, two from the National Library of Australia (NPLAN and PANDORA) and one from Finland, the National Repository Library. The two Australian projects can be considered preservation cooperatives: one to preserve the nation's newspapers and one to preserve Internet publications on Australia. The other three cooperative projects are in the area of archiving or storage: the Washington Research Library Consortium (WRLC) has a successful protected titles program; Information Alliance brings three separate regional academic institutions together to build shared collections of "little-used" materials; and CONSORT consists of four Ohio colleges who cooperate to create a shared remote storage facility.

The description and analysis of opportunities, barriers, and best practices in cooperative collection development that follow are derived from the qualitative responses of the interviewees from each project to a set of over 20 questions (see Appendix 2). The findings from the interviews for each of the three categories are organized into three areas of analysis: formation and founding; decision making, organization and administration; and funding and infrastructure.

OPPORTUNITIES, CHALLENGES, AND BEST PRACTICES IN COOPERATIVE COLLECTION DEVELOPMENT

1. Formation and Founding

1.1 Selection

For the six projects/programs that are concerned with selection and purchase of non-electronic materials, a common element that contributed to their strong foundation was a positive history of sharing resources and of cooperation. A tradition of collaboration gave the participants of the area studies' projects, in particular, "confidence and trust" to enter into agreements that would define and delimit their local holdings. Communication and transparency were critical to maintaining the trust once these selection projects were started. These cooperatives also pointed to the importance of commitment from the highest levels in the early stages. At the very least, there needs to be a perception from the top administrators that collaboration is good for the institution. The higher up the impetus came from to establish a cooperative collection development program, the more likely the chances that it will succeed. Director-level commitments, for example, put Latin American Research Resources Project (LARRP) on solid ground early. New monies, from grants or elsewhere, can also be a decisive element of success for getting a collective on solid footing. LARRP, for example, obtained

a foundation grant that served as seed money that drew initial participants in unexpected numbers.

A well-defined focus and explicated goals combined with the ability
to be flexible were essential even in the early stages of the shared selection cooperatives. The need for flexibility and agility were reinforced
when initial decisions or actions had to be changed or overturned. CRL,
for example, started with four programs and dropped two that were unworkable, centralized cataloging and coordination of collection policies. The other two founding programs, cooperative acquisitions and
storage of less demanded materials, have been successful for over half a
century. These cooperatives also pointed out the need to share the goal
of creating a "collective library." The East Coast Consortium of Slavic
Library Collections accepted that they could share the cost of acquisitions without sacrificing depth and breadth of collections once the participants adopted the principle of a shared library. ICCMP, however,
made the very important observation regarding the establishment of
their cooperative, that successful cooperation can help define and refine
the participant's individual missions and goals. For all these cooperatives that are based on shared selection, especially the area study projects, the division of collecting responsibilities needs to be well defined
and coherent in a way that is easily comprehensible to both selectors
and administrators.

Just as a tradition of cooperation is an element of a successful start,
the existence of longstanding allegiances or loyalties to institutions outside of the current cooperative can impede its success. Traditional relationships need to be transcended so they do not skew the priorities of the
participating institutions. Strong individual personalities with competing agendas can create tension and work against the cooperative effort.

Another barrier that is confronted early on in this type of cooperative
is the unequal distribution of commitment, effort, and money among the
institutional partners. TRLN pointed out that one of the greatest challenges in defining selection responsibilities is separating out core areas
for each campus from those that can be distributed among the partners.
Some early acquisitions decisions had to be reversed as procedures and
guidelines were not fully tested. LARRP warned that going into the un-
charted waters of distributed collection development takes more time
than one bargains for. They did not realize initially that they did not
have a great enough mix of knowledge about metadata, cataloging, and
document delivery, for example, in the early formation of the project
and that consultants would have helped to avoid some poor decisions.
Logistical barriers should be anticipated. For example, cooperatives

whose membership spans different states will confront additional state regulations for purchasing and sharing monies. In addition, in these types of projects in which efficient ILL is key, it became clear early on that costs for sharing in a distributed model can simply not be controlled in an agreement.

1.2 Shared Electronic Licensing

Strategic use of acquisition funds, commitment to communication, and a structure for input are all part of the best practices that put these consortia on a solid foundation.

For the consortia that license and build shared electronic collections, a tradition of cooperation was just as important as for the print selection cooperatives. NERL, SCELC, and CDL each had a history and "culture" of cooperation in a prior arena. The founders of SCELC, composed of small private academics, saw early participants appreciating the opportunities of "banding together" and becoming part of a "system." Common goals were articulated from the beginning among these projects. Impetus and resources flowing from the top administrators of the institution were widely pointed to as a critical element in establishing the consortia. For example, the University of Southern California's University Librarian brought vision and funding that was necessary to SCELC's beginning. USC, as the single institution with a mission, continued to drive the agenda and solidified SCELC in the early years. The founding director of the CDL provided vision and political connections that led this program to a solid start. He persuaded the president of the University of California system of the vision of a California Digital Library, who in turn championed it during its fledgling years.

Strong founding leaders understood the necessity of centralized funding for establishing a shared electronic collection. Both CDL and OhioLINK realized early on how a separate additional funding line brought immediate credibility to the initiative. They spoke to the need to leverage central funding to create common ground. It provided an "impetus for cooperation" (OhioLINK) and brought the unbelievers and doubters to see the benefits of cooperation. LALINC's Board of Regents also realized the importance of bringing separate funding to the table to get buy-in of a shared collection program.

A deliberate pace and careful building of an advisory structure were important elements to achieve widespread support and buy-in. CCLA, the statewide consortium for community colleges in Florida, cited the advisory committee structure as necessary from the beginning. No small challenge for a statewide consortium of 28 institutions, the advisory structure allowed for input from all sizes of colleges. LALINC noted that a well thought-out committee structure with representation of various constituencies contributed to getting members to cooperate from the beginning. Planning for the CDL also was a process that involved all stakeholders from the system, not just librarians. While the CDL director knew planning could not bog down, he needed to allow time for widespread input. After 18 months of planning, the CDL had gained the confidence of the campuses. OhioLINK indicated that the pace of adoption and expansion needs to be deliberate. A slow pace will not overwhelm the members. Almost all mentioned the important practice of communicating early and often and of the necessity to make clear *why* one database was selected over another. Getting information out quickly and efficiently and making sure it gets read were a constant battle, but one worth fighting. The more complex the organization is, the more the need for "constant and redundant" communication.

NERL began and has remained the least structured of these consortia. NERL's history underscores that economic necessity and opportunity are powerful preconditions for a cooperative collection development program. NERL's founding, in fact, came about because vendors were offering discounts for consortia.

A challenge for the electronic resources cooperative was the difficulty local institutions had in overcoming their parochialism and thinking "globally" or in a statewide way. Moving beyond known boundaries and a fear of change and loss of control were barriers for a number of these consortia. Even in a system that is a corporate entity, such as the University of California, there also exists "the deep suspicion to centralized solutions" at the campuses. OhioLINK noted the problems of its members in adjusting to models of shared funding, common agendas, and single time frames. CCLA found that early on local needs were raised, even when they might be in opposition to the combined need of 28 community colleges. As the selection group mentioned, CCLA members learned the need to be flexible and adaptable to time lines that might not be ideal. Large multi-type consortia such as LALINC had to work hard to reconcile opposing needs and interests of its diverse membership. OhioLINK adopted a strategy of focusing on general reference resources because of the universal appeal of these as opposed to specialized resources. And as with those in the shared selection category, obtaining commitments from everyone to make the effort seem equitable was a challenge and contributed to the suspicion of the viability of the centralized model.

1.3 Access, Storage, and Preservation

A tradition of cooperation, shared vision and goals, and a flexible structure were important elements of a successful foundation for the Access, Storage, and Preservation Group. The CONSORT libraries in Ohio spoke of their cooperative being a "natural outgrowth" of elements that had been in place for some time. The fact that these libraries had a track record of successful programs in cataloging, information literacy, and government documents helped to give their selection-for-storage cooperative program a solid and optimistic start. However, CONSORT also undertook the strategy to articulate the need for an explicit agreement on a common purpose and the vision behind it. Serious preparatory work to define and publicize the program gained buy-in. Washington Research Library Consortium (WRLC), which involves seven independent institutions, had been working together for a number of years on reciprocal borrowing and document delivery when they launched their "protected titles" project. The project thus seemed like a "natural step" to take. NPLAN, involving a commitment by the state libraries of Australia to preserve and provide access to the country's historic back file of newspapers, depended on a history of successful cooperation that gave the participants a desire to get off to a good start. They understood that there was a common problem of some urgency—the disappearance of Australian historical newspapers. The members shared an enthusiasm and passion for saving the newspapers that gave them all a sense of mission.

These cooperatives tended to set up a formal structure and set of goals, yet kept their set of objectives loose enough to adapt. This proved a successful strategy. As with other cooperatives the flexibility allowed libraries to commit without tight requirements and rigid accountability. PANDORA, composed of eight institutions, took on the daunting task of building a selective archive of their national heritage from the Internet. The most important tactic in the beginning was just to make a start. Starting small and solving problems one at a time rather than trying to have everything in place, proved successful for PANDORA.

These types of cooperatives were less likely than the other two to have access to additional funding sources, and they pointed to the lack of supplemental resources and funding as raising skepticism towards the cooperative project. Though not as pervasive as in the shared electronic projects, there was resistance by selectors to this kind of cooperative collection development. Information Alliance, the cooperative of three separate universities, found it a challenge to cultivate support from selectors whose participation was critical. For a task as enormous as PANDORA's–to build a shared national repository from the ground up–the absence of new money was a huge barrier. This group testified to the fact that it takes time to build staff support and to gain acceptance. The lack of the right expertise and the proper level and range of skills also proved a barrier in this arena of cooperation as in others.

2. Decision Making, Organization, and Administration

2.1 Selection

For those cooperatives that must build shared collections of monographs and serials, it is essential that individuals making decisions are committed to the idea of cooperation. What undermines commitment is both losing the glow after the cooperative is launched and the competition for the time of individual selectors, who have to balance commitments to the project and their local duties. SACWest made the compelling point that in these kinds of cooperatives, the goals of the cooperatives and the individual institutions cannot be at cross purposes or in competition if the shared program is to succeed. One project noted that local needs must be perceived as being satisfied first before cooperative projects are built.

Decision making for the selection cooperatives is governed by standing agreements, guidelines for eligible materials, a nomination and voting process, or some combination of the above. The process for decision making for all but the most loosely structured projects involved a review or coordinating committee that recommended or evaluated purchase proposals. The ad hoc and loosely structured decision-making procedures were cited as allowing institutions the opportunity to work autonomously to meet institutional as well as consortia needs and goals. They cited the importance of the cooperative structure allowing for representation of the partner institutions and the use of the vote in the selection of materials as the best means to achieve that. LARRP noted that they created a "level playing field" for decision making by combining collection development librarians and library directors into a coordinating committee. The East Coast Consortium of Slavic Library Collections employs a rotating chair who coordinates meetings and projects. This model has proved very successful as information on vendors, acquisitions, and statistics gets shared and projects get moved along. Despite the variety of the structures and processes for selection decision among these cooperatives, they all felt they had been flexible enough to adapt over time, whether to growing membership or new technology. Adaptation included adding working groups, selector groups, or centralized support staff. Flexibility in the decision-making process was echoed by all as necessary for making distributed collection building work. However, one cooperative noted that it is important to control the number of projects at any given time and to monitor the progress and communicate on that progress.

Communication and education remain a constant challenge. It was also clear that mechanisms to facilitate communication among selectors were essential. Communication devices ranged from web-based databases and templates to face-to-face meetings. Regular meetings were cited by one cooperative as providing the opportunity for librarians to share and develop ideas and to cultivate the goodwill necessary for cooperative projects. The cooperative needs to be more than a buying club but include educating people about the benefits of cooperation for all stakeholders. These cooperatives cited a number of barriers they confronted in the area of administration of their projects: the lack of institutional support, lack of comparable data from different institutions, lack of voter response, the difficulty of identifying the decision maker at an institution, lack of motivation, and the failure for members to meet obligations. These projects also had to guard against the negative impact of staff turnover on the ongoing commitment to cooperation. It should also be noted that the commitment to representative decision making slows the process of decision making.

2.2 Shared Electronic Licensing

· The structure for decision making for shared electronic cooperatives ranges from the simplistic "pay to play" model to the hierarchical committee organization. The most elaborate structures are designed to support a decision model based on consensus, not voting. NERL is the closest to a pure buying club and is thus quite nimble in responding to vendor opportunities or member demands for resources. Yale provides the organizational home to NERL and three years ago hired a program coordinator who handles negotiations and billing. Like SCELC, members are either in or out of a deal so it is not necessary to reach a consensus. They have an annual meeting and rely on a listserv and closed website to discuss purchases. The less structured the decision making the more imperative that individuals respond quickly and share in the work. There are downsides to staying loosely and simply organized. For NERL, disparity in size and financial capability make it a challenge to meet the demands of the small affiliates while not hurting the interests of the core members.

At the other end of the spectrum, CDL, CCLA, and OhioLINK have elaborate committee structures. These committees establish guidelines and criteria, evaluate projects, and make recommendations. Effective means for communication and for guaranteeing input are essential. CDL has put in considerable effort to realize a successful bottom-up process for identifying resources to license. Each subject area is represented by a bibliographer or selector group with a liaison to a steering committee for shared purchases. These groups are surveyed each year on resources of interest and then licenses are negotiated by the central CDL staff. The CDL director can make decisions to commit funding without oversight of a board, but works closely with the advisory committees to reach consensus. OhioLINK members also have a committee that has responsibility for selection and has the authority to create working groups or consult selector groups. The committee will consider an aggregation of databases as well as resources on a case by case basis. LALINC, as a consortium of library directors, sanctions a committee of reference librarians to select resources for shared licensing. SCELC also uses a product review committee of front line librarians to make selection decisions that are then implemented by the executive director. For the projects that are not as "lean and mean" as NERL, the commitment to broad input and participation and an open atmosphere of decision making overcame the downsides of committee bureaucracy.

As with other types of cooperatives, member institutions need to hold a statewide or consortium wide perspective in selection that is over and above the interests of a single institution. This is one reason the CDL has created shared principles that are documented and promulgated. The lack of a shared philosophy among the NERL members creates what OhioLINK has worked hard to prevent–"never having all the libraries wanting to do something at the same time." OhioLINK noted that as members perceive the benefits of cooperation through wise selection, there is a willingness to take more risks–to trust in the cooperative body. At the same time, OhioLINK reiterated the importance of a big pot of centralized funds to acquire widely enough so that all members can find something to support and appreciate. If the deal is big and broad enough, all libraries can see something in it to their advantage.

An important organizational aspect of the complex consortia is the existence of a separate centralized staff that carries out the negotiating, licensing and acquisition functions. CCLA noted that the existence of a centralized office for negotiating and licensing promotes a "worry free" atmosphere for participation and this certainly would be echoed by the others in the group. Those with centralized administrative staff point to the importance of its participation as an active and equal partner in the enterprise of building electronic resources. The central staff of OhioLINK, for example, serves on taskforces and monitors subject groups, besides doing the yeoman work of data collection and analysis as a basis for decisions. Turf battles have been avoided because the participants who make the decisions don't have to worry about the money. Yet, for those with centralized staff, there will never be enough staff to carry out negotiations for all the electronic resources that the partners want.

Whether having a simple or complex structure of decision making, these cooperatives have adapted their procedures and organization over time as membership grew or more sophisticated technology was made available. SCELC, which started out making decisions in a "poker game fashion," has successfully made their structure more elaborate in order to accommodate the exponential growth in its number of members. It has incorporated as a non-profit with by-laws, an executive director, and an executive board, which gives the program structure and direction. In this reorganization, SCELC established a reserve fund that allows funding of the executive director to handle negotiations. SCELC warned that one outcome of growth and formalization is apathy among members about governance. But SCELC suggests that it is impossible to remain a pure "buying club" because issues of vendor and staff education and program evaluation soon arise. LALINC, like SCELC, learned that while you can start out with an informal structure you soon need to have central leadership and a paid staff. CDL has seen standing committees come and go, a resource liaison structure implemented, and a second level of licensing with its own procedures implemented. Clearly the ability to adapt and change with relative ease is a part of the longevity of these successful cooperatives.

Establishing good working relationships with vendors is something the majority of these cooperatives pointed out as important. In most cases this means educating them to the specific needs and wants of the particular consortium and the need to adapt licenses to different situations. Credit is given to vendors who are willing to work with these consortia to make the packaging of resources sensible. SCELC noted that it would be impossible to succeed as they have without having "trained" the vendors to the unique and particular characteristics of their small, private institutions. Consortia will face a wide variety of vendor style and practice which calls for flexibility and ability to adjust to every new negotiation. CCLA spoke for all these cooperatives in citing the importance of paying attention to standards and trends in good consortia practice, in particular to the International Coalition of Library Consortia's (ICOLC's) work.

2.3 Access, Storage, and Preservation

Decision making for these types of cooperatives is driven very much by the local collection development policies and practices of the partners. For these kinds of cooperatives, a predominant challenge for policy making and implementation was that participating libraries had varying institutional cultures and organizational structures. Since channels of communication are different at each institution it is important to share as much information as possible and share widely.

For a national cooperative project like Australia's NPLAN, success or failure rides on the individual partners' responsiveness to the national plan to preserve the states' newspapers. NPLAN bemoans the varying levels of commitment to take action, make resources available, and to place value on their newspaper collections. The loosely defined obligations and lack of shared responsibility mean partners lack the perception of "owning" the cooperative project. The result is both a lack of "organizational readiness" to respond and failure to address important issues, like digitization as part of the preservation strategy. Another interesting observation of NPLAN is that a centralized project that respects partners' autonomy means that an uphill battle is faced in getting agreement on selection priorities. Thus, while the federated structure has allowed considerable local action in terms of microfilming for the project, the lack of rigor has contributed to a "backlog of business-critical issues." The knowledge of collections and knowledgeable preservation personnel also determine how successful participation is by a given state. However, the loose structure has allowed the partners to participate at a slow pace that suits them.

PANDORA, on the other hand, is very much a top-down structure with the National Library of Australia calling the shots, developing selection guidelines, providing staffing, and developing tools for common use. One advantage of a centralized funding and decision-making model, PANDORA points out, is that it simplifies the development of the program. The collection development officers (CDOs) of the three institutions that form the Information Alliance (IA) manage the project, consulting with selectors. The IA pointed to the relatively quick decision-making potential of their model in which CDOs coordinate the projects and make decisions. One challenge is being supportive of the selector's input. The limited roles of selectors means that they do not necessarily think of the shared repository as a working option for collection management.

The two "last copy" projects require formalized collaborative decision making. CONSORT selection for storage and last copy is controlled by a Memorandum of Agreement. But they use a collection development committee that reports to the library directors for ongoing policy and procedural issues. CONSORT found that it was important to solicit faculty input and have them participate and support the decisions for storage selection criteria. They also learned that after a few years it was impossible to operate without a coordinator to assist with communication and implementation. They successfully pursued a grant to fund a coordinator for three years. Selection decisions for the WRLC last-copy journal project is managed to a great extent by a representative Collection Development Advisory Committee, while a centralized staff and budget take care of information technology and operations of the off-site storage facility. WRLC's library directors constitute the primary operating committee. They solicit input, follow well understood criteria for selection, review on a five-year cycle, and review all requests for cancellation.

3. Funding and Infrastructure

3.1 Selection

Shared selection consortia depend on commitment of local funding to the cooperative program. The availability of local collections dollars to put toward the collaborative selection projects is essential. In practice these take the form of membership fees, grants, or local resources committed to the program. These funds were either pooled for purchases by the central agency (CRL, LARRP) or ponied up to pay invoices for specific purchases or services by the individual institutions (TRLN, ECC, SACWest). Only ICCMP provided an independent, centralized line of funding for projects approved through the review and advisory structure.

As LARRP stated explicitly, the advantage of combining local funding toward a cooperative program is that the leveraging of resources realizes a far greater provision of access to materials. Pooled or co-funded projects that cross state lines do face legal and administrative hurdles. Different state regulations affect how money can be spent to support programs at state institutions. The "pay to play" model has a wonderful simplicity to it and avoids the barriers of varying budget cycles. The disparity of budget size, however, means that institutions in this kind of a cooperative program participate on an uneven, ad hoc basis. If a project gets started on grant money, strategies for moving to permanent funding are necessary if the project is to mature and stabilize. One consortium spoke to the advantage of central state funding: it negates the need for membership fees and broadens participation. There is agreement on the key services that make cooperative collection development work among the shared selection cooperatives. Collections must be visible through a union catalog, a web finding aid, through web page summaries/descriptions, or cataloged in the online catalogs of individual institutions. CRL's dues-paying members expect easy bibliographic access to the materials. CRL cites the web as a critical technology for members to identify the consortium's holdings. Available data about the holdings of cataloged and uncataloged collections inform collective decision making as well as support end-user access.

Reciprocal interlibrary loan agreements are critical to the success of these programs. Arrangements for interlibrary loan must be in place whether charges apply or not. The granting of extended loans for research material to partners in the consortium or cooperative is an important practice. A key component of the infrastructure is the availability and accessibility of technical expertise and support. LARRP observed that if one of the member institutions is offering its technical support group to the centralized efforts of the consortium it is best if it is based in the library, so that the technologists are familiar with bibliographic data and records. Finally, ICCMP highlighted the importance of "training/teaching." Part of any new bibliographer's training addresses the benefits of cooperative collection management.

3.2 Shared Electronic Licensing

Funding models and strategies varied from simplistic to sophisticated. NERL lauded the simplicity and efficiency of the "pay to play" model. It most directly responds to local needs. Obviously, this model reduces the capacity of individual institutions to affect everything from prices to strategies. The "lean and mean" model requires only a website and listserv for communication.

The large statewide consortia in this group have developed funding models that are the most sophisticated and complicated among the types of cooperatives. CDL and LALINC follow a co-investment model, with varying portions coming from the central, state supported funding line. CDL uses the centralized funds strategically in cost-share models that allow small campuses to afford co-investment and to make consortial purchases worthwhile for the big campuses. They have also developed a Tier 2 program that allows participants to use CDL program personnel, but not funds, to pursue licenses. Both CDL and OhioLINK license a large number of electronic journal packages wherein individual campuses commit to maintain a base dollar amount and the consortium leverages that amount with modest central funds. Compelled to adapt to shrinking state resources for a central pool of funding, OhioLINK has developed a diverse set of funding strategies, integrating central and local funds. They have used the "war chest" approach where pooled local resources are matched by central funds to buy sets of databases. They have developed a second tier for more selective buying, where institutions "pay to play." Finally OhioLINK has developed what they call an "NPR" model. Basically, institutions make commitments to resources that OhioLINK can no longer afford to subscribe to but that they can't do without. If the total amount committed is greater than the current cost, members pay OhioLINK rather than the vendor and the databases are made available to everyone. All of these statewide consortia note that their strategic use of separate funds contributes to the acceptance of cooperation and the willingness of participants to commit resources of their own. Central funds also allow flexibility from one budget year to the next. In restrictive budget years, OhioLINK points out, cooperation doesn't mean you can "avoid the grim reaper. But you can minimize his harvest."

A commitment to developing the technology that makes discovery and delivery beyond the "library walls" seamless, has been a fundamental factor in the success of the big electronic resources consortia. Features of this infrastructure include: a centralized library system, union catalog, database integration, article level linking from A&I databases, statewide document delivery service, and an ability to authenticate remote users. OhioLINK's development of its own tools, rather than buying off-the-shelf solutions defined by vendors, is not only cheaper but it has made its resources and services highly integrated. CDL has used the same strategy and makes clear that the advantages of investing in technical expertise are that it allows the development and use of tools that add tremendous functionality for the user. CDL has concentrated investment on their infrastructure. Sophistication and customization do not come without a cost to participants. Membership in these consortia requires that campuses commit resources for local trouble shooting, coordination, and communication.

3.3 Access, Storage, and Preservation

WRLC, IA, and CONSORT, the last copy and shared storage repository cooperatives, tend to rely on local staffing to implement their programs. Participating in cooperative collection development is perceived as an additional burden on local collection management resources. As one of these cooperatives looks ahead to moving off of grant funding they anticipate an uphill battle to sell joint collection development at the price of some local funding.

As with other types of cooperatives, the technological infrastructure that allows for quick identification and retrieval of resources is essential to the viability of the storage and preservation cooperatives. A union catalog that contains the records for materials in the shared projects is essential. Conversely, the absence of this type of infrastructure can prove a huge handicap. CONSORT expended time and resources on workarounds because one of their members was not part of the union catalog. Patron-initiated borrowing and an efficient document delivery system, including courier services among campuses, were pointed to as basic to the success of shared storage projects. (CONSORT even commented that the fact that campuses were within driving distance made remote storage more palatable.)

NPLAN admitted that availability of central funds to the participants would have proved a great boon to increasing the level of activity. It would have enabled them to exert a better quality of control and coordination of programs. Participation is uneven because partners depend on their own funding. NPLAN points to an interesting lesson they've learned with the microfilm preservation project. Because they did not make explicit basic infrastructure obligations of the participants, they are confronting certain risks that could have been avoided. These include inadequately checked film, storage facilities that do not meet optimum conditions for preservation masters, and inadequate storage facilities for paper copies. A shared storage facility for newspapers is being considered very cautiously by NPLAN, because of the lack of willingness by partners to store newspapers centrally.

Finland's NRL is successful because it is funded from the Minister of Education and the ongoing costs are less than 1% of the acquisitions budgets of all the university libraries in Finland. The availability of a sophisticated archive system at no cost to the partners has made the central funding model of PANDORA irresistible and the project successful.

CONCLUSION

A fine line exists between circumstances or elements that promote success in cooperative collection development and best practices or methods. At the risk of crossing that line, it can be said that successful cooperative collection development projects or programs seem to have a propitious foundation when three conditions exist: a history and tradition of successful cooperation; a commitment among participants to provide funding to the cooperative project, regardless of whether new monies are available or whether they emanate from local or central resources; and a shared commitment to the cooperative mission. The value of a track record in a cooperative effort cannot be overstated in forming a basis for trust and the willingness to take risks and to move beyond the local to the global perspective. A "culture" of cooperation underlay the success of the cooperatives regardless of how simple or complex the goals and structure of the project were. For the types of cooperatives that were involved in building either print or electronic shared collections, two factors played an important role in their viability: vision and impetus for cooperation emanated from the highest ranks of the institution and new money flowed into the cooperative project.

There were also barriers that impeded cooperative collection development and needed to be overcome as part of a best practices approach. Perhaps the biggest challenge for all types of cooperatives was the variable levels of motivation, effort, and commitment that exist among partners. Administrators of cooperatives had to be able to adapt to this disparity, which manifests itself in indifference and lack of participation. Unequal access to funds and lack of supplemental funding hurt the cooperative effort. Finally, the battle between competing local and collective goals and concerns was constant.

While there were a number of laudable activities that were common among some or many of the cooperatives, there seem to be four categories in which all three types of cooperatives displayed best practices: communication and consultation; goals and focus of projects; flexibility and adaptability; and technological infrastructure.

Communication and Consultation

No practice seemed more important in all areas and stages of the three types of cooperatives than an effective system of communication and consultation. This included the following: a deliberate pace to allow time for consultation and buy-in during the foundation; an advisory committee structure that obtained broad input from and cultivated the support of line selectors and librarians; a practice of transparent decision making; and a commitment to consensus.

Goals and Focus

All the cooperatives defined goals and articulated the focus of their cooperative project in the context of the common good. These goals were promulgated and in some cases became part of the formal training of campus selectors. The more complex cooperative organizations strategically shaped funding, acquisitions, and infrastructure decisions in order to meet the defined goals of the cooperative effort. Finally, the cooperative goals were shaped to be in sync with the partners' local goals.

Flexibility and Adaptability

Even the consortia with the most complex administrative structure were willing and able to be flexible in their objectives. They adapted to the circumstances of fluctuating budgets, expanding membership, uneven commitment and involvement among partners, and changing technologies. Adjustments were made in every arena of activity, from the decision-making structure to the cost sharing models for participants.

Technological Infrastructure

Finally, all three types of consortia put resources into the technological infrastructure as an essential element for cooperative collection development and management. The infrastructure of services that proved sufficient for cooperative collection development in the past–the union catalog, ILL, document delivery–is no longer sufficient for these types of cooperatives. Linking and integration, remote authentication, and desk-top delivery are part of the basic infrastructure for discovering, managing, and delivering the shared collection. The cooperatives demonstrated their understanding of the importance of information technology by ensuring that they had adequate technological expertise and support.

The factors and practices that facilitated or retarded cooperative collection development for the 18 cooperatives in this study have largely confirmed what earlier studies have found. However, this study points out that one factor of the new dynamics and economies of cooperative collection development is the growing complexity and sophistication of consortia in the area of electronic resources. There is one type of behavior among such consortia who license resources that received little emphasis in previous studies of best practices: pervasive strategic action. Such action was seen in a range of activities, whether in the use of collection funds, deployment of staff, design of infrastructure, or vendor relations. It is important to analyze further the activities of such strategic cooperative development projects as constricting funding for collections and space makes it imperative that we build, preserve, and manage shared collections collaboratively.

BIBLIOGRAPHY FOR COOPERATIVE COLLECTION DEVELOPMENT

Armstrong, Kim and Bob Nardini. "Making the Common Uncommon? Examining Consortial Approval Plan Cooperation." *Collection Management* 24 nos. 1/2 (2000): 45-55.

Association of Research Libraries. Office of Management Studies. *Cooperative Collection Development.* SPEC Kit, 111. Washington, DC: Association of Research Libraries, Office of Management Services, 1985.

Branin, Joseph J. "Cooperative Collection Development." In *Collection Management a New Treatise*, edited by edited by Charles B. Osburn, Ross Atkinson, 81-110. Greenwich, Connecticut: JAI Press Inc., 1991.

_____. "Shifting Boundaries: Managing Research Library Collections at the Beginning of the Twenty-First Century." *Collection Management* 23 no. 4 (1998): 1-17.

Bril, Patricia L. "Cooperative Collection Development: Progress from Apotheosis to Reality (in the U.S.)." In *Collection Management in Academic Libraries*, edited by Clare Jenkins and Mary Morley, 235-58. Aldershot, Hants, England: Gower, 1991.

Brown, Doris Rahe. "Cooperative Collection Development: The Illinois Experience." In *Collection Management for the 1990s: Proceedings of the Midwest Collection Management and Development Institute, University of Illinois at Chicago, August 17-20, 1989,* edited by Joseph J. Branin, 141-7. Chicago: American Library Association, 1993.

Chapman, Liz. "Buying Shares in Libraries: The Economics of Cooperative Collection Development." *IFLA Journal* 24 no. 2 (Mar. 1998): 102-6.

Cochenour, Donnice and Joel S. Rutstein. "A CARL Model for Cooperative Collection Development in a Regional Consortium." *Collection Building* 12 no. 1-2 (1993): 34-53.

Dannelly, Gay N. "The Center for Research Libraries and Cooperative Collection Development: Partnerships in Progress." *Collection Management* 23 no. 4 (1998): 37-45.

Diedrichs, Carol Pitts. "Designing and Implementing a Consortial Approval Plan: The OhioLINK Experience." *Collection Management* 24 nos. 1/2 (2000): 15-44.

Dominguez, Patricia Buck and Luke Swindler. "Cooperative Collection Development at the Research Triangle University Libraries: a Model for the Nation." *College & Research Libraries* 54 (Nov. 1993): 470-96.

Dorst, Thomas J. "Cooperative Collection Management." *Illinois Libraries* 71 (Jan. 1989): 3-64.

Dowler, Lawrence. "The Research University's Dilemma: Resource Sharing and Research in a Transinstitutional Environment." *Journal of Library Administration* 21 no. 1/2 (1995): 5-26.

Drummond, Rebecca Carter, Anne Page Mosby, and Mary Hovas Munroe. "A Joint Venture: Collaboration in Collection Building." *Collection Management* 14 no. 1/2 (1991): 59-72.

Erickson, Rodney. "Choice for Cooperative Collection Development Among Three Academic Libraries in Minnesota and North Dakota." *Library Acquisitions* 16 no. 1 (1992): 43-9.

Evans, G. Edward. "Management Issues of Consortia. Part Two." *Library Management* 23 no. 6-7 (2002): 275-286.

Fedunok, Suzanne. "A Perspective on U.S. Cooperative Collection Development Science Serials and Electronic Journals in Academic Libraries." *INSPEL* 31 no. 2 (1997): 47-53.

Filstrup, E. Christian, Jordan M. Scepanski and Tony K. Stewart. "An Experiment in Cooperative Collection Development: South Asia Vernaculars Among the Research Triangle Universities." *Collection Management* 24 nos. 1/2 (2000): 93-104.

Harloe, Bart, ed. *Guide to Cooperative Collection Development.* Chicago: American Library Association, 1994.

Hazen, Dan C. "Cooperative Collection Development: Compelling Theory, Inconsequential Results? (Seven Case Studies)." In *Collection Management for the 21st Century,* edited by G. E. Gorman, and Ruth H. Miller, 263-83. Westport, Conn.: Greenwood Press, 1997.

_____. "Dancing with Elephants: International Cooperation in an Interdependent (But Unequal) World." *Collection Management* 24 nos. 3/4 (2000): 185-213.

Heady, Donna M. "Cooperation Works! Successful Models of Cooperative Collection Development: Report of a Program at the 1995 ALA Conference." *Library Acquisitions* 20 (Summer 1996): 190-192.

Hewitt, Joe A., and John S. Shipman. "Cooperative Collection Development Among Research Libraries in the Age of Networking: Report of a Survey of ARL Libraries." *Advances in Library Automation and Networking* 1 (1987): 189-232.

Holley, Robert P. "Cooperative Collection Development: Yesterday, Today, and Tomorrow." *Collection Management* 23 no. 4 (1998): 19-35.

Hruska, Martha and Kathy Arsenault. "Back to the Future: Building the Florida Library Research Consortium." *Collection Management* 24 nos. 1/2 (2000): 79-85.

Johnson, Peggy. "When Pigs Fly, or When Access Equals Ownership." *Technicalities* 12 no. 2 (February, 1992): 4-8.

Kisling, Vernon N. Jr., Stephanie C. Haas, and Pamela S. Cenzer. "Last Copy Depository: Cooperative Collection Management Centers in the Electronic Age." *Collection Management* 24 nos. 1/2 (2000): 87-92.

Kreimeyer, Vicki R. "Washington's Cooperative Collection Development Project: Library Information and Resources for the Northwest." *PNLA Quarterly* 53 (Spring 1989): 26-8.

Mirsky, Phyllis, R. Bruce Miller, and Karl Lo. "From Farmington Plan to the Pacific Rim Digital Library Alliance: New Strategies in Developing International Collections." *Collection Management* 24 nos. 3/4 (2000): 241-50.

Moore, Mary Y. "Washington State's Cooperative Collection Development Project." *Journal of Interlibrary Loan & Information Supply* 2 no. 3 (1992): 33-8.

Naru, Linda A. "The Role of the Center for Research Libraries in the History and Future of Cooperative Collection Development." *Collection Management* 23 no. 4 (1998): 47-58.

Niessen, James P. and Susanne F. Roberts. "Challenges and Constraints for History Selectors." *Collection Management* 24 nos. 1/2 (2000): 149-73.

Nye, James and David Magier. "International Information Exchange: New Configurations for Library Collaboration in South Asian Studies." *Collection Management* 24 nos. 3/4 (2000): 215-39.

O'Connor, Steve and Stephen Pugh. "Collaborative Purchasing: A Model for Financially Straitened Times." *Collection Management* 24 nos. 1/2 (2000): 57-77.

Perrault, Anna H. "The Printed Book: Still in Need of CCD." *Collection Management* 24 nos. 1/2 (2000): 119-36.

Pettas, William A. and Henry Bates. "Cooperative Collection Development: An Inexpensive Project in Northern California." *Collection Management* 11 no. 1/2 (1989): 59-67.

Ritter, Marian. "Four Paradigms for Sharing Library Resources." *College & Research Libraries News* 52 no. 6 (June 1991): 366-8.

Sartori, Eva Martin. "Regional Collection Development of Serials." *Collection Management* 11 no. 1/2 (1989): 69-76.

Schaffner, Bradley L. "Specialized Cooperative Efforts in Collection Development: An Analysis of Three Slavic Programs." *Collection Management* 24 nos. 3/4 (2000): 263-80.

Shubert, Joseph F. "Coordinated Collection Development for the Purpose of Resource Sharing." *Collection Management* 7 no. 1 (Spring 1985): 75-83.

Shreeves, Edward. "Is There a Future for Cooperative Collection Development in the Digital Age?" *Library Trends* 45 (Winter 1997): 373-90.

Smith, Geoff. "Cooperative Collection Development: A UK National Library Perspective." *Collection Management* 24 nos. 3/4 (2000): 251-62.

Soete, George J. and Karin Wittenborg. "Applying a Strategic Planning Process to Resource Sharing: The Changing Face of Collaborative Collection Development Among the University of California Libraries." *Advances in Library Resource Sharing* 2 (1991): 51-9.

Soete, George J., comp. *Collaborative Collections Management Programs in ARL Libraries.* SPEC Kit, 235. Washington, DC: Association of Research Libraries, Office of Leadership and Management Services, 1998.

Soete, George J. "Planning Models for Library Resource Sharing." Paper presented at the Pacific Neighborhood Consortium Conference, Bangkok, Thailand, January, 1995. Available at http://www.sinica.edu.tw/info/event/pnc/htdocs/soete.html.

Sohn, Jeanne G. "Cooperative Collection Development: A Brief Overview." *Collection Management* 8 (Summer 1986): 1-9.

Thompson, Ann. "Getting into a Cooperative Mode: Making Cooperative Collection Development Work." In *Collection Management for the 1990s: Proceedings of the Midwest Collection Management and Development Institute, University of Illinois at Chicago, August 17-20, 1989,* edited by Joseph J. Branin, 127-34. Chicago: American Library Association, 1993.

Wolf, Milton T. "Cooperative Collection Management: Online Discussion." *Collection Management* 23, no. 4 (1998): 59-93.

Wolf, Milton T. and Marjorie E. Bloss. "The Whole Is Greater Than the Sum of Its Parts." *Collection Management* 24 nos. 1/2 (2000): 105-18.

APPENDIX 1

COOPERATIVE COLLECTION DEVELOPMENT PROJECTS INTERVIEWED BY THE BEST PRACTICES WORKING GROUP

The Best Practices Working Group selected 18 model cooperative collection development projects for in-depth interviewing. Six were chosen in each of 3 categories: Selection and Purchase of Non-Electronic Material Projects, Shared Electronic Purchasing Projects, and Storage, Access, and Preservation Projects. (While most of the projects chosen could fit in multiple categories, each was interviewed in one category only.) The majority of the selected projects came from the survey work done by the Cooperative Collection Development Mapping Project Working Group (this group also arose from the 1999 Aberdeen Woods Conference). The Mapping Project Working Group was charged to develop a "tree of possible" CCD models and to develop a website database of current CCD. The results of the group's work can be found at: http://www.crl.edu/awcc2002/ccdsurveyresults.htm which also contains links to original responses to the mapping survey. The brief descriptions of the selected projects below include, when possible, the names of project participants or links to project member lists.

THE PROJECTS SELECTED FOR IN-DEPTH INTERVIEWS

Selection and Purchase of Non-Electronic Material Projects

Illinois Cooperative Collection Management Program
(http://www.niulib.niu.edu/ccm/)

Person interviewed: Arthur Young
    Description: The Illinois Cooperative Collection Management Program (ICCMP) was formed with the primary goal of enriching and strengthening "the collective information resources available to the customers of the consortium libraries and to the citizens of the State of Illinois" (Soete Plan, 1996). ICCMP is organized around three guiding principles: Cooperative Collection Management; Resource Sharing; and Continuing Professional Education. A list of participating libraries can be found at: http://www.niulib.niu.edu/ccm/ ccmlibr.html.

TRLN Cooperation for the General Collections
(http://www.trln.org/)

Person interviewed: Patricia Dominguez
Description: The goals of the TRLN Cooperative Collection Development Program are to enhance the collections of member libraries (Duke University, University of North Carolina at Chapel Hill, North Carolina State University, and North Carolina Central University) and provide better service to users by sharing access to specialized and expensive resources that do not need to be duplicated on individual campuses.

East Coast Consortium of Slavic Library Collections
(http://www.princeton.edu/~nshapiro/eastconsrt.html)

Person interviewed: Nadia Zilper
Description: The East Coast Consortium of Slavic Library Collections presently numbers ten member institutions: Columbia, Cornell, Dartmouth, Duke, Harvard, The New York Public Library, New York University, Princeton, University of North Carolina at Chapel Hill, and Yale. The Consortium's work has included the following topics: collection development and acquisitions, including efforts to prevent needless duplication of serial and other periodical-like materials; collection description, assessment, and preservation, and the pursuit of coordinated grant-funded projects in these areas, including the creation of a cooperative preservation Slavic and East European area studies group, under the auspices of the Center for Research Libraries; the preparation of informative literature intended to assist and promote area studies research at member institutions; the electronic publication of a Union List of Newspapers; and identification and evaluation of electronic resources for the Slavic and East European studies field.

SACWest (South Asia Consortium West)
(http://library.berkeley.edu/SSEAL/SouthAsia/sacwest/)

Person interviewed: Merry Burlingham
Description: SACWest's mission is to share acquisition responsibility for materials from or about South Asia and to work toward cooperative activity for reference and web-based resources. University of California at Berkeley, University of California, Los Angeles, University of Hawaii at Manoa, University of Texas at Austin, and University of Washington, Seattle are all members of SACWest.

Center for Research Libraries Purchase Proposal Program
(http://www.crl.edu/content.asp?l1=3&l2=17)

Persons interviewed: Carol Stukey and Mary Wilke
   Description: The Center for Research Libraries (CRL) is an international not-for-profit consortium of colleges, universities, and libraries that makes available scholarly research resources to users everywhere. The mission of CRL is to foster and advance scholarly inquiry through cost-effective, cooperative programs that provide reliable access through traditional and electronic means to unique and unusual collections of library materials that are in all appropriate formats, international in scope, and comprehensive in disciplines. Lists of participating libraries can be found at: http://www.crl.edu/info/crlmem.htm.

Latin Americanist Research Resources Project
(http://www1.lanic.utexas.edu/query/participating_libraries.jsp)

Person interviewed: Eudora Loh
   Description: The Latin Americanist Research Resources Project (LARRP) is a cooperative initiative that seeks to improve access to the array of research resources published in Latin America. Its goals are to restructure access to collections and resources on a comprehensive scale and to improve electronic access and document delivery systems for Latin Americanist resources. Through the concerted reallocation of library collection budgets, enhanced coverage of "non-core" materials is provided in an inter-connected network of collections. The participating Libraries are ARL institutions (http://www.lanic.utexas.edu/query/participating_libraries.jsp) and two non-ARL members: the Felipe Herrera Library of the Inter-American Development Bank and Florida International University. In 2000/2002, five Latin American Partner Institutions (http://lanic.utexas.edu/project/arl/lapartners) were invited to join the project under the provisions of a United States Department of Education grant.

Shared Electronic Purchasing Projects

Statewide California Electronic Library Consortium (SCELC), Inc.
(http://scelc.org)

Person interviewed: Rick Burke
   Description: The Statewide California Electronic Library Consortium (SCELC) was established in 1986 to develop resource-sharing relationships among the libraries of private academic and research institutions in California. The consortium seeks to explore issues related to electronic and digital infor-

mation and to promote the creation, access, use, management and maintenance of this information for the benefit of faculty and students in SCELC institutions. A list of consortium members can be found at: http://www.usc.edu/isd/partners/orgs/scelc/scelc_consortium.html.

California Digital Library (http://www.cdlib.org)

Person interviewed: Beverlee French
   Description: Founded in 1997, the California Digital Library (CDL) is a collaborative effort of the ten campuses of the University of California and is responsible for the design, creation, and implementation of systems that support shared collections of the University. CDL assists in the transition of University collections to the digital environment through the cooperative licensing and acquiring of shared electronic content, development of systems and technology to enhance shared collections, and the provision of tools and infrastructure to transform scholarly communication.

NERL: NorthEast Research Libraries consortium
(http://www.library.yale.edu/NERLpublic)

Person interviewed: Ann Okerson
   Description: The NorthEast Research Libraries consortium (NERL) comprises 21 academic research libraries with the common objectives of access and cost containment, joint licensing, and possible joint deployment of electronic resources. A list of members can be found at: http://www.library.yale.edu/NERLpublic/NERLMembers.html.

College Center for Library Automation (http://www.ccla.lib.fl.us)

Person interviewed: Lisa Close
   Description: CCLA's mission is to provide service and leadership in statewide automated library and information resources to enhance the educational experience at Florida's community colleges. This mission is accomplished by providing access to shared information resources; ensuring effective use of technology through training, support, and consultation; researching and implementing suitable new technologies; and providing library advocacy for issues of concern to community college libraries. A list of Florida's community colleges libraries can be found at: http://www.ccla.lib.fl.us/libraries/colleges/comm_colleges.asp.

Louisiana Academic Library Information Network Consortium (LALINC)
(http://www.lsu.edu/ocs/louis/about/about8.html)

Person interviewed: Ralph Boe
Description: Louisiana Academic Library Information Network Consortium (LALINC) is comprised of all public and private academic library directors in Louisiana. The LALINC committees (Executive, Information Literacy, Preservation & Disaster Preparedness, Research and Development, Resource Development, Staff Development) help investigate potential initiatives and guide LOUIS (the Louisiana Library Network) in the design and implementation of statewide library endeavors which have been approved by the Louisiana Library Network Commission.

OhioLINK–Ohio Library and Information Network
(http://www.ohiolink.edu)

Persons interviewed: Tom Sanville and Carol Diedrichs
Description: The Ohio Library and Information Network, OhioLINK, is a consortium of Ohio's college and university libraries and the State Library of Ohio. Serving more than 80 institutions, OhioLINK's membership includes 17 public universities, 23 community/technical colleges, 39 private colleges and the State Library of Ohio. OhioLINK offers user-initiated, non-mediated online borrowing through its statewide central catalog. It also provides a delivery service among member institutions to speed the exchange of library items. OhioLINK has cooperatively licensed over ninety research databases covering a variety of disciplines as well as licenses to full-text journals. A list of members can be found at: http://www.ohiolink.edu/members-info/mem-links.php.

Access, Storage, Preservation

WRLC Protected titles program (http://www.wrlc.org)

Person interviewed: Lizanne Payne
Description: The Washington Research Library Consortium (WRLC) is a regional resource-sharing organization established by seven universities in the Washington, D.C. metropolitan area to expand and enhance the information resources available to their students and faculty. The Protected Titles Program coordinates the retention of core journals ("protected titles" program). A list of members can be found at: http://www.wrlc.org.

Information Alliance (http://www.lib.utk.edu/~alliance)

Person interviewed: John Haar
Description: The Libraries of the University of Kentucky, the University of Tennessee, Knoxville and Vanderbilt University have embarked on an alliance

between the organizations to strengthen library user access to regional information resources, and link information experts formally and informally. The Information Alliance IRIS project fosters broad collection development and access for its members. A user of any of the libraries has the benefit of three major research collections, each of which has unique strengths. IRIS maximizes dollars spent on information by the three cooperating institutions through signing cooperative license agreements with vendors for databases; jointly purchasing expensive, but infrequently used materials; and cooperatively archiving and preserving little used books and journals.

CONSORT Cooperative Collection Development Project
(http://www.wooster.edu/library/oh5/cccd/default.html)

Person interviewed: Margo Curl
Description: This is a project of four members (The College of Wooster, Denison University, Kenyon College, Ohio Wesleyan University) of the Five Colleges of Ohio with the shared CONSORT online catalog. The purposes of the project are to maximize the strength, currency, and diversity of the individual and consortial collections and to reduce the need for building additional library space on the individual campuses.

National Repository Library (http://www.nrl.fi)

Person interviewed: Pentti Vattulainen
Description: The Repository Library is meant to be a repository to be shared by all libraries in Finland as the most economical way of storing library material. The basic function of the Repository Library is to receive and store the material transferred from other libraries and to offer the material for the use of other libraries.

National Plan for Australian Newspapers (NPLAN)
(http://www.nla.gov.au/preserve/nplan.html)

Person interviewed: Colin Webb
Description: NPLAN is a cooperative activity aimed at collecting, locating, preserving and making accessible all published Australian newspapers. Optimally an original print copy is preserved in an Australian library. Each state library assumes primary responsibility for the newspapers published in its state. NPLAN is a cooperative initiative of all seven State Libraries and of the National Library of Australia.

PANDORA: Preserving and Accessing Networked Documentary Resources of Australia
(http://pandora.nla.gov.au/index.html)

Person interviewed: Margaret Phillips
  Description: The PANDORA Project was set up to further the initiative of the National Library of Australia to ensure long-term access to significant Australian online publications. Its aims include establishing an archive of selected Australian online publications, and developing policy and procedures for the preservation and provision of access to Australian online publications, and developing a proposal for a national approach to the long-term preservation of these publications.

APPENDIX 2

BASE QUESTIONS USED FOR THE BEST PRACTICES INTERVIEWS

Selection and Purchasing of Non-Electronic Materials Questions

1. Formation/founding

  a. What factors in this area contributed to success of the project or cooperative entity?
  b. What barriers did you face and/or overcome in founding the project?
  c. What lessons did you learn?

2. Decision making on selection and management of hard copy Serial/Monograph titles?

  a. What kind of structure and process do you have in place for selection?
  b. What elements have contributed to success of the selection and management process?
  c. What kind of structures and process do you have in place for user feedback and input?
  d. How has the structure and process changed over time?
  e. What particular barriers have you faced and/or overcome?
  f. What lessons have you learned?
  g. What factors in this area contributed to success of the project?

3. Organization and authority

    a. What kind of management structure is in place and how has it changed over time?
    b. How are decisions made?
    c. How has this contributed to success of the cooperative project?
    d. What lessons have been learned of things to avoid or overcome in such a structure?

4. Funding

    a. Describe the decision process of actually purchasing the titles. Does one member buy abc titles and another buy xyz titles? Or is money jointly contributed to a central pool and invoices are paid from this?
    b. Describe the funding strategy and how it has changed?
    c. How has the funding strategy contributed to the success of the project?
    d. What barriers had to be overcome and what lessons have been learned?

5. Technological Infrastructure and Services to support shared acquisition

    a. What are the important elements of the infrastructure? How is it decided where to store the titles (e.g., common remote site storage with borrowing privileges for all members in project, one library stores abc titles, another xyz titles, etc.)?
    b. What are the important elements of services (e.g., union catalog, desk top delivery, no charge ILL to other members in project, special loan periods for returnables to other project members)?
    b. How has this contributed to success of project?
    c. What lessons have you learned in this area (e.g., how is it worked out when one library has the item out on loan to a second library and a third library (in the cooperative group) wishes to borrow the item)?

Shared Electronic Purchasing Questions

1. Formation/founding

    a. What factors in this area contributed to success of the project or cooperative entity?
    b. What barriers did you face and/or overcome in founding the project?
    c. What lessons did you learn?

2. Decision making on selection and management of electronic acquisitions

    a. What kind of structure and process do you have in place for selection?
    b. What elements have contributed to success of selection and management process?

   c. What kind of structures and process do you have in place for user feedback and input?
   d. How has the structure and process changed over time?
   e. What particular barriers have you faced and/or overcome?
   f. What lessons have you learned?
   g. What factors in this area contributed to success of the project?

3. Organization and authority

   a. What kind of management structure is in place and how has it changed over time?
   b. How are decisions made?
   c. How has this contributed to success of the cooperative project?
   d. What lessons have been learned of things to avoid or overcome in such a structure?

4. Funding

   a. Describe the funding strategy and how it has changed.
   b. How has the funding strategy contributed to the success of the project?
   c. What barriers had to be overcome and what lessons have been learned?

5. Technological Infrastructure and Services to support shared acquisition

   a. What are the important elements of the infrastructure and services (e.g., union catalog, digital asset management system, desk top delivery, directory)?
   b. How has this contributed to success of project?
   c. What lessons have you learned in this area?

Access, Storage, and Preservation Questions

1. Formation/founding

   a. What factors in this area contributed to success of the project or cooperative entity?
   b. What barriers did you face and/or overcome in founding the project?
   c. What lessons did you learn?

2. Decision making on selection and storage of materials

   a. What kind of structure and process do you have in place for selection? For storage?
   b. What elements have contributed to success of the selection and management process?

   c. What kind of structures and process do you have in place for user feed-back and input?
   d. How has the structure and process changed over time?
   e. What particular barriers have you faced and/or overcome?
   f. What lessons have you learned?
   g. What factors in this area contributed to success of project?

3. Organization and authority

   a. What kind of management structure is in place and how has it changed over time?
   b. How are decisions made?
   c. How has this contributed to success of the cooperative project?
   d. What lessons have been learned of things to avoid or overcome in such a structure?

4. Funding

   a. Describe the funding strategy and how it has changed.
   b. How has the funding strategy contributed to the success of the project?
   c. What barriers had to be overcome and what lessons have been learned?

5. Technological and physical infrastructure and services support shared storage and access?

   a. What are the important elements of the infrastructure and services (e.g., union catalog, storage facility, digital asset management system, desk top delivery, directory, etc.)?
   b. How has this contributed to success of the project?
   c. What lessons have you learned in this area?

Measuring Success
of Cooperative Collection Development: Report of the Center for Research Libraries/ Greater Western Library Alliance Working Group for Quantitative Evaluation of Cooperative Collection Development Projects

Stephen Bosch
Lucy Lyons
Mary H. Munroe
Anna H. Perrault
Chris Sugnet

SUMMARY. This report of the Working Group for Quantitative Evaluation of Cooperative Collection Development identifies ways of evaluating

Stephen Bosch is Materials Budget, Procurement, and Licensing Librarian, University of Arizona Library, 1510 East University, PO Box 210055, Tucson, AZ 85721-0055 (E-mail: boschs@u.library.arizona.edu). Lucy Lyons is Bibliographer for Collection Analysis and Planning, Northwestern University Library, Evanston, IL 60208 (l-lyons@northwestern.edu). Mary H. Munroe is Associate Dean, Collections and Technical Services, Northern Illinois University, DeKalb, IL 60115 (E-mail: mmunroe@niu.edu). Anna H. Perrault is Associate Professor, School of Library and Information Science, University of South Florida, Tampa, FL (E-mail: perrault@chuma1. cas.usf.edu). Chris Sugnet, MLS, MA, is Director, Collection Development and Management Division, University Libraries, University of Nevada, Las Vegas, Box 457038, Las Vegas, NV 89154-7038 (E-mail: csugnet@ccmail.nevada.edu).

[Haworth co-indexing entry note]: "Measuring Success of Cooperative Collection Development: Report of the Center for Research Libraries/Greater Western Library Alliance Working Group for Quantitative Evaluation of Cooperative Collection Development Projects." Bosch, Stephen et al. Co-published simultaneously in *Collection Management* (The Haworth Information Press, an imprint of The Haworth Press, Inc.) Vol. 28, No. 3, 2003, pp. 223-239; and: *The New Dynamics and Economics of Cooperative Collection Development* (ed: Edward Shreeves) The Haworth Information Press, an imprint of The Haworth Press, Inc., 2003, pp. 223-239. Single or multiple copies of this article are available for a fee from The Haworth Document Delivery Service [1-800-HAWORTH, 9:00 a.m. - 5:00 p.m. (EST). E-mail address: docdelivery@haworthpress.com].

http://www.haworthpress.com/web/COL
Digital Object Identifier: 10.1300/J105v28n03_03

through quantitative measures the success of cooperative collection development activities. Following a literature review, the group developed four basic groups of performance measures including: resources or input data (numerical data like FTE, staff, items purchased, items in collections, etc.); financial data (library/group expenditures, unit costs, etc.); use data (use of electronic, print, or near print, documents delivered, etc.); and user satisfaction data. On the basis of a modified balanced scorecard approach, specific performance measures and underlying data points are identified that could be effective in measuring cooperative collection development efforts and determining if a cooperative collection development project reduced unit costs, increased access to information resources, and resulted in increased use and user satisfaction. *[Article copies available for a fee from The Haworth Document Delivery Service: 1-800-HAWORTH. E-mail address: <docdelivery@ haworthpress.com> Website: <http://www.HaworthPress.com> © 2003 by The Haworth Press, Inc. All rights reserved.]*

KEYWORDS. Cooperative collection development–evaluation, cooperative collection development–statistics, quantitative measures, performance measures, Center for Research Libraries, Greater Western Library Alliance, library assessment, user satisfaction, Aberdeen Woods Conference

Cooperative collection development is an important strategy libraries have used to maximize local resources. One question that is always associated with the topic has been, "How do we know if a cooperative project has actually benefited our library?" The Working Group for Quantitative Evaluation of Cooperative Collection Development was asked to develop methods for answering this question. The Aberdeen Woods Conference on Cooperative Collection Development (AWCCCD) held in November 1999 was the genesis of this project. The scope of the conference was to discuss current initiatives in cooperative collection development and to seek ways to expand the scope of this activity. The conference was intended to produce outcomes that would provide a foundation for future developments in cooperative collection development. Four working groups were established to implement projects identified by conference participants as important to future cooperative collection development. This was one of those groups.

For the purposes of these initiatives, cooperative collection development was defined as any collaborative activity characterized by planned, coordinated collection development and/or management. All collaborative enterprises, even informal working arrangements, are eligible for inclusion as long as they are active and viable. This definition of cooperative collection development encompasses consortia that purchase electronic databases as well as collaborative digitization projects.

As the project was getting underway, Adrian Alexander (the Director of the Greater Western Library Alliance (GWLA), at that time the Big Twelve Plus), believed that this project could be a good opportunity for collaboration between CRL and GWLA. GWLA was undertaking several cooperative collection development projects and was developing processes for shared purchasing of electronic resources. GWLA would need to develop quantitative performance measures for the emerging initiatives if the new efforts were to be effectively assessed. After consultation with CRL and GWLA this project became a joint CRL/GWLA effort. Volunteers were drawn from both GWLA and CRL Aberdeen Woods Conference participants. The working group started with ten members but has now dropped to the current seven members. Those members were Steve Bosch (Chair), Steve Atkins, Mary Munroe, Lucy Lyons, Anna Perrault, Karen Schmidt and Chris Sugnet.

INITIAL PROCESSES FOR THE WORK OF THE GROUP

The working groups were expected to accomplish their work mainly through the use of e-mail and telephone conference calls. This proved to be a barrier at times since it is sometimes difficult to schedule busy professionals for conference calls, and e-mail is not a good tool for reaching clarity on complex issues. The first step taken by the group was to review the literature concerning performance evaluation and quantitative measures activity in the library field. There is not a substantial body of information relevant to libraries, but several other national and international library groups were developing similar projects. The working group focused attention on the Association for Research Libraries New Measures Initiatives, in particular the Association of Research Libraries E-Metrics Study (see http://www.arl.org/stats/newmeas/emetrics/index.html). The ARL initiative was intended to address two basic needs: to shift library statistics from the collection of simple input measures to the development of statistics that measure outcomes that impact important programs, and to be able to benchmark best practices that maximize the use of resources. Also, the group reviewed similar activity by the International Federation of Library Associations (IFLA) IFLANET, Internet & Networking, Surveys and Statistics (http://www.ifla.org/II/stats.htm), as well as the Equinox Library Performance Measurement and Quality Management System Project in Great Britain (http://equinox.dcu.ie/).

Once the group had developed an understanding of the issues that might be involved in the project, a basic definition of what would constitute a successful cooperative collection development project was developed. What constitutes a successful cooperative collection development project? A general description might assert that a successful cooperative collection development project reduces unit costs, and increases access to information resources, resulting in increased use and user satisfaction.

From this basic definition, the Group then began the process of crafting test performance measures. As much as possible, the focus of efforts was on outcomes using a modified balanced scorecard approach. Normally, the balanced scorecard is a performance management method that incorporates information from four perspectives: feedback from customers, internal business data, learning and growth of the organization, and financial success. For the purposes of this project, learning and growth were not considered major performance issues, at this time. As the nature of cooperative collection development changes and shifts from an activity based on projects to an activity that has become part of continuing operations, this could change. The group developed four basic groups of performance measures including:

* Financial–library/group expenditures, unit costs, etc.
* Resources or input data–numerical data like FTE, staff, items purchased, items in collections, etc.
* Use–use of electronic, print, or near print, documents delivered, etc.
* User satisfaction.

Within these basic groups, the following specific performance measures and underlying data points were identified by the group as those that would be most effective in measuring cooperative collection development efforts and those that would be the most effective at determining if a cooperative collection development project reduced unit costs, increased access to information resources, and resulted in increased use and user satisfaction.

FINANCIAL

Financial measures look at the effective use of resources to achieve the goals of the project. An important measure will be the overall decline in the unit cost/per use of the resource per FTE. To determine this cost, it will be especially important to measure costs before the cooperative collection development project (if possible) and after. Some data points may not be directly related to dollars, but are important to determining the cost effectiveness of a project.

Performance Measures

PM F.1   Unit costs per use per FTE students (or other user base) per individual institution versus unit costs per use per FT students (or other user base) per consortia or cooperating group

PM F.2   Unit costs per FTE staff per individual institution versus unit costs per FTE staff per consortia or cooperating group

Data Types/Points

F 1.   Total FTE students served
F 2.   Total FTE per professional library staff
F 3.   Items processed per library staff FTE
F 4.   Total library expenditure per items processed
F 5.   Documents delivered per library staff FTE
F 6.   Total library expenditure per document delivered
F 7.   Total library expenditure per titles in stock
F 8.   Total library expenditure per FTE
F 9.   Library staff expenditure and operating costs per FTE
F 10. Acquisition costs per FTE
F 11   Cost/use of electronic full-text journals (local and consortial)
F 12. Cost/use of electronic reference sources (local and consortial)
F 13. Cost/use of electronic books (local and consortial)
F 14. Cost/use of journals (local and consortial)
F 15. Cost/use of near print sources (local and consortial)
F 16. Cost/use of books (local and consortial)
F 17. Cost/use of ILL items delivered to internal customers (local and consortial)
F 18. Cost/use of ILL items delivered to external customers (local and consortial)
F 19. Library expenditures for information technology overhead including bibliographic utilities, networks, and or consortia
F 20. External expenditures (on behalf of a library) for information technology bibliographic utilities, networks, and or consortia

RESOURCES/NUMBER

Expanded access to resources, enhanced collection strengths, and access to more unique resources are not measures that are easily defined, as there are qualitative aspects that are hard to measure. This area has been divided by format (serial and non-serial) since there are some basic differences between the two types of measures. Since cooperative collection development is the focus of the measures, most of the data would be collected and reported on a consortial level rather than for single institutions. Despite this, most of the measures would be compared to baseline data for the unit of measurement which in many cases would be data from individual institution. Stated more simply, most of this data would be gathered for the group (number of staff, subscriptions, etc.) but the data needed to compare changes probably will be gathered at the institutional level.

Performance Measures

PM N.1   % increase in the overall number of information resources available to the target population for the target subject area

PM N.2   % increase in the number of information resources that represent primary materials that are now available to the target population for the target subject area

PM N.3   % increase in documents delivered or made available through ILL per FTE (target population) during a year

Data Types/Points

Non-Serial Titles (Near-Print Materials)

N1.   Number of non-serial titles by subject and time period

N2.   Ratio of titles to number of users

N3.   Ratio of titles to number of uses

N4.   Number of unique titles by subject and time period

N5.   Mean number of holding libraries per title (on the average how many libraries hold each title)

N6.   Median age of collections by subject (for subjects in which currency is important)

Serials

N7.   Number of subscribed to electronic full-text journals (individually and through consortia)

N8.   Number of current print journal subscriptions (individually and through consortia)

N9. Number of electronic journals provided by cooperative agreements

N10. Number of electronic reference sources and databases including full-text databases (individually and through consortia)

N11. Number of document delivery transactions (per individual institution and through consortia)

USE

If the success of a cooperative collection development project is characterized by increased use, it becomes necessary to develop the means to measure use of the information resources that are targets for the project. There are many definitions for use, and it will be necessary to develop common terms for projects. Increased use could occur in several areas including: use of electronic resources, circulation or in-house use of print or near print collections, interlibrary loan, etc. Use of electronic resources is still an area that lacks universal acceptance of definitions. A good source of information for this area is the document *Guidelines for Statistical Measures of Usage of Web-Based Information Resources* produced by the International Coalition of Library Consortia (ICOLC–see http://www.library.yale.edu/consortia/2001webstats.htm). Another source of information will be forthcoming from the National Information Standards Organization (NISO) in NISO Z39.7-2002 *Standard for Information Services and Use: Metrics & Statistics for Libraries and Information Providers–Data Dictionary*. The standard is on draft trial, and there is no guarantee that this standard will be adopted, but the document is still valuable (see http://www.niso.org/emetrics).

Performance Measures

PM U.1   Documents delivered/ILL per library staff FTE

PM U.2   Documents delivered/ILL per FTE student during a year

PM U.3   Use of electronic resources compared to number of electronic resources

PM U.4   Use of electronic resources compared to costs for electronic resources

PM U.5   Use of print/near print compared to number of titles in the collection

PM U.6   Use of print/near print compared to the cost of the collection

Data Types/Points

U1. Total population served
U2. Use of electronic journal/full-text collection
U3. Use of electronic reference sources
U4. Use of electronic books
U5. Use of journal/full-text collection
U6. Use of near print collection
U7. Use of books
U8. ILL items delivered to internal customers
U9. ILL items delivered to external customers

USER SATISFACTION

Information concerning user satisfaction is some of the hardest data to correctly gather and use. Generally, the best data comes directly from the users. Surveys are always costly in terms of staff time and costs, but using data from user satisfaction surveys can help demonstrate accountability. Can a cooperative collection development project be successful if the user population doesn't use it or express some satisfaction with the effort? Some variables that impact perceptions of quality and service are best discovered through direct interaction with customers. Some of the data types may not be incorporated into the current performance measures listed below, but some data that describes activities like instruction and reference services may be very important variables in use and satisfaction.

Performance Measures

PM US.1 % increase in overall user satisfaction
PM US.2 80% of users surveyed express satisfaction with information resources supplied through a cooperative collection development project

Data Types/Points

US1. Trends in use of electronic journal/full-text collection over time
US2. Trends in use of electronic reference sources over time
US3. Trends in use of electronic books over time
US4. Trends in use of journal/full-text collection over time

US5.   Trends in use of near print collection over time
US6.   Trends in use of books over time
US7.   Focus groups that measure user satisfaction with library services
US8.   Surveys of satisfaction with document delivery services
US9.   Trends in use of electronic reference sources over time
US10. Trends in use of print reference sources over time (reshelving studies)
US11. Number of reference questions received over time
US12. Number of correct reference answers received (unobtrusive studies)
US13. Trends in use of electronic reference desk or virtual reference services
US14. Number of students involved in formal BI per FTE students during a year
US15. Measures of use of library resources in freshman, sophomore or capstone courses (studies using readers and student papers including control and instruction groups)

NEXT STEPS

After crafting draft performance measures and data types, the group then reviewed the activity of the other CRL project teams to determine if there was information they had developed that would inform our efforts. The Current Cooperative Collection Development Mapping Project, charged to develop a "tree of possible" cooperative collection development models and develop a website database of current projects, had useful information concerning current cooperative collection development activities. The projects listed in this mapping were organized by our project into 9 broad groups for cooperative collection development including: Shared Personnel, Shared Resources via ILL, Shared Collection Development Programs, Shared Electronic Resources, Shared Reference, Duplicate Exchange, Off Site Storage/"Last Copy" Projects, Preservation, and Shared Digitization Projects. The Group plans to craft "tool boxes" for each of the areas identified above that can be used as a template for developing quantitative measures. The "tool box" would provide a broad outline describing how to go about establishing procedures for measuring the effectiveness of cooperative collection development projects. It would include performance measures relevant to an area, data types and definitions as well as suggested methodologies for gathering data. A sample follows:

DRAFT TEMPLATE FOR A SET OF MEASUREMENT TOOLS FOR SHARED DIGITIZATION PROJECTS

A Shared Digitization Project would include any collaborative activity that is characterized by planned efforts that results in materials from individual institutions being reformatted or created in a digital format and made available to a broader group of institutions. All collaborative enterprises, even informal working arrangements, are eligible for inclusion as long as they are active and viable. This definition encompasses consortia.

SPECIFIC PROJECT ORIENTED PERFORMANCE MEASURES (PM) FOR THE EVALUATION OF A SHARED DIGITIZATION PROJECT

PM 1. % change in the number of digital resources made available to users through the project. The resources should be tracked by category (could include serial, non serial, near-print, electronic, etc.), by subject, and by time period for the target area of the digitization project. (N4 Time1 – N4 Time2) / N4 Time1

PM 2. Unit costs, per use, per FTE user base, per individual institution versus unit costs per use per FTE user base for all digitization project participants. (F3 + F5 + F9 / U1 / N1) compared to (F4 + F5 + F10 / U2 / N2)

PM 3. Unit costs per FTE project staff per individual institution versus unit costs per FTE project staff per other digitization arrangements. (Baseline costs) (F4 / N14) / (F4 / N15)

PM 4. % change in the ratio of the number of titles made available to the number of users for the target area of the digitization project. (N4 Time1 – N4 Time2) / N4 Time1) compared to N2

PM 5. % change in the ratio of the number of titles to the number of uses for the target area of the digitization project. (N4 Time1 – N4 Time2) / N4 Time1) compared to U2

PM 6. Total library expenditures for support for the digitization project F3 + F5 + F9

PM 7. Total library expenditures for staffing, processing, etc., in support of the target area prior to digitization project F3 + F5 + F9

PM 8. Items processed per library staff FTE N4 / N15

PM 9. Shelf space made available compared to project costs
        N19 / F3 + F5 + F9
PM 10. Use compared to access records created or linked U2 / N16
PM 11. Use compared to public relations/education costs U2 / F11
PM 12. User satisfaction with information resources in target area
        of the digitization project US1
PM 13. User satisfaction with available digital resources in the
        target area compared to unit costs US1 compared to (F3 +
        F5 + F9) or (F4 + F5 + F10)

BY THE PERFORMANCE DATA TYPES FOR USED MEASURES DRAFTED FOR AN EVALUATION OF A SHARED DIGITIZATION PROJECT

FINANCIAL

Data Types/Points

F 1. Total FTE students served
F 2. Total FTE per professional library staff
F 3. Items processed per library staff FTE
F 4. Total library expenditure per items processed
F 5. Documents delivered per library staff FTE
F 6. Total library expenditure per document delivered
F 7. Total library expenditure per titles in stock
F 8. Total library expenditure per FTE
F 9. Library staff expenditure and operating costs per FTE
F 10. Acquisition costs per FTE
F 11. Cost/use of electronic full-text journals (local and consortial)
F 12. Cost/use of electronic reference sources (local and consortial)
F 13. Cost/use of electronic books (local and consortial)
F 14. Cost/use of journals (local and consortial)
F 15. Cost/use of near print sources (local and consortial)
F 16. Cost/use of books (local and consortial)
F 17. Cost/use of ILL items delivered to internal customers (local
      and consortial)
F 18. Cost/use of ILL items delivered to external customers (local
      and consortial)
F 19. Library expenditures for information technology overhead
      including bibliographic utilities, networks, and or consortia
F 20. External expenditures (on behalf of a library) for information
      technology bibliographic utilities, networks, and/or consortia

RESOURCES/NUMBER

Data Types

N1. Total FTE students/faculty/customers served local
N2. Total FTE students/faculty/customers served co-operating group or consortia
N3. Total FTE library staff
N4. Items processed (could be items cataloged or linked, items digitized, etc.
N5. Documents delivered
N6. Documents delivered in target area
N7. Titles in stock–locally held (useful to organize by subject and by publishing date)
N8. Titles available through shared collections (useful to organize by subject and by publishing date)
N9. Serial subscriptions (print or electronic)–local
N10. Serial subscriptions (print or electronic)–consortia
N11. Units purchased (print or electronic)–local
N12. Units purchased (print or electronic)–consortia
N13. Number of library computer workstation hours available
N14. Library staff assigned to project, local
N15. Library staff assigned to project, co-operating group or consortia
N16. Number of access records created or records linked
N17. Items committed to target project–locally held (useful to organize by subject and by publishing date)
N18. Items in target project available through shared collections (useful to organize by subject and by publishing date)
N19. Shelf space made available through the removal of materials from local collections

USE = INCREASED USE, CIRC, ILL, ONLINE, ETC.

Data Types

U1. Use of electronic resources (could be e-journals, full-text databases, abstracting and indexing (A and I) or other reference databases, e-books, or other digital resources, etc.), local. Use should be defined based on ICOLC guidelines

U2. Use of electronic resources (could be e-journals, full-text databases, A and I or other reference databases, e-books, or other digital resources, etc.), co-operating group or consortia. Use should be defined based on ICOLC guidelines

U3. Use of print or near print collections, local

U4. Use of print or near print collections, co-operating group or consortia

U5. ILL/document delivery items delivered to internal customers

U6. ILL/document delivery items delivered to external customers

U7. Percentage of information requests submitted electronically (could be ILL requests, reference, purchase requests, etc.)

U8. Library computer workstation use rate

U9. Rejected electronic sessions as a percentage of total attempted sessions

U10. Reference transactions local

U11. Reference transactions provided external customers

U12. Use of print reference collections (re-shelving studies)

U13. Number of correct reference answers received (unobtrusive studies)

U14. Number of students receiving bibliographic instruction, or other similar library-based training

Data Collection Procedures

It was recognized that a set of procedures would need to be developed to assist in the implementation of a measurement project. For each data type there would need to be an outline that defined the data element and described how to gather the information. A sample is provided below.

TEMPLATE Data Collection Procedures

N1   Number of non-serial titles by subject and time period

Definition: The number of monographic titles, definition for title as follows:

Title: a single physical unit of any printed, typewritten, handwritten, mimeographed, or processed work, distinguished from other units by a separate bibliographic record or description, which has been cataloged, classified, and made ready for use, and which is typically the unit used to charge circulation transactions.

Subject: The classification system used to develop subjects should be identified. The following subject classification systems are preferred: Dewey Decimal Classification (DDC), Library of Congress (LC), National Library of Medicine (NLM), or the Universal Decimal Classification (UDC) and its twenty-five groups as set forth in the UNESCO recommendations. If an index is not arranged by subject, the organization of the index will still need to be described.

Time Period: For the sake of comparability with other measures, the preferred time period would be determined based on the reporting needs. The selected period should conform to regular intervals such as fiscal year, calendar year, or imprint year. The rationale for the selection of the base period should be provided.

Implementation

Collected by: Local systems

Frequency: As needed to support reporting on progress of the project.

Procedures: Include in volume counts duplicates and bound volumes of periodicals. For purposes of this measure, unclassified bound serials arranged in alphabetical order are considered classified. Exclude microforms, maps, nonprint materials, and uncataloged items. If any of these items cannot be excluded, please provide an explanatory footnote in the "Footnotes" section of the report. Include government document titles that are accessible through the library's catalogs regardless of whether they are separately shelved. "Classified" includes documents arranged by Superintendent of Documents, CODOC, or similar numbers. "Cataloged" includes documents for which records are provided by the library or downloaded from other sources into the library's card or online catalogs. Documents should, to the extent possible, be counted by the number of unique records used to catalog the documents.

IMPORTANT: Title counts should not be considered the same as volume counts or piece counts. They are very different. If a volume count becomes necessary, it may be estimated through sampling a representative group of title records and determining the corresponding number of volumes, then extrapolating to the rest of the collection. Or, as an alternative, an estimate may be made using the following formulae: 52 document pieces per foot / 10 "traditional" volumes per foot = 5.2 document pieces per volume. If either formulas or sampling are used for deriving your count, please indicate in a footnote.

Subject organization needs to be agreed to by all project members prior to gathering the information. Subject divisions provide the outline for the collection process. The overall classification system has to be negotiated as well as the level to which the subject will be divided. Enter all subject classifications in the study on the data collection forms.

Time period is also defined (annual based on calendar, quarterly based on fiscal year, etc.) prior to gathering the volume counts. Indicate the date or time period to which the count is applicable in the "Title Count Source Date" column in Figure 1 below:

FIGURE 1. (for N1) Sample Number/Subject/Time Report Form

Name of Co-operative Project: _____

Subject Classifications	Participating Institutions				Time of Count
	Volumes (Participant A)	Volumes (Participant B)	Volumes (Participant C)	Volumes (Participant, Etc.)	

SUMMARY OF THE PROJECT TO DATE

A large portion of basic data types are standard data like expenditures, use, number of volumes or items, staffing, FTE, etc. These types of data have been collected regularly by libraries in the past. What's changing in the area of gathering library statistics is that these data points are being combined with others to form measures for performance, not just statistics. Different measures are the products of several variables not just a simple number–e.g., cost per use compared to FTE or other user base.

Using the balanced scorecard management approach, it is important to look at use, and user satisfaction as well as all the other measures. Feedback from customers is important in developing the customer's perspective on performance.

These combined measures are more likely to indicate success than simple input or output measures. For example, the success of a project is much more clearly indicated by the measures: use of the resources increased 17% while unit costs dropped 3% and users indicated 90% satisfaction with the program, as opposed to the simple measure, the library made 15,000 additional titles available to customers.

Cost per use is an important component of the performance measures. A product or service may cost more in a cooperative collection development project due to wider participation and a wider availability of information. If the use increases more than costs, then a reduced cost per use was achieved. For example: a library participates with a group in a shared collections project. They are responsible for providing a defined set of materials to all members participating. The standard costs of purchasing and processing the resources would need to be combined with the costs of delivering the materials to participants. For the program to be successful the total costs compared to use should decrease. Also, overall use should increase by at least the same percentage as the user base. If there were 150% more users in the group, then similar numbers should be seen for increases in use. If not then the program needs to be reviewed to understand why it hasn't achieved minimum market penetration. Outreach, marketing (PR), bibliographic access, or library instruction could all be variables contributing to lack of use.

Cost per use has been an elusive figure to develop especially for electronic resources. The problems of gathering comparable use data was a significant barrier discovered in the ARL E-metrics program and will also present difficulties for cooperative collection development projects. However, since some cooperative collection development projects are limited in scope it may be easier to craft common definitions for "use" for the specific project and gather comparable data. Gathering comparable use data from 2-3 vendors may be possible. Trying to develop common data for the entire marketplace is impossible at this time.

NEXT STEPS

- The group is working with the Greater Western Library Alliance to develop base line data on the cost effectiveness of the consortial purchase of electronic information resources.

- The group is also looking for other groups that may want to pilot a measurement project.
- The group plans to build customized tools for the pilots and provide definitions, methodologies and data gathering templates that can be used in the pilot measurement projects.
- Based upon feedback from the pilot projects, the group will craft complete "toolboxes" and make these available to all interested parties.

BIBLIOGRAPHY

Bertot, J. (1999). "Developing National Network Statistics and Performance Measures for U.S. Public Libraries: Models, Methodologies and Issues" In *Proceedings of the 3rd Northumbria Conference on Performance Measurement in Libraries and Information Services* (pp. 3-10). Newcastle Upon Tyne: Information North for the School of Information Studies, University of Northumbria at Newcastle.

Bertot, John Carlo. "Measuring Service Quality in the Networked Environment: Approaches and Considerations" *Library Trends*, Spring 2001, Vol. 49 Issue 4, 758-775.

Bertot, J. C.; McClure, C. R.; & Ryan, J. (2001). *Statistics and Performance Measures for Public Library Networked Services*. Chicago, IL: American Library Association.

Cook, Colleen; Heath, Fred M. "Users' Perceptions of Library Service Quality: A LibQUAL+ Qualitative Study" *Library Trends*, Spring 2001, Vol. 49 Issue 4, 548-584.

Corcoran, Mary. "But Enough About Me, What About the Users?" *Online*, Nov/Dec 2001, Vol. 25 Issue 6, 90-92.

Cullen, Rowena. "Perspectives on User Satisfaction Surveys" *Library Trends*, Spring 2001, Vol. 49 Issue 4, 662-686.

Flanagan, Pat; Horowitz, Lisa R. "Exploring New Service Models: Can Consolidating Public Service Points Improve Response to Customer Needs?" *Journal of Academic Librarianship*, Sept. 2000, Vol. 26 Issue 5, 329-338.

Luther, Judy. "NISO Forum on Library Statistics" *Information Today*. June 2001, Vol. 18 Issue 6, 52-53.

McClure, Charles R.; Lopata, Cynthia. "Assessing the Academic Networked Environment" *Journal of Academic Librarianship*, July 1996, Vol. 22 Issue 4, 285-289.

Poll, R., Te Boekhorst, P. et al. 1996. *Measuring Quality: International Guidelines for Performance Measurement in Academic Libraries*. Munchen: K.G. Saur. (IFLA Publications 76).

Willemse, John. "Performance Assessment in IFLA and United Kingdom Academic Libraries" *South African Journal of Library & Information Science*, Dec. 1998, Vol. 66 Issue 4, 161-165.

Young, Ann-Christe "Performance Measures." *College & Research Libraries News*, March 1998, Vol. 59, 207.

Digitizing Geosciences Information Proposal and Report for the Center for Research Libraries Working Group on Cooperative Collection Development in Science and Technology

Diane E. Perushek

SUMMARY. A Center for Research Libraries working group on coopera-tive collection development in the sciences and technology identified the geosciences as a domain whose current and historical publications make ideal candidates for a digitization demonstration project, due to their utility and the diverse nature of their text, tables and images. State geological sur-veys engage in some of the most important and practical fieldwork under-taken by geologists. State geological surveys and maps have had a critical impact in the discovery, exploration, use and conservation of natural re-sources. As a consequence, close to 2,000 selected publications from the states of Illinois, Pennsylvania, Texas and Wyoming were chosen for the scope, quality and variety exhibited in them. The eighteen-month digiti-zation pilot project will, upon conclusion, design a self-sustaining model for a continuation program. *[Article copies available for a fee from The Haworth Document Delivery Service: 1-800-HAWORTH. E-mail address: <docdelivery@ haworthpress.com> Website: <http://www.HaworthPress.com> © 2003 by The Haworth Press, Inc. All rights reserved.]*

Diane E. Perushek is University Librarian, University of Hawai'i Library, Univer-sity of Hawai'i at Manoa, Honolulu, HI 96822 (E-mail: perushek@hawaii.edu).

The author would like to give credit to Vernon N. Kisling, Jr., Stephanie Haas, and Paul Kirk for writing Appendix 6, entitled "Archiving Print Publications in the Digital Age."

[Haworth co-indexing entry note]: "Digitizing Geosciences Information Proposal and Report for the Cen-ter for Research Libraries Working Group on Cooperative Collection Development in Science and Technol-ogy." Perushek, Diane E. Co-published simultaneously in *Collection Management* (The Haworth Information Press, an imprint of The Haworth Press, Inc.) Vol. 28, No. 3, 2003, pp. 241-262; and: *The New Dynamics and Economics of Cooperative Collection Development* (ed: Edward Shreeves) The Haworth Information Press, an imprint of The Haworth Press, Inc., 2003, pp. 241-262. Single or multiple copies of this article are avail-able for a fee from The Haworth Document Delivery Service [1-800-HAWORTH, 9:00 a.m. - 5:00 p.m. (EST). E-mail address: docdelivery@haworthpress.com].

KEYWORDS. Scientific and technical literature, geosciences, scholarly publishing–cooperation, digital archives, Aberdeen Woods Conference

BACKGROUND AND CHARGE

This proposal and report are an outgrowth of the discussions at the Center for Research Libraries (CRL)/Association of Research Libraries (ARL) Aberdeen Woods Conference of 1999 that focused on materials in science and technology. As a result the Working Group on Cooperative Collection Development in Science and Technology was formed to explore possible cooperative ventures.[1] Their final report and recommendations were submitted to CRL in July 2002.

The working group crafted a charge to identify areas on which to concentrate any of the following activities: acquisition and deacquisition, archiving, preservation, assessment of current and previous cooperative projects, identification of granting agencies who may fund the group's recommendations and partners who may wish to investigate archiving with a library organization. Appendix 3 lists the myriad databases and tools we consulted in fulfilling our charge.

Through a series of meetings and conference calls leading to a survey of global scholarly communication in the sci-tech field, the group decided to break down its sizable charge into parts. The desire was to capitalize on the noteworthy work already undertaken by such organizations as SPARC, Earthscape, BioOne and the Digital Library Federation, without duplicating their efforts. Realizing that one could not tackle all of the sciences, it was decided that the geosciences offered unique opportunities. The group concluded that the archiving of materials, especially electronic but including print as well, was the most urgent need in this discipline.

The reasons for choosing the geosciences are as follows:

1. The scope of the field is broad yet manageable for a project.
2. The project could scale out to global proportions because significant and groundbreaking research is carried on in all parts of the world, including developing countries.
3. An analysis using Institute for Scientific Information's (ISI) *Journal Citation Report* (*JCR*) yielded a finite number of titles that could be archived, published by both commercial and society publishers, and governmental organizations at all levels.
4. Researchers in this field value and routinely use older materials as well as newly published ones.
5. Published materials include maps and other images that would offer challenges for electronic archiving.

6. We believed that some publishers would be suitable partners for a project that sought to archive materials electronically.
7. There was evidence that funding agencies might be found for such a project.
8. Because many journals in the geosciences are published only in print, the recommendations could cover print and born-digital titles.

METHODOLOGY

Through a thorough review of the *GeoRef Priority Titles* and *JCR* impact factors and total citations, the Group initially selected eight titles to recommend for archiving. Of the eight, two are published by commercial vendors, and the others by association or society publishers. Some of the publishers already are known to be committed to archiving their electronic titles and collaborating with libraries in this commitment, while others have less formalized approaches to perpetual access and archiving. Thus the level of challenge differs with the publisher as well as with the content.

In the realm of print archives, the Group did not want to overlook the importance of maintaining print collections though this is regarded as a second interest at this time because libraries have a long tradition of maintaining print repositories. However, the Group did note the precarious future of materials from developing countries in general and Russia and the former Soviet republics in particular. Because CRL has made concerted efforts over an extended period of time to collect Russian Academy of Sciences (RAS) materials, we offer a recommendation for ensuring the future collection and retention of RAS publications as a supplementary suggestion.

Over the months during which the Group deliberated about geosciences archives, a number of pertinent reports and programs appeared. Some of them may serve as background in carrying out the recommendations below, as is the case with the *E-Journal Archive DTD Feasibility Study* issued in December 2001 by the Harvard University Library Office for Information Systems E-Journal Archiving Project, reports of the LOCKSS Project, and other more recent reports. The Working Group advises, for example, that the geosciences archiving project follow currently accepted standards for markup language, authentication, etc., rather than undertake to write proprietary standards for this project.

A RELATED PROJECT

One concurrent program caused the Group to change the project proposal in midstream. Unknown to the working group until well into its task, a parallel initiative to form an online geosciences journal repository was being spearheaded by a group of important geosciences societies. Dr. Sharon Mosher, a geosciences faculty member at the University of Texas at Austin, is the Geological Society of America member on the multi-society organizing committee. She provided us with details about this new initiative. Other members of this alliance are the American Association of Petroleum Geologists (AAPG), the Geological Society of America (GSA), the Society for Exploration Geophysics (SEG), the Geological Society of London (GSL), the Mineralogical Society of American (MSA), the Society for Sedimentary Geology (SEPM), and, pending final board approval, the American Geological Institute (AGI). Eventually this organizing group hopes to include a significant number (30-40) of the world's geosciences societies achieving broad representation of all subjects in the geosciences.

The proposed multi-society geosciences electronic journal aggregate would consist of peer-reviewed, high-quality journals chosen from across all the earth and space sciences, and would include non-U.S. based journals. Nonprofit, professional societies and specialized publishers issue these journals. Several market surveys by the organizing group have led them to agree that such an aggregate is both financially and technically feasible. Our CRL Working Group fully supports this goal. We believe that it will be successful and result in significantly enhanced electronic, full-text access and a secure archive for many core geosciences journals.

A PROJECTED STATE GEOSCIENCES PUBLICATIONS ARCHIVE

Recognizing that the societies' efforts include journals that were originally targeted by the CRL Working Group project, the Group decided to review other types of publications in the geosciences to determine which would complement the geosciences journals aggregate. The decision became one that re-focuses CRL's efforts on the digital conversion and archiving of the publications of selected state geological surveys. Dr. Mosher supported this direction, which could lead the eventual implementers to explore ways in which the two projects might be linked.

State geological surveys engage in some of the most important and practical fieldwork undertaken by geologists. State geological surveys and maps have had a critical impact in the discovery, exploration, use and conservation of natural resources. State, territorial and federal geographical and geological resource surveys were established in the early days of the American republic to inventory and manage the natural wealth of the country. This mission for these state and federal agencies persists today, often with additional responsibilities to conserve land and water resources, to plan for environmentally sound land use, to assess changes in erosion, the impact of climate changes, and natural hazard risks. Most agencies are also charged with the role of informing and educating their citizenry about natural resources.

Scientists and researchers, students, policymakers, legislators and others in governmental agencies and commercial enterprises use the publications of these agencies. This primary geosciences source literature together with the theses and dissertations that cite these publications merits the attention that improvements in full-text access and preservation will deliver. Patterns of use indicate that earlier published materials retain their value as both historical benchmarks and sources of information for comparative studies of changes in, for example, resource availability and landscape use. A few preservation projects of this material have been undertaken for northern California, Florida and Texas. Information about state geological surveys is available from the agency and most importantly from *GeoRef*, the major indexing source for the geosciences.

RECOMMENDATIONS

In the proposal "Preliminary Proposal to Create a Persistent Archive of Geosciences Literature," in the following section, the Group recommended the establishment of a pilot project to explore the feasibility of converting, archiving and delivering serial publications of U.S. state geological surveys in digital form at cost. This pilot will require the creation of new organizational and technical partnerships in order to master the complexities surrounding such a digital project. The Group also acknowledges that the library and research communities' confidence in digital reformatting and archiving programs depends as much on the existence of secure and redundant print archives as on the adherence to standards and best practices for digital archives. It will be important to identify and maintain one or more locations as dependable sources for access to and preservation of geological survey publications. There are a number of candidates for this role including the U.S. Geological Survey library, state geology agencies and the academic community. In the past, the Center for Research Libraries has played a strong role in the acquisition of and access to state publications. The Center could serve an important and appropriate role as a trusted print archive for this particular digital project.

The recommendations in the proposal that follows this report are designed not expressly or exclusively for CRL to undertake, as they may or may not fit CRL's mission as a membership organization. They are offered as an emergent plan for any organization with an interest in the geosciences and the preservation and online archiving of some of their most select materials.

PRELIMINARY PROPOSAL TO CREATE A PERSISTENT ARCHIVE OF GEOSCIENCES LITERATURE

Executive Summary

The proposed project seeks to form an electronic archive of geosciences materials published by four states spanning the U.S. The three major elements of the project are: (1) test the feasibility of digitizing print materials interspersed with maps, foldouts, charts, varied color, etc.; (2) create a trusted digital and print archive of materials vital to the geosciences which to now have not been so targeted; (3) create an accessible digital resource with appropriate interface and indexing that will be distributed at an affordable price.

Content and Scope

Currently there are many projects afoot that experiment with the establishment of a permanent online repository of research. From the many projects are evolving standards and guidelines that will shape the trusted electronic archives of the future. In addition, of vital importance to both scholars and libraries is the content made so readily available in the repositories. One area of science and technology offers unique challenges and global potential for archiving: the geosciences.

The geosciences as a discipline are only beginning to receive attention for archiving though there are thousands of active journals and other publications recording important geosciences research all over the world, issued by commercial publishers, governments, and societies. A collaboration of six or seven society publishers and university faculty in the U.S. and U.K. has recently announced a proposal to publish online and digitize archives of their publications that will be searchable through *GeoRef*. The idea in the current proposal is similar but not identical, as we propose to conduct a demonstration project that will speedily create an online persistent archive of state field trip guidebooks, conference proceedings, state survey publications, etc., from four states in distinct geographical regions of the United States. As some of the materials will be under copyright, the project will resolve copyright issues with the state agencies. Once digitized, these publications, which date from 1866 to 2001 will be made available at minimal cost to subscribers.

The partners in this demonstration project will be the state publishers, university libraries, scientists, and the Center for Research Libraries (CRL). The Working Group, commissioned in 2000 by CRL to design a program in cooperative collection development in the sciences, has already identified the states of Illinois, Pennsylvania, Texas and Wyoming as ideal samples for this project. Because of their contributions to geosciences, the quality of their publications and the impact of activities in each state on research, they make excellent candidates for materials to be digitally preserved and disseminated to scholars the world over. The objective of the project is to digitize at least one completed series for each of the four states in order to create sufficient digital content both to stand alone as a primary resource for scholars in the field, and also to form the base for a larger future project.

Rationale

Geosciences were chosen for a variety of reasons. It is a broad field of interest to scholars in a number of disciplines, to commercial enterprises and governments at all levels. Groundbreaking research is carried on throughout the world, including developing countries whose publications have not yet entered the digital age. Researchers use older materials as well as newly published ones; thus an archive will be of enduring interest. The plates, tables, foldout maps, etc., found in these publications are still a challenge to digitize successfully. Finally, many periodicals in the geosciences are still available only in print format, thus presenting excellent examples for comparison and varied approaches to archiving. State materials were chosen because they constitute a sizable, important body of resources that have not yet been targeted for large-scale digital archiving. Moreover, the actual paper publications, once digitized, could become part of the Center for Research Libraries collection, which is a noted repository for state publications of various sorts. Thus, a paper backup would exist and be accessible to scholars and researchers.

Each of the chosen states offers unique research activities in the broad discipline of geosciences. The titles we propose to digitize will not overlap with other digital archive projects such as the one mentioned above (cited in the *Geoscience Information Society Newsletter* which will archive titles from AAPG, GSA and SEC [195, April 2002]). This U.S.-U.K. group is concentrating on journal archiving, and has expressed an interest in the current project as a complement to theirs. Should the proposed demonstration project be a success, a collaborative project with the U.S.-U.K. group to digitize books or other scholarly resources might ensue.

Work Plan

Project management, fiscal management and technological services will be overseen by CRL. Librarians and scientists from two universities in the Carnegie Foundation Doctoral/Research Universities–Extensive category, both known for their programs in geosciences and their library holdings in these areas, will conduct the actual work of the project including organizing, metadata, high-integrity caches, data format, user interface, copyright negotiating, standards, and marketing, taking into account both the problems common to all journal archives and those unique to materials in the geosciences, such as the large number of maps and foldouts. The actual digitization of the materials, which represent a wide range of resources from a score of selected bulletins, reports, guidebooks and circulars, will be carried on at the Center for Research Libraries or outsourced to a vendor such as Digital and Preservation Resources. By the end of the project, whose duration is estimated to be eighteen months, the partners will have produced an archive accessible to all, based the archive on accepted guidelines with broad application for similar projects, and planned the perpetuation of the initiative on a cost recovery basis. Negotiations with the state publishers will be critical, as this is an area where some potential archivers have failed in the past. The work of archiving the resulting database will be assumed by the project partners. Moreover, if the project is successful, issues relating to the maintenance of an expanded digital and print archive will be pursued in a future project.

CRL will appoint an advisory board made up of faculty who are editors of the selected journals, publishers, science librarians, including a liaison to the Geoscience Information Society, and CRL staff. The board will offer suggestions regarding interface, retrieval, pricing models, usage statistics, as well as provide a test group for the archive as it develops.

Outcomes

One important outcome of the project is the near-free delivery of data and research to students and researchers the world over. Another will be the development of a pricing model to recover the cost to continually add to the archive, maintaining, updating and refreshing the trusted archive, and responding to new formats as they arise. Finally, the project will introduce the Center for Research Libraries as a player in digital archiving. CRL, a massive print repository that counts 200 of America's most important research libraries among its members, has been the sponsor of a variety of area studies digitization projects over the past decade. With the proposed geosciences online state repository, CRL will branch into an area where immediate access to information is essential and, for the first time, provide a permanent home to digitized data. It will provide an alternative to existing long-term archiving efforts such as LOCKSS (Lots of Copies Keep Stuff Safe) with its forty-six test sites. Currently sufficient experimentation has been carried on by such groups as BioOne, Earthscape, the Digital Library Federation and the Research Libraries Group that the demonstration project can adopt existing standards for mark-up language, authentication, etc.

NOTES

1. The group comprised Christian Filstrup, Julia Gelfand, Vernon Kisling, Jane Kleiner, D. E. Perushek (chair), Chestalene Pintozzi, Melissa Trevvett (CRL liaison), and Kathleen Zar. Each of them contributed to the creation of this report.

Preliminary Proposal to Create a Persistent Archive of Geosciences Literature

PROPOSED BUDGET

Project management staff ($50,000 per year)	$75,000
Equipment (server, PCs, scanners, printers, software, disk storage)*	$165,000
Digitization technician ($30,000 per year to digitize approx. 134,000 pp. of state publications)*	$45,000
Metadata creation, scanning check ($40,000 per year)	$40,000
Interface design	$5,000
Travel to conferences (3 trips)	$4,500
TOTAL	$334,500

If outsourcing digitization to a commercial vendor is more cost-effective, such will replace the equipment budget and on-site digitization technician.

TIMETABLE

Month 1-4
Hire staff, gather publications, purchase equipment, negotiate contract with publishers
Months 3-15
Digitization
Months 3-18
Create metadata, check accuracy of scanning
Quarterly beginning in Month 6
Disseminate information about project in newsletters, journals
Month 12
Design self-sustaining model for continuation program
Month 15-18
Evaluation

APPENDIX 1

Center for Research Libraries Working Group on Cooperative Collection Development in Science and Technology

Proposed Project Titles

State	Series	Dates	# of Pubs	# of Pages (rounded or estimated)	Other Materials
Illinois	Bulletins	1906-2001	106	18,000	figures, maps, plates, tables
Illinois	Circulars	1906-2001	560	14,000	figures, maps, plates, sections, tables
Illinois	Reports of Investigations	1924-1968	221	9,300	charts, figures, maps, plates, tables
Illinois	Worthen Reports	1866-1882	11	6,200	figures, plates, maps
Pennsylvania	General Geology Reports	1931-1993	75	8,100	plates, maps
Pennsylvania	Mineral Resource Reports	1922-1996	98	13,800	plates, maps
Pennsylvania	Water Resource Reports	1933-1998	68	7,000	plates, maps
Texas	Guidebooks	1958-2001	28	2,917	figures, maps, plates, tables
Texas	Mineral Resource Circulars	1930-1994	85	1,900	figures, tables
Texas	Reports of Investigations	1946-2001	263	20,500	figures, plates, tables
Texas	UT Bulletins (geologic)	1915-1964	120	19,400	figures, maps, plates, tables
Wyoming	Bulletins	>1911-2000	71	7,920	figures, maps, tables
Wyoming	Memoirs	1968-1993	5	1,400	figures, maps
Wyoming	Reports of Investigations	1934-1998	53	3,600	color photographs, figures, maps
Totals			**1764**	**134,037**	

APPENDIX 2

Center for Research Libraries Working Group on Cooperative Collection Development in Science and Technology

Detailed Information on a Subset of State Geosciences Titles

ILLINOIS:

Bulletin 100–*Structural Features in Illinois*, W. John Nelson, 1995, 144 pages.
Bulletin 95–*Handbook Illinois Stratigraphy*, H. B. Willman et al., 1975, 261 pages.
Bulletin 10–*Mineral Content of Illinois Waters*, Edward Bartow et al., 1909, 192 pages.
Report of Investigations 220–*Chemistry, Uses, and Limitations of Coal Analyses*, O. W. Rees, 1966, 55 pages.
Report of Investigations 184–*Illinois Building Stones*, J. E. Lamar and H. B. Willman, 1955, 25 pages.
Worthen Report–*Economical Geology of Illinois*, A. H. Worthen, 1882, 3 volumes, 1752 pages.

PENNSYLVANIA:

Mineral Resource Report 50–*Atlas of Pennsylvania's Mineral Resources*, 4 parts, 174 pages, loose-leaf folio with maps.
Mineral Resource Report 6–*Bituminous Coal Fields of Pennsylvania*, George H. Ashley, James D. Sisler, and John F. Reese, 4 parts with maps.
Water Resource Report 1–*Ground Water in Southwestern Pennsylvania*, Arthur M. Piper, Margaret Dorothy Foster, and Charles Spaulding Howard, 1933, 406 pages.

TEXAS:

Guidebook 5–*Geology of the Llano Region and Austin Area*, Virgil E. Barnes, 1963, 73 pages.
Guidebook 24–*Tertiary and Quaternary Stratigraphy and Vertebrate Paleontology of Parts of Northwestern Texas and Eastern New Mexico*, 1990, 128 pages.
Mineral Resource Circular 23–*Faulting in Northwestern Houston County*, Texas, H. B. Stenzel, 1943, 9 pages.
Mineral Resource Circular 29–*Index to Mineral Resources of Texas by Counties*, Elias Howard Sellards, 1944, 21 pages.
UT Bulletin 1916, no. 44–*Review of the Geology of Texas*, J.A. Udden et al., 1916, 164 pages.
UT Bulletin 1869–*The Geology of East Texas*, E.T. Dumble, 1920, 388 pages.

WYOMING:

Bulletin 68–*The Geology of Wyoming's Precious Metal Lode and Placer Deposits*, W. D. Hausel, 1997, 229 pages.
Memoir 5–*The Geology of Wyoming*, A. W. Snoke et al., 1993, 3 volumes, 937 pages.
Report of Investigations 20–*A Stratigraphic Evaluation of the Eocene Rocks of Southwestern Wyoming*, Raymond Sullivan, 50 pages.
Report of Investigations 38–*Geothermal Resources of the Wind River Basin*, Wyoming, B. S. Hinckley and H. P. Heasler, 1987, 30 pages.

APPENDIX 3

Data Collected for Journal Archive in the Geosciences

1. SUBJECT HEADINGS–GEOSCIENCES JOURNALS

2. JCR Year and Edition: 1999 Science

3. JCR Year and Edition: 2000 Science

4. 1999 and 2000 JCR Total: Publishers from Top 200 by Impact Factor and Top 200 by Total Cites for 1999 and 2000

5. 1999 and 2000 Unique Publishers: lists all publishers included in 1999 and 2000 JCR geosciences journals reports

6. GEOREF Priority Titles: lists journals given priority indexing by GeoRef

7. PUBSCIENCE: Primary GeoScience Related Titles

8. PUBSCIENCE: Index to 67 of 462 Related Geosciences Journals

9. ALL GEOSCIENCE JOURNALS: lists all geosciences journals from JCR 2000 with full titles, citation data, impact factors, immediacy indices, number of articles published, and cited half life

10. GeoScience Plan and Related Federally Funded Projects

11. Geosciences: Sources of Potential Funding

12. Selected Government Publications in Earth Sciences–North America, South America, Central America, Australia, and New Zealand: lists representative government publications in the geosciences

13. Print Archiving of Russian and Soviet Republic Publications

14. Geosciences and related fields librarians/bibliographers

APPENDIX 4

Literature Review

This literature review explores the themes that are central to our charge:

1. how geosciences is treated in the professional and scholarly literature and how primary users of the geosciences literature use it
2. trends in the usage of that literature
3. key people, organizations and issues

According to the ISI *Journal Citation Reports* for 2000 in the subject categories "Geology and Geosciences, Interdisciplinary," there are 149 journals that are included in the data analysis. Those journals produced a total of 11,894 articles that year and 28 journals produced more than 100 articles each, with three titles producing more than 500 each. The average citation impact factor was .9519 with 14 journals having an impact factor of 2.0 or greater. Thus, one can conclude that a very few journals contain the most highly cited articles and they tend to be published by two major international professional societies.

Geosciences has both a very scholarly/research and a very active practice side with a significant number of publications issued by local, regional and national associations. With technology playing a greater role in both the research and practice side, it is clear that specialization contributes to the nature of publishing trends in recent years as does the increase in interdisciplinarity and relevance to many other interests and subjects. It is also very clear that dissertations and theses play a significant role in the literature of geosciences. Maps and other inserted items also are critical sources of information and are appended in various ways until digital formats can now incorporate them more successfully.

There is also an increase in interest to support women and promote diversity in the subject areas of geosciences and geography as documented in the literature. Preservation and archival work is an effort underway by many libraries and societies as the latter are releasing more of their content electronically and concerns associated with digital preservation grow. Lifespan of the geosciences literature indicates that older reports and data are very important to the geosciences as the primary study of comparing regions and specific interests over time is among the critical emphases.

Information literacy has a weaker tradition in the geosciences than in other science disciplines. The explanation of this is less clear, except to say that enrollment in both undergraduate and graduate courses in the geosciences is less than in the life sciences, physical sciences of chemistry, physics or mathematics and basic engineering and computer science. Since 1995, enrollments appear to be increasing. As one writer indicates, "Perhaps more than any other scientific discipline, the earth sciences require an extremely diverse array of material, including books, reports, journals, government documents, maps and other types of data from every country in the world" (Lamb, 1998).

APPENDIX 4 (continued)

Organizing that information and making it accessible via standard indexing and abstracting services is still not optimal for all topics. Still, only two tools appear to cover the range of materials, and they are the Science Citation Index (including the Current Contents updates) and *GeoRef.* New spheres of interest incorporate new research methodologies, including spatial mapping and information technology, or GIS. The literature survey reveals that there are many challenges for geology librarians because the nature of their work changes as their users' dependence on information not only expands but is more universal and multidisciplinary, and utilizes multiple formats. Citations noted reflect publications from the very late 1980s, but are more consistent for the past decade.

REFERENCES

Applegate, D., "Are the Geosciences Keeping Up?" *Geotimes,* Vol. 44, #2, February 1999, 13, 35.

Bichteler, Julie, "Geologists and Gray Literature: Access, Use and Problems," *Science & Technology Libraries,* Vol. 11, Spring 1991, 39-50.

Bichteler, Julie, "Geoscience Libraries of the Future: Predictions for the Next Decade," *Proceedings of the 24th Annual Meeting of the Geoscience Information Society,* 1990, 97-106.

Butkovich, Nancy J., "Discussion of the Use of Foreign Language Sources in Geological Journals," *Proceedings of the 25th Annual Meeting of the Geoscience Information Society,* 1991, 99-109.

Butler, J., "The Year 2000 Challenges: Special Issue for the Journal of Computers and Geosciences," *Computers & Geosciences,* Vol. 26 # 6, July 2000, 615-616.

Butler, J.C., "Internet Resources for the Geosciences," *Computers & Geosciences,* Vol. 21 #6, July 1995, 727-729.

DeFelice, Barbara, "Cooperative Collection Development and Preservation Projects in the Geosciences," *Proceedings of the 24th Geoscience Information Society Meeting,* 1990, 57-63.

Derksen, Charlotte R., and O'Donnell, Jim, "What We Did/What We Do/What We'll Do: Geoscience Information Centers in a Time of Change, 1970-2000," *Proceedings of the 29th Meeting of the Geoscience Information Society,* 1995, 1-11.

Derksen, Charlotte R. and Noga, Michael M., "The World of Geoscience Serials: Comparative Use Patterns (at Stanford and UCLA)" in *Proceedings of the 26th Annual Meeting of the Geoscience Information Society,* 1992, 15-62.

Geitgey, Judy A., "Government Documents in the Geosciences: An Annotated Bibliography," *PNLA Quarterly,* Vol. 50, Spring 1986, 28-31.

Haner, Barbara E. and O'Donnell, Jim, Eds., "Changing Gateways: The Impact of Technology on Geoscience Information Exchange" *Proceedings of the 29th Meeting of the Geoscience Information Society,* 1994.

Haner, Barbara E., "Government Information Recorded in Core Serials of the Geological Sciences," *Government Publications Review,* Vol. 17, August 1990, 341-355.

Haner, Barbara E., "Guidebook Citation Patterns in the Geologic Journal Literature: A Comparison Between 1985 and 1967," *Proceedings of the 24th Annual Meeting of the Geoscience Information Society*, 1990, 159-169.

Hanson, Dena F., Ed., "International Initiatives in Geoscience Information: A Global Perspective," *Proceedings of the 26th Annual Meeting of the Geoscience Information Society*, 1992.

Hauck, Roslin V. et al., "Concept-Based Searching and Browsing: A Geoscience Experiment," *Journal of Information Science*, Vol. 27 #4, 2001, 199-201.

Holoviak, Judy C., "Publishers' Decisions in the Field Trip Guidebook Business," *Proceedings of the 24th Annual Meeting of the Geoscience Information Society*, 1990, 199-203.

Kidd, Claren M., "Schemes for Redistributing Geological Literature," *Proceedings of the 26th Annual Meeting of the Geoscience Information Society*, 1992, 75-87.

Lamb, Melisa, A., "Geoscience Information Needs of the Researcher and Educator," Presented at the Geological Society of America 1998 annual meeting. Noted in *Abstracts with Programs, Geological Society of America*, Vol. 30 #7, 1998, 197-98.

Lamont, Melissa, "Managing Geospatial Data and Services," *Journal of Academic Librarianship*, Vol. 23 #6, November 1997, 469-473.

Larocque, A.C.L., "Challenges and Rewards of Graduate Studies in the Geosciences: A Woman's Perspective," *Geoscience Canada*, Vol. 21 #3, September 1994, 129-132.

Lerud, Joanne, "The Geoscience Information Professional in the Brave New Information World," *Proceedings of the 30th Annual Meeting of Geoscience Information Society*, 1996, 1-4.

Li, Yuwei, "Development of Spatial Information Technology and Methods of Geology," *Earth Science Frontiers*, Vol. 5, #2, 1998, 335-341.

Manson, Connie J., "How Long Is Long? A Statistical Analysis of the Longevity of Geoscience Information," Presented at the Geological Society of America, 1999 annual meeting. Noted in *Abstracts with Programs of Geological Society of America*, Vol. 31, #7, 1999, 163.

Manson, Connie, J., "Types and Uses of Geologic Literature: A Statistical Analysis of 100 Years of Citations on the Geology of Washington State," *Proceedings of the 26th Annual Meeting of the Geoscience Society*, 1992, 175-193.

Muhongo, D. et al., "Perspectives for Geosciences in the 21st Century," *Episodes*, Vol. 24 #1, March 2001, 3-8.

Musser, Linda R., "Earth System Science: The Real Environmental Science," *Proceedings of the 31st Meeting of the Geoscience Information Society*, 1997, 1-3.

Newman, Linda P., and Pausch, Lois, M., "Written in the Stones: Expanding the Boundaries of Geoscience Literature," *Proceedings of the 31st Meeting of the Geoscience Information Society*, 1997, 45-54.

Payne, Kathryn and Merriam, Daniel Francis, "Impact of Geoscience Specialist Journals: A Study in Use Patterns." *Proceedings of the 27th Annual Meeting of the Geoscience Information Society*, 1993, 57-63.

Payne, Kathryn and Merriam, Daniel Francis, "Use of the Proceedings of International Conferences and Symposia in Geology as Determined by Citation Analysis," *Proceedings of the 26th Annual Meeting of the Geoscience Information Society*, 1992, 165-173.

APPENDIX 4 (continued)

Schejbal, Ciirad, "How to Estimate Costs of Geoscience Information: Either Based on Calculated Expenses or on Final Users Demand," *Proceedings of the 5th International Conference of the Geoscience Information Society*, 1996, 80-88.

Scott, Sally J., "Interdisciplinary Use of Science Information Science by Geology Faculty and Graduate Students: Implications for Library Services (at the University of Wyoming)," *Proceedings of the 31st Meeting of the Geoscience Information Society*, 1997, 5-15.

Scott, Sally J., "Method for Evaluating Preservation Needs of Oversized Illustrations in Geology Theses (at UCLA)," *Proceedings of the 25th Annual Meeting of the Geoscience Information Society*, 1991, 137-146.

Smith, James G., "Future Publication Plans of the U.S. Geological Survey: Paper Plans, Electronic Dreams," *Proceedings of the 31st Meeting of the Geoscience Information Society*, 1997, 37-44.

Walker, Richard D., "The Geoscience Journal: Its Role, Past, Present and Future," *Proceedings of the 24th Annual Meeting of the Geoscience Information Society*, 1990, 87-95.

Wick, Constance S., "Preservation of Geoscience Library Collections: Current Conditions and Future Trends," *Proceedings of the 25th Annual Meeting of the Geoscience Information Society*, 1991, 147-155.

Wimberly, Mary Kate, "Supporting Women in the Geosciences," Paper Presented at the Geological Society of America, South Central Section, 34th Annual Meeting, and noted in *Abstracts with Programs of Geological Society of America*, 32, #3, March 2000, 45.

Wishard, Lisa, "Activities of the Geoscience Information Society Preservation Committee," in Science Editing and Information Management; Proceedings of the Second International AESE/CBE/EASE Joint Meeting, Sixth International Conference on Geoscience Information and 32d Annual Meeting of the Association of Earth Science Editors. *Proceedings of the International Conference on Geoscience Information*, Vol. 6, 1999, 43-49.

Yocum, Patricia B. and Almy, Gretchen S., "Information Literacy in the Geosciences: Instructional Methods and Basic Competencies," Presented at Geological Society of America 1999 annual meeting. Noted in *Abstracts with Programs of Geological Society of America*, Vol. 31, #7, 1999, 197.

Zipp, Louise, S., "Identifying Core Geologic Research Journals: A Model for Interlibrary Cooperative Collection Development (in Iowa)," *Proceedings of the 29th Meeting of the Geological Information Society*, 1995, 59-65.

APPENDIX 5

JCR Data Analysis of 8 Selected Geosciences Journals

AMERICAN MINERALOGIST
ISSN: 0003-004X

	# of Articles by Year[1]	Total Cites[2]	Cited Journal[3]	Impact Factor[5]
All Years			8058[4]	
2001	169	8058	55	1.806
2000	222	7345	319	1.862
1999	216	7066	472	1.842
1998			442	2.124
1997			358	1.888
1996			431	
1995			307	
1994			281	
1993			260	
Rest of Years (prior to 1990)			4861	

[1] Total number of articles in all issues for volume year.
[2] Number of times article cited from all years in given year.
[3] Number of times articles published in given year(s) cited articles in given journal.
[4] Total for all years available–recorded from latest (2001) data available.
[5] A measure of the frequency with which the "average article" in a given journal has been cited in each year.
Helps to evaluate a journal's relative importance.

GEOPHYSICAL RESEARCH LETTERS
ISSN: 0094-8276

	# of Articles by Year	Total Cites	Cited Journal	Impact Factor
All Years			21309	
2001	1151	21309	385	2.516
2000	1016	19940	1945	2.719
1999	915	17980	2913	2.306
1998			3146	2.290
1997			2013	2.180
1996			1912	
1995			1624	
1994			1256	
1993			969	
Rest of Years			4324	

APPENDIX 5 (continued)

JOURNAL OF GEOPHYSICAL RESEARCH
ISSN: 0148-0227

	# of Articles by Year	Total Cites	Cited Journal	Impact Factor
All Years			84449	
2001	2105	84449	620	2.609
2000	2045	80663	4253	2.600
1999	2178	77792	6764	2.701
1998			7614	2.577
1997			7178	2.416
1996			6143	
1995			5075	
1994			4923	
1993			4113	
Rest of Years			34042	

METEORITICS & PLANETARY SCIENCE
ISSN: 0026-1114

	# of Articles by Year	Total Cites	Cited Journal	Impact Factor
All Years			1244	
2001	117	1244	87	2.559
2000	120	1206	313	3.168
1999	91	550	227	1.879
1998			301	3.690
1997			177	2.301
1996			135	
1995			1	
1994			0	
1993			0	
Rest of Years			3	

PALAEOGEOGRAPHY PALAEOCLIMATOLOGY PALAEOECOLOGY
ISSN: 0031-0182

	# of Articles by Year	Total Cites	Cited Journal	Impact Factor
All Years			3861	
2001	193	3861	137	1.449
2000	183	3590	224	1.467
1999	180	3570	302	1.601
1998			252	1.150
1997			331	1.319
1996			272	
1995			248	
1994			296	
1993			152	
Rest of Years			1459	

PALAEONTOLOGY
ISSN: 0031-0239

	# of Articles by Year	Total Cites	Cited Journal	Impact Factor
All Years			1333	
2001	57	1333	13	0.731
2000	52	1190	30	0.964
1999	52	1157	46	0.879
1998			71	0.908
1997			55	0.607
1996			47	
1995			48	
1994			45	
1993			52	
Rest of Years			872	

TECTONICS
ISSN: 0278-7407

	# of Articles by Year	Total Cites	Cited Journal	Impact Factor
All Years			3343	
2001	56	3343	17	2.526
2000	63	3124	129	2.260
1999	72	2978	212	2.221
1998			188	2.444
1997			197	2.242
1996			326	
1995			267	
1994			235	
1993			221	
Rest of Years			1343	

WATER RESOURCES RESEARCH
ISSN: 0043-1397

	# of Articles by Year	Total Cites	Cited Journal	Impact Factor
All Years			12885	
2001	284	12885	82	1.757
2000	314	12051	400	1.640
1999	339	12511	747	2.061
1998			731	2.107
1997			744	1.648
1996			797	
1995			685	
1994			852	
1993			655	
Rest of Years			6485	

APPENDIX 6

Archiving Print Publications in the Digital Age

Vernon N. Kisling, Jr. is Collection Management Coordinator, Marston Science Library; Stephanie Haas is Assistant Director, Digital Library; and Paul Kirk is Geosciences Librarian, Marston Science Library, George A. Smathers Libraries, all at the University of Florida.

Although the recent emphasis of sci-tech publishers and libraries, as well as this working group, has been on archiving publications digitally, we need to clarify exactly what that means and how it relates to the overwhelming amount of print material. Although it improves access, searching and distribution, for the foreseeable future digital archiving will neglect a large portion of the existing print publications and will continue to be an ineffective preservation technique. Despite common belief, the virtual library is still a long way off, and the preservation aspects of digital formats will remain problematic for some time to come. Simply relying on the digitization of a small number of random publications is not a sufficient response to cooperative collection management of sci-tech publications. We need to provide a comprehensive and balanced approach to accessing, preserving and storing the sci-tech literature. As part of this overall effort, we need to deal with the enormous amount of print publications, especially now when libraries are shifting to digital formats and transforming shelving space to computer and patron space.

Libraries should continue their role as information repositories and should not rely on publishers to assure the long-term survival and usability of their publications. Valuable historic data is retained in today's ordinary print collections, which will become tomorrow's special collections. For as long as we can, we need to archive and preserve print publications for whatever purpose they may serve in the future, even after this material is eventually microfilmed or digitized. However, there is no need for every library to have copies of these publications and many libraries should have the option to withdraw titles in order to save space. This option to withdraw titles should not be made in isolation since the expedient, uncoordinated withdrawal of titles is not an acceptable solution.

A compromise to this all or nothing situation is to establish a system of regional depositories that would be responsible for archiving print publications in specific subjects or those that are of regional interest. These depositories could be existing libraries or they could be storage facilities supported by regional library consortia. The regions could be multi-national, national, multi-state, or statewide. While these efforts would be voluntary, coordination and a union catalog of titles archived would be needed to make the system effective. Each depository would be responsible for "last copies" of titles for their region (specialized titles may not be found in each region while other titles would be found at several regions for needed redundancy, for improved access at the local level, and interlibrary loans services–this ILL service would insure that digital services maintain competitive pricing in their print and download costs). This arrangement should allow other libraries in the regions to remove archived titles from their shelves in an appropriate manner.

In the United States, this arrangement of archival depositories should be done through state or regional library partnerships such as the existing consortia. Academic research libraries in particular need to begin this process by deciding which subject areas and regional publications they feel responsible for. These many local efforts should be coordinated through the use of a union catalog maintained at a national institution such as CRL. For an international case study see this report's Appendix on *Print Archiving of Russian and Soviet Republic Publications*.

Through the use of regional ("last copy") depositories for archiving print publications, microfilming for preserving print publications, and digital formatting for easy access to print publications, libraries could provide well-balanced, cooperative collection management of print publications. Eventually, only the most serious researchers may need the original paper formats of our print publications, but we are a long way from that situation, and until then we need to archive and preserve our scientific heritage (most of which is still in print) as best we can.

Print Archiving of Russian and Soviet Republic Publications

Appendix to: "Archiving Print Publications in the Digital Age"
Vernon N. Kisling, Jr., Stephanie Haas, and Paul Kirk

Providing regional depositories for archiving print publications, microfilming for preserving print publications, and digital formatting for improved access to print publications work together to provide a well-balanced cooperative collection management of print sci-tech materials. As an example of how this might be done at the international level, one can consider archiving Russian and Soviet Republic print publications.

APPENDIX 6 (continued)

Russian and Soviet Republic sci-tech publications constitute an important body of literature, but one that has limited distribution and very few titles in digital format. In addition, these countries probably have little infrastructural support for archiving, preserving or digitizing their publications. Therefore, efforts should be made to assist these countries with these activities, especially archiving since it will take longer to microfilm and digitize these materials.

National and regional depositories should be established among these countries in a cooperative way with the Russian Academy of Sciences (RAS). Each depository, which would be located at existing libraries or at facilities supported through library consortia, should accept responsibility for archiving print publications in specific subject areas, as well as the depository's national and regional publications. In addition to these depositories, international depositories at major libraries in other countries could serve as secondary, or mirror, archives for the Russian/Soviet Republic publications. Coordination of the international depositories should be the responsibility of the Russian Academy of Sciences in cooperation with international institutions such as CRL.

To begin with, support for the RAS efforts to archive, preserve and digitize their print sci-tech publications should be done in partnership with CRL, which has already established ties with RAS. In addition, libraries such as the United States Geological Survey library could serve as an international depository for their geosciences publications while other specialized libraries could serve as archival depositories for other subjects (such collections may already exist and could serve as the foundation of an international depository system). Having additional copies of Russian and Soviet sci-tech publications in the United States and Europe would ease the burden on the Russian/Soviet Republic libraries and would make international access easier.

As an initial step, on behalf of U.S. researchers, CRL and/or ARL should inventory American collections to establish a union catalog of existing Russian/Soviet Republic journal and report holdings. There should also be an inventory of library collections with significant Russian/Soviet publication holdings in specific subjects. RAS should also establish a union list of published Russian/Soviet journals and reports. Then CRL could work with RAS to develop a plan for establishing and coordinating a system of regional, national and international depositories. Included in this plan should be recommendations on how underrepresented publications would be distributed among the depositories. Once this foundation of archival depositories is functional (or in the process of becoming functional), CRL and RAS should determine preservation and digitization needs, and develop a mechanism by which it would be possible for other libraries and funding agencies to help with these longer-term needs.

Index

Page numbers followed by "f" indicate a figure.

AAPG. *See* American Association of
　　Petroleum Geologists
　　(AAPG)
AAU. *See* Association of American
　　Universities (AAU)
Aberdeen Woods Conference, 64,185,
　　224,242
Access, Storage, and Preservation
　　Group, 198
Adaptability, in CCD, 209
African Newspaper Union List Project
　　(AFRINUL), 139
African Studies Association (ASA), 139
Africana Librarians Council (ALC), 139
AFRINUL. *See* African Newspaper
　　Union List Project (AFRINUL)
AGI. *See* American Geological
　　Institute (AGI)
ALC. *See* Africana Librarians Council
　　(ALC)
Alexander, A., 225
American Association of Petroleum
　　Geologists (AAPG), 244
American Geological Institute (AGI),
　　244
American Mathematical Society, 96
AMPs. *See* Center for Research Libraries
　　Area Studies Microform
　　Projects (AMPs)
Andrew W. Mellon Foundation, 34,37,
　　38,129,136. *See also*
　　Collection management
　　strategies, in digital
　　environment
　behavior data in, 42
　cost data in, 42-43

grant for, phases of, 41
implementation of, 41
journal selection by, criteria for, 40
objectives of, 39-40
preference data in, 42
use data for, 42
Antiquarian Bookman, 78
Archiving Print Publications in Digital
　　Age, 260-261
ARIEL, 161
Arizona State University, 190
ARL. *See* Association of Research
　　Libraries (ARL)
Armstrong, K., 80
"arXiv e-Print archive," 168
ASA. *See* African Studies Association
　　(ASA)
Association for Research Libraries
　　(ARL) E-Metrics Study, 225
Association for Research Libraries
　　(ARL) New Measures
　　Initiatives, 225
Association of American Universities
　　(AAU), 135,136,149
　Task Force of, 136
Association of Asian Studies, 142
Association of Research Libraries
　　(ARL), 26,135,136,149,154
Atkins, S., 225
Atkinson, R., 3
Aurelius, M., 78
Australian National University, 130

Barron's, 95
Bibliographic access, in campus
　　libraries, 59